HEMINGWAY'S SUN VALLEY
Local Stories behind His Code, Characters, and Crisis

HEMINGWAY'S
Sun Valley

Local Stories behind His Code,
Characters, and Crisis

By
PHIL HUSS

Published by The History Press
Charleston, SC
www.historypress.com

Hemingway's Sun Valley: Local Stories behind His Code, Characters, and Crisis
Copyright 2020 by Phil Huss
All rights reserved.

Front Cover: Hemingway with a stringer of mallard ducks after a morning of hunting on Silver Creek. *Magnum Photos.*
Back Cover: Hemingway at his typewriter in Sun Valley. *The Community Library, Ketchum, Idaho.*

First published in 2020
Manufactured in the United States
ISBN: 978-1-46714-581-7
Library of Congress Control Number: 2020934329

Notice: The information in this book is true and complete to the best of our knowledge. It is offered without guarantee on the part of the author or The History Press. The author and The History Press disclaim all liability in connection with the use of this book.

No part of this book may be reproduced or transmitted in any form whatsoever without prior written permission from the publisher except in the case of brief quotations embodied in critical articles and reviews.

Contents

Dedication		vii
Acknowledgments		ix
Preface		xi
Foreword By Mariel Hemingway		xvii
Introduction to the Code		xix
1	Complete Tasks Well	1
	Sun Valley Stories: Completing Tasks Well	*2*
	Novels and Short Stories: Completing Tasks Well	*10*
2	Value Mentors and Community	24
	Sun Valley Stories: Valuing Mentors and Community	*24*
	Novels and Short Stories: Value Mentors and Community	*33*
3	Value Nature as an Ethical Arena	42
	Sun Valley Stories: Valuing Nature as an Ethical Arena	*43*
	Novels and Short Stories: Value Nature as an Ethical Arena	*50*
4	Find Faith in Love	82
	Sun Valley Stories: Find Faith in Love	*82*
	Novels and Short Stories: Find Faith in Love	*89*
5	Self-Assess	120
	Sun Valley Stories: Self-Assess	*120*
	Novels and Short Stories: Self-Assess	*124*
6	Develop Experiential Knowledge	135
	Sun Valley Stories: Develop Experiential Knowledge	*135*
	Novels and Short Stories: Develop Experiential Knowledge	*142*

7	Embrace the Present	148
	Sun Valley Stories: Embrace the Present	*148*
	Novels and Short Stories: Embrace the Present	*150*
8	Speak through Actions	163
	Sun Valley Stories: Speak Through Actions	*163*
	Novels and Stories: Speak through Actions	*167*
	Poetry	*172*
9	Take Responsibility for Wrongs	177
	Sun Valley Stories: Take Responsibility for Wrongs	*177*
	Novels and Short Stories: Take Responsibility for Wrongs	*183*
10	Avoid Self-Pity	190
	Novel and Short Stories: Avoid Self-Pity	*190*
	Sun Valley Stories: Avoid Self Pity	*197*
	First Suicide Attempt: April 21, 1961	*207*
	Second Suicide Attempt: April 24, 1961	*208*
	Third Suicide Attempt: April 25, 1961	*209*
	Fourth and Final Suicide Attempt: July 2, 1961	*209*
	Reflection	*213*
Appendix		214
Endnotes		219
Bibliography		231
Index		235
About the Author		241

Dedication

"What do you value most?"
—Ernest Hemingway in *A Farewell to Arms*

My answer:
My love for my wife, Chrissie, and our two children, Nils and Gretel.

Acknowledgments

My first acknowledgment of gratitude must be for my wife, Chrissie, whose enduring love and support mean everything to me.

Of course, I am grateful to Ernest Hemingway for providing such wonderful short stories and novels that inform my thinking and enhance my classroom discussions. And I am grateful to him for showing us all how to balance life of the mind and a life of adventure.

I am indebted to writers and researchers who have allowed me to bring the Idaho Hemingway stories to life: Lloyd Arnold, Tillie Arnold, Dorice Taylor, and Larry Morris.

I am also indebted to The Community Library of Ketchum, Idaho and the support of the library's executive director, Jenny Emery-Davidson, and regional history director, Mary Tyson. Mary provided an archive of interviews with local friends, hunting partners, and acquaintances of Ernest Hemingway, and these proved to be rich ore.

To publish this book, I had to demonstrate local support from vendors. The following individuals generously provided financial support by purchasing advanced copies of the book: Terry Ring of Silver Creek Outfitters, Whit Atkinson of Atkinsons' Market, Jenny Emery-Davidson of The Community Library, Ben Pettit of Sun Valley Community School, Scott Schnebly of Lost River Outfitters, and Dave Whorton of the Tugboat Institute. This outpouring of support from owners of local businesses and nonprofits was both encouraging and edifying and proved to be one of the best parts of the process of writing and publishing this book.

I also appreciate John Lundin, who after listening to my lecture at The Community Library on the Hemingway code in the Idaho stories, recommended my book to Arcadia Publishing and The History Press. And I am appreciative of my editor, Artie Crisp, for taking an interest in my work.

Finally, I am forever grateful for my students at Sun Valley Community School for sustaining my love for the life and works of Ernest Hemingway through lively discussions. And I appreciate their collaboration with me in distilling the principles of the Hemingway heroic code through nearly twenty years of reading their English papers on Hemingway.

Preface

"A hell of a lot of state, this Idaho, that I did not know about," remarked Ernest Hemingway during his first visit to Sun Valley in 1939. Coming back from a pronghorn hunt in the Pahsimeroi Valley and looking back at the Sawtooth Valley and the headwaters of the Salmon River from atop Galena Summit, Hemingway also told a hunting companion, "You'd have to come from a test tube and think like a machine to not engrave all of this in your head so that you never lose it."[1]

THE VIEW FROM GALENA SUMMIT: THE SAWTOOTH VALLEY AND THE HEADWATERS OF THE SALMON RIVER *By Charles Knowles – Flickr: Galena Summit Idaho, CC BY 2.0 https://commons.wikimedia.org/w/index.php?curid=19829662.*

Agreed. I have lived in the Wood River Valley (home to the towns of Sun Valley, Ketchum, Hailey, and Bellevue) for twenty years at the writing of this book. I have run many of its rivers, backpacked through many of its mountains, hunted ducks on Silver Creek, and fished lots of its waters, but I still know there is "a hell of a lot of... Idaho that I" do not know about. But I do know that both Ernest Hemingway's legacy and the impression this vast, wild country of Idaho leave upon us are deeply "engraved" indeed. Hemingway's cultural legacy is alive and well in the Wood River Valley. There is an annual Hemingway Festival each September at The Community Library in Ketchum, and it attracts scholars, indebted authors, friends of the family, and general readers from all over the globe. Sun Valley Lodge's suite 206, where Hemingway wrote chapters of *For Whom the Bell Tolls*, is a destination for Hemingway enthusiasts, his bust on Trail Creek Memorial, with his eyes looking out over the trout stream and the cottonwoods, honors his love of the area, and his grave in the Ketchum Cemetery is surrounded by the graves of his wife, Mary, his children, and his closest hunting companions and friends. A monument to his hunting adventures on Silver Creek has the epigraph to *The Sun Also Rises* etched into it. His house just outside of the mountain town of Ketchum remains in almost the same condition as when Ernest tragically ended his life there on July 2, 1961.

I came to know Hemingway as a young man when I read his *Old Man and the Sea* at the age of nine. It was my first real book. As a boy who would often disappear alone with a fishing rod and a faded, yellow bucket to ply the streams of western Pennsylvania for fingerling trout, the story of catching a giant marlin was a marvel. After moving to the Wood River Valley in 2000 to teach English at Sun Valley Community School, an independent school, I taught and still teach a course called "Hemingway." In this course, we read a wide selection of his short stories and novels: *In Our Time*, *The Sun Also Rises*, *A Farewell to Arms*, *For Whom the Bell Tolls*, and *The Old Man and the Sea*. We also study the local stories about Hemingway's time in Sun Valley as windows into understanding the characters in his most famous texts. This is the subject matter of this book.

Hemingway's Sun Valley

Ernest Hemingway lived a larger-than-life existence everywhere he went: Italy, France, Spain, Key West, Africa, Cuba, and Sun Valley, Idaho. Ambulance driver in World War I, journalist in the Spanish Civil War, correspondent in World War II, novelist, hunter, and fisherman, Hemingway was a man of action and was happiest combining his love of writing with his love for adventure. Some of his happiest days were here in Sun Valley, where he wrote a significant portion of *For Whom the Bell Tolls* and hunted with a group of local hunting guides. Why was Hemingway here in Sun Valley? What were his days like? And how does his life in Idaho help us understand some of the seminal novels and stories of the twentieth century?

Hemingway was invited to the Sun Valley Resort and was offered free room and board at the Sun Valley Lodge in exchange for the rights to use his image on the resort's publicity materials. Between 1939 and 1947, Hemingway spent five fall seasons in Sun Valley. With his new best-selling novel, *For Whom the Bell Tolls*, and new crew of close friends from his hunting adventures, these five falls were some of the best times of his life. University of Idaho Hemingway scholar Marty Peterson remarked, "I think [Hemingway] was in search of the vanishing frontier. I think he was in search of a place where he could have some anonymity, where the hunting and fishing was still good. And he found that in Central Idaho."[2] But how do the stories of his adventures in Idaho, of his connections to the local people, of the only place *he* ever purchased a home in America inform our understanding of the man, his writing, and this place?

This book proposes to answer this question by connecting Ernest Hemingway's life in Sun Valley to the specific principles of the code of conduct he developed in his most admired characters in his stories and novels. Many of the code principles Hemingway developed about how to live well were learned in his experiences during his time spent writing, hunting, and falling in love in and with Sun Valley. The principles of the Hemingway heroic code manifest in the mentors and heroes of his stories and novels, but many of the code principles he crafted in his fictionalized characters emerged through the friends and memorable moments he made in the Wood River Valley—the Idaho frontier.

A coded hero or heroine in the works of Ernest Hemingway is a character who is emotionally, physically, or psychologically "destroyed, but not defeated," who dies with self and code principles intact, and who keeps the random, negative consequences of life at bay by running an order through the chaos of life. While the concept of the Hemingway hero with a stiff upper lip, grace under pressure, and willingness to remain steadfast to a just cause even if (and especially if) the end goal is futile is familiar to many readers of Hemingway, this book proposes to add more specificity to the Hemingway heroes both in his life and in his written work. While one may be vaguely familiar with the notion of a Hemingway code, this book proposes to codify the specific principles of the code to enable a reader to assess the successes and failures of his friends and his characters and Hemingway himself in living up to the mutually enhancing principles of the code. It is an informing belief of this book that characters and friends who, at times, fail to follow the principles of the code are just as instructive as those who follow them. Understanding the code principles through how they emerge or fail to emerge in various characters and friends and in Hemingway's life is very helpful in appreciating Hemingway's works as a whole.

The design of the book is simple. Each code principle receives a separate chapter. Each code principle receives a working definition, an exploration of moments related to the principle in Hemingway's life here in Sun Valley, and a canvassing of relevant moments related to the principle from the stories and novels. In my readings and teachings over the years, my students and I have been able to codify the Hemingway heroic code of conduct as follows: complete tasks well, value mentors and community, value nature as an ethical arena, find faith in love, self-assess, develop experiential knowledge, embrace the present, speak through actions, take responsibility for wrongs, and avoid self-pity.

It is rare for any one character or friend to follow all of these principles (Robert Jordan in *For Whom the Bell Tolls* almost does), but when one looks at the heroic characters, the favored mentors in the novels, and the admired friends in his life, it becomes evident that these code principles are to be sought after and admired when followed. In this age when contemporary iconic figures, from athletes to actors to politicians, repeatedly fail to behave in admirable ways, having a code to follow and heroes who live by a code are all the more important for readers, especially younger readers. It has been a labor of love to connect the life, works, and legacy of the author I love to the Wood River Valley—a place I love.

Foreword
By Mariel Hemingway

I grew up in the Wood River Valley. It has always been my home, regardless of where else I may have received my mail or laid my head. But let me be clear, it was grandfather, Ernest Hemingway's love for this place that inspired my father to move his entire family from Mill Valley, California to this extraordinary community.

Father left a stock-broking business in San Francisco to come to Sun Valley where he had met his wife, my mother, Puck (a native Idahoan). He chose to pursue his passion for living life in the outdoors. He dropped the suits, the 9-5 job and donned khakis, corduroy, and fishing vests for the majority of his remaining life here (35 years). He became Idaho's Fish and Game Commissioner and fly fished most every spring and summer day. He then hunted every day throughout the fall. I was four-years-old when we arrived and have known no other place like I know Ketchum and Sun Valley. Certainly, Ernest ignited my father's passion for this place. My father then very deliberately bred that passion into our little family of my mother, sisters and me.

My childhood is beautifully wrapped in the splendor of the valley's unique gifts. I have always been mesmerized by the valley's take on nature. I personally know our valley by the different smells of the seasons. The smell of damp, clammy, earth covering the past is a sign that spring is here, heralding the promise of new growth. Summer enters at first, warm smelling with a mix of spring newness and a blast of daily heat which by summer's end burns the nostrils midday. Who could deny that punch of hot earth, rocks, drying sage and relentless wind? And then finally when fall arrives, the air is cool and the sage is at the peak of pungency. Oh! And our skies! During the fall, our sky is as blue as any sky you've ever seen. The contrast of blue sky with a few puffed up white clouds and a golden grassed earth is when you know you have entered HEMINGWAY COUNTRY. I use this moniker because a lot of older locals who used to know my grandfather and my friends at The Community Library have coined the phrase to represent Ernest Hemingway's connection to the Wood River Valley, Sun Valley and the still small town of Ketchum. Papa (a common nickname of my grandfather's) is our mentor here. I say that not only because he is Ernest Hemingway, the icon and my grandfather, but because it is what we who love it here all feel. We love the valley and we love that Papa loved it and saw it all rough and unfinished. It is not majestic at first glance; it is rugged, part desert-part mountain and only after a while do you see its hidden elegance gazing right at you. All of us who live here relate to my grandfather's understanding of it. Whether or not you fly fish or hunt doesn't matter because it's the terrain, the smell, the sky, and the people of Hemingway Country that make it solid and important to us all.

 Although I never knew my grandfather (he died four months before I was born), I have felt his presence daily and I still do. *Hemingway's Sun Valley: Local Stories behind His Code, Characters, and Crisis* also allows us to feel his presence through its recounting of the adventures he had and the friends he made in the Wood River Valley. When I am on the trails or sitting at the edge of a stream, I feel him and I appreciate what he represents to this place I call home. He represents an honesty and courage of living that the Valley imprints on your soul.

Introduction to the Code

HEMINGWAY'S FAMILY CREST USED TO MARK HIS SUITCASES AND FURNITURE. *Author's collection*.

The above is a photo I took of the Hemingway family logo. This one appeared on a leather suitcase in the master bedroom of the Hemingway home in Ketchum, Idaho. There is an identical logo on the back of a Cuban leather chair at the desk in the master bedroom. Interpret it as you will, but I see mountains, an arrowhead, and rivers or flowing water. Some see mountains, a deer hoof, and rivers or flowing water. Either way the mountains form the rivers, and the rivers in turn supply the lakes and sea with the water to return to the mountains in the form of snow. And the circle that keeps all within it in equilibrium captures this cycle. And the natives at the center: whether it is Native Americans in the form of an arrowhead or deer in the form of a hoof, both are endemic to the mountain-river ecosystem. Both live in it in greater harmony than modern man with his outsize impact on the sustainability of intact ecosystems.

What is the connection to the Hemingway code? Hemingway wanted to indicate ownership of his suitcases, chairs, and desks with a logo that conveys an order, an equilibrium between mutually enhancing elements in an ecosystem. This is the Hemingway code: mutually enhancing principles lead to an order that keeps chaos without and within at bay. And these principles lead to the development of the native, empirical, natural self.

In *Death in the Afternoon*, Hemingway includes extensive self-referential passages about writing and life. In one of his most famous passages, he writes:

> *There are some things which cannot be learned quickly, and time, which is all we have, must be paid for their acquiring. They are the very simplest things, and because it takes a man's life to know them the little new that each man gets from life is very costly and the only heritage he has to leave.*[3]

This passage encapsulates his paramount goal in creating literary characters who became heroes by living according to self-imposed code principles. The "heritage" we, as readers, receive from these illustrative moments in which mutually enhancing code principles manifest is "how to live in the world," as Jake Barnes puts in *The Sun Also Rises*.

"In life, one must (first of all) endure," stated Hemingway in the familiar masculine, matter-of-fact tone that is parodied and pilloried today.[4] But those familiar with the Hemingway concept of "arrested development" know what Hemingway means by "endure." Arrested development is a concept that appears in name in *The Sun Also Rises*, but it is illustrated through many of his texts. For Hemingway, arrested development is a way of describing individuals who have never had physical, emotional, or psychological setbacks in life and so could not learn and grow from them. Hemingway most often developed characters who suffer from arrested development because they fail to learn and grow from physical, emotional, or psychological trauma. In *The Sun Also Rises,* Robert Cohn is the classic exemplar of arrested development. Excessively self-satisfied that he slept with Lady Brett Ashley, Cohn fails to see that Brett does not and will not love him, that his "chaps" are mocking him incessantly to his face, and that his current lover, Frances, manipulates him. He does not learn and grow from setbacks. But coded mentors do: Count Mippipopolous in *The Sun Also Rises* is in love with life because he nearly lost his life, ninety-four-year-old Count Greffi in *A Farewell to Arms* is "careful" about love, because he lost his wife, and Anselmo in *For Whom the Bell Tolls* is aware that he will need to perform some "civic penance" in the future for the fellow Spaniards he kills in the Spanish Civil War.

To endure is not just to tolerate the setbacks in life but also to learn and grow from them to "get strong in the broken places."

This is not to say that Hemingway encouraged self-reflection to the point of self-obsession and solipsism. In the most recent biography of Hemingway and the first by a woman, Mary Dearborn writes, "The so-called Hemingway code—a tough, stoic approach to life that seemingly substituted physical courage and ideals of strength and skill for other forms of accomplishment—increasingly looked tiresome and macho."[5] She follows this honest contemporary take on the seemingly dated Hemingway code with questions: "Should we still read Hemingway? Are his concerns still relevant?" Yes. And yes.

Aristotle's *Nicomachean Ethics* focuses on developing the integrity of the agent, the person committing the action, in order to improve the virtues of the individual and the moral status of the community. Instead of obsessing over the ideas in the action (deontological moral philosophy) or the greater good of the ends achieved by the action (teleological moral philosophy), Aristotle encouraged readers to self-reflect on the mutually enhancing virtues that would flourish in the individual if s/he were to commit to an action for the virtues embodied in the action. Human obsession with character traits, with virtues, with aspirational principles in order to become our better selves has been and should always be a part of how we strive to become better agents in the world.

In his book *The Road to Character* (2016), David Brooks addresses the recent nadir of self-centeredness encouraged by the contemporary toxic cocktail of instantaneous communication speeds that disallow self-reflection, social media self-aggrandizement, and "a broadcasted personality that seeks social approval."[6] Brooks offers an antidote to self-obsession by encouraging us to foster traits that will be celebrated more in our eulogies than in our resumes. He is riding a recent interest in character, in "character education," and fostering virtues in others. In the vein of Aristotelian virtue ethics, Brooks argues that "character is built in the course of your inner confrontation…(it) is a set of dispositions, desires and habits…slowly engraved during the struggle against your own weakness. You become more disciplined through a thousand small acts of self-control, sharing, service, friendship, and refined enjoyment…people of character are capable of long obedience in the same direction."[7] Ernest Hemingway was deeply interested in writing about fictional characters who followed a set of unspoken principles, struggled against their own weaknesses, and emerged disciplined through a long obedience to these principles. Most importantly, Hemingway developed characters who followed principles based upon admirable virtues, regardless of the positive or negative outcomes achieved by following these principles. This book endeavors to codify the unspoken principles that constitute a Hemingway hero.

The existence of an unspoken code of conduct in Ernest Hemingway's texts begs the question: *Why is there a need for the principles of a code?* Well, the answer to this question lies in a mixture of both Hemingway's life experiences and the texts that found germination in the rich soil of his adventurous life.

While Hemingway was never actually a commissioned soldier, he experienced four wars: World War I (WWI), the Greco-Turkish War, the Spanish Civil War, and World War II (WWII). As a volunteer ambulance driver for the Italian Red Cross in WWI and received a trench-mortar wound in his leg, he was a journalist who covered all of the other wars. Why did he keep going back to war after witnessing the atrocities and codeless behavior he so vividly depicts in his short story collection *In Our Time* and in *A Farewell to Arms*?

Hemingway was fascinated by the emergence of character that manifests in others and himself when life is threatened. As is exhibited in his fascination with bullfighting, boxing, and big-game hunting, Hemingway knew that the courage to follow the unspoken code of completing tasks well regardless of one's ability to affect a positive outcome is most often shown when one's life and the lives of others are threatened. While Hemingway wrote candidly about the cowardice and ineptitude of matadors in *In Our Time* and *Death in the Afternoon* and big-game hunters in "The Short Happy Life of Francis Macomber", he also wrote about the soldiers, matadors, and big-game hunters who did what they needed to do in a life-threatening moment and how they felt edified by the experience. It is only in the context of codeless behavior— the shooting of the minister during a firing squad in a chapter of *In Our Time*, the bad sticking of the bull by the young matador in a chapter of *In Our Time*, and the chaos of the retreat from Caporetto in *A Farewell to Arms*— that the honorable, coded moments of gain clarity and prominence. As the omniscient narrator recalls about WWI veteran Harold Krebs in the famous short story "Soldier's Home" in *In Our Time*:

> *All of the times that had been able to make him feel cool and clear inside himself when he thought of them; the times so long back when he had done the one thing, the only thing for a man to do, easily and naturally, when he might have done something else, now lost their cool, valuable quality and then were lost themselves.*[8]

The salient point here is that Krebs's performance of the action he needed to do to save himself and others during the war "when he might have done something else" *once* made him feel "cool and clear inside himself." Krebs took great pride in self-assessing and knowing that he controlled what he could control, was an "instrument to his duty," and performed an action that embraced the present and exhibited courage through his actions. The sad statement that these memories no longer have their "valuable qualiti(es)" and "were lost" speaks to the emotional numbing of post-traumatic stress disorder (PTSD) experienced by many soldiers during and after war. In the context of the undisciplined behavior of war and in life, to be witness to or to perform "the one thing, the only thing for a man to do" fascinated Hemingway as both observer and participant.

Robert Penn Warren's seminal 1947 essay "Hemingway" first outlined the emergence of a code in the heroic characters in Hemingway's stories and novels. It is instructive to recall Warren's description of Hemingway heroes as "defeated on their own terms." Warren goes on to mention the unspoken code of the heroes as individuals (both men and women) who

> maintain...an ideal of themselves...formulated or unformulated, by which they have lived. They represent some notion of a code, some notion of honor...which distinguishes (them) from people who merely follow their random impulses and who are, by consequence, messy.[9]

Warren captures Hemingway's belief that a hero follows an ideal set of mutually enhancing code principles in order to develop and maintain "honor," especially when one realizes that following a self-imposed way of conducting oneself may not result in the accomplishment of one's desired goal nor even the preservation of one's life. While Warren's essay framed the notion of a heroic code and heroic hero in Hemingway's works and referenced courage, wisdom, and perseverance as admirable heroic qualities, the essay, in my view, does not codify the code principles of the Hemingway hero in satisfying detail. This book proposes to be more detailed about the specific code principles and how they emerge in his best characters. And it will do so chapter by chapter:

Chapter One: Complete Tasks Well
Chapter Two: Value Mentors and Community
Chapter Three: Value Nature as an Ethical Arena

Chapter Four: Find Faith in Love
Chapter Five: Self-Assess
Chapter Six: Develop Experiential Knowledge
Chapter Seven: Embrace the Present
Chapter Eight: Speak through Actions
Chapter Nine: Take Responsibility for Wrongs
Chapter Ten: Avoid Self-Pity

It is important to address the reckless, chaotic, unjust actions Ernest Hemingway witnessed at war and imaginatively depicted in his texts to grasp the need for a self-imposed code of conduct. Of the many "shitty" titles (Hemingway's adjective at the top of the title list) for *A Farewell to Arms*, the most instructive one is *The Sentimental Education of Frederic Henry*. While this happily did not make the cut (along with *I Committed Fornication in Another Country and Now the Wench is Dead*), the notion that Frederic Henry was "sentimental" about war is instructive, for his experiential knowledge gained from war disabuses him of his preconceived and naïve belief that war is replete with heroic, honorable, "valorous conduct."

Hemingway's early texts about war contain myriad examples of characters who fall short of "valorous conduct." A quick recollection of undisciplined, reckless, unheroic moments will suffice in establishing the context for the need for a self-imposed code of conduct after the war. In Hemingway's first depiction of war in *In Our Time*, British soldiers brag about "potting Germans" as if it were a game, American soldiers are drunk out of fear of being shot on their way to the front, a firing squad shoots a soldier in the head after his legs collapse from his debilitated state, and Greek soldiers break the legs of their mules and toss them into the harbor so the Turks will not put to them use after the Greek evacuation from Turkey. In Hemingway's second war text, *A Farewell to Arms*, Frederic Henry watches Passini's stump of a leg twitch from a mortal shell before Passini dies, and Aymo is killed by a bullet that is shot by his fellow Italians and that pierces the back of his neck; Frederic attempts to plug the holes in Aymo's neck and face, but Aymo dies in his arms. In addition, in *A Farewell to Arms*, Bonello surrenders to become a prisoner of war during the retreat, Frederic Henry shoots Italian sergeants when they refuse to help remove the vehicle Frederic stuck in the mud, and the Battle Police both kill high-ranking Italian officers for allegedly deserting their troops and threaten Frederic's life as he jumps in the Tagliamento River to escape the codelessness of war.

While there were moments of heroism and valor, most of what Frederic Henry witnesses during WWI is far from admirable. Nick Adams is shot in the spine as he watches his friend take his last breath in *In Our Time*. Frederic Henry has his kneecap blown off and receives a fractured skull from a mortar while he is eating cheese and drinking wine. And Ernest Hemingway received a debilitating leg injury during WWI while he was handing out chocolates to wounded Italian soldiers. Both Frederic Henry and Ernest Hemingway receive the Italian Silver Medal for being wounded and acting heroically at war (Frederic's is promised), but neither takes any pride in the "false abstraction" of the heroism represented in the medals.

Robert Penn Warren captures the notion that people "of your party" have a "discipline, a style, a code."[10] The priest and Count Greffi in *A Farewell to Arms* and the proprietor of Hotel Montoya, Count Mippipopolous, and Pedro Romero in *The Sun Also Rises* and Anselmo and Pilar in *For Whom the Bell Tolls* and Santiago and Manolin in *The Old Man and the Sea* have "a self-imposed discipline…to redeem the incoherence of the world: they attempt to impose some form upon the disorder of their lives. The technique of the bullfighter or sportsman, the discipline of the soldier, the fidelity of the lover" are admired by the protagonists of these texts and by Hemingway in his life, particularly within "the family" of hunting guides and friends he surrounded himself with in Sun Valley, Idaho.[11]

In *A Farewell to Arms*, Frederic later says to his lover, Catherine Barkley, "I know where I stand (on bravery). I've been out long enough to know. I'm like a ball-player that bats two hundred and thirty and knows he's no better."[12] Both Frederic and Hemingway learn through the experience of war that the moments at war when they performed or witnessed the performance of "the one thing, the only thing for a man to do" that could make them feel "cool and clear inside (themselves)" were far and few between the moments of recklessness, disorderliness, and chaos. Suffering emotionally and psychologically from witnessing the horrors of war, Hemingway developed a heightened respect for imposing a code of conduct in his actions in his life and became increasingly fascinated with developing characters who valued and followed the unspoken, self-imposed principles of the code. In Robert Penn Warren assessment of Hemingway's characters, he writes, "In the God-abandoned world of modernity, man can realize an ideal meaning only in so far as he can define and maintain the code."[13]

Raised a Congregationalist in Oak Park, Illinois, Hemingway was an altar boy, but his faith in God diminished through the atrocities he witnessed in war and as a journalist covering war. His most overt indictment of faith, of the idea of Divine Providence, occurs in a bizarre essay / short story sketch called "The Natural History of the Dead." In this piece, Hemingway mocks Mungo Park who, while starving in the African desert, finds faith in God by witnessing a desert flower. "Can the Being who (brought forth this flower) look with unconcern upon the situation and suffering of creatures formed after his own image?" reflects Mungo Park. In "The Natural History of the Dead," Park then finds himself guided to safety by the hand of God. But Hemingway's narrator wryly proceeds to ask, "Let us therefore see what inspiration we may derive from the dead on a battlefield."[14] The bloated, black-and-yellow bodies of the dead soldiers, the quick death from small shards of shrapnel, and the skull fragments of women who were blown to pieces in an Italian munitions factory (a gruesome spectacle Hemingway witnessed) removed any notion that the narrator or the reader could can have faith in God, in Divine Providence, in the mysterious ways of our Lord. So "in the God-abandoned world of modernity" and modern warfare, what replaces the innate human need for faith in an order outside oneself? A self-imposed code.

The interior monologue of the old man in the short story "A Clean Well-Lighted Place" captures this realization well; the narrator states, "It was all nothing and man was nothing too. It was only that and light was all it needed and a certain cleanness and order."[15] A "certain cleanness and order" can be achieved at war and after war through controlling actions that will "distinguish him from people who merely follow their random impulses and who are, by consequence, messy." The old man in "A Clean Well-Lighted Place," like many Hemingway characters, is a "man who hungers for the certainties and meaningfulness of a religious faith but cannot find in his world a ground for that faith."[16] It will take a lifetime of both living and failing to live by a self-imposed code and a panoply of fictional characters who live and fail to live by a self-imposed code for Hemingway to arrive at the "grounds for a faith" not in God but in man at his best.

But this begs another question: how does one arrive at the code principles upon which to live? Hemingway had "a great contempt for any type of solution arrived at without the testings of immediate experience."[17] Echoing the definition for the code principle "develop experiential knowledge," Robert Penn Warren argues that the answer to developing a code derives from one of the essential code principles: value what you know from experience. Hemingway has no time for people who "are ignorant. Stupid…Uninformed. Inexperienced, stupid from inexperience," as Frederic Henry says of Rinaldi.[18] Hemingway's heroic characters learn to value love by losing it, to self-assess by learning the shallowness of accepting meritless criticism and false praise from others, to speak through actions by witnessing people who would rather talk about what they have done or will do than do the thing that needs to be done. "It takes a man's life to know them and the little new that each man gets from life is very costly and the only heritage he has to leave," writes Hemingway in *Death in the Afternoon*. So the answer to how one develops a discipline of conduct lies in vigilant attention to one's actions in life and the actions of others. That is, how to live lies in living life with unrelenting, continuous self-awareness.

1

COMPLETE TASKS WELL

Maintain self-discipline and honor in completing tasks even if (especially if) this may not result in achieving the proposed end goal.

[Robert Jordan] was completely integrated now and he took a good long look at everything…As the officer came trotting now on the trail of the horses of the band he would pass twenty yards below where Robert Jordan lay. At that distance *there would be no problem.* [He] lay behind the tree, holding onto himself very carefully and delicately to keep his hands steady.[19]

    In this moment from the Spanish Civil War novel *For Whom the Bell Tolls*, Robert Jordan—the most coded of all the Hemingway heroes—prepares to hold off the enemy as best he can even though he has a broken leg. While we never get to witness Jordan completing this task well, we know that he does. When one thinks of Ernest Hemingway's heroes in his most famous texts, the ability of these characters to pour themselves into a task, to lose their self-consciousness in the completing of the task, and to strengthen their "selves" through adhering to the unspoken "rules of the game" comes to mind. Nick Adams expertly fly-fishing in "Big Two-Hearted River." Pedro Romero gracefully wearing down a bull in *The Sun Also Rises*. Santiago carefully placing his lines at specific depths and fending off the sharks as best he can in *The Old Man and the Sea*. And the moment above: Robert Jordan holding off the enemy while he lies on the pine forest with a broken leg in *For Whom the Bell Tolls*. First, let's look to the definition of the most commonly referenced Hemingway code principle: completing tasks well. It is helpful to realize that Hemingway created characters who maintain self-discipline and honor through the means by which they complete tasks, even if (especially if) this may not result in achieving the proposed end goal. In Hemingway's worldview, there is a victory even if one is ultimately unsuccessful in completing the larger task if one completes the necessary task at hand well.

SUN VALLEY STORIES: COMPLETING TASKS WELL

During Ernest Hemingway's first visits to Sun Valley, he poured himself into the task of writing *For Whom the Bell Tolls* well. In 1939, local Sun Valley Resort hunting guide and author *of Hemingway: High on the Wild*, Lloyd Arnold recalled, "The following dawn the work on (*For Whom the Bell Tolls)* continued as scheduled and it went better in the mountain cool than it had in months of heat in a hotel in Havana. (Hemingway) said he was on the rough of Chapter 13 and had worked the name Sun Valley into it. We lifted brows. How could he do it, time-wise? Hemingway grinned and replied, "'The freedom of fiction.'"[20] He wrote many chapters of *For Whom the Bell Tolls* in suite 206 of the Sun Valley Lodge and published it on October 21, 1940, completing this task well.

Scribner's sold 491,000 copies in six months. Paramount film studio offered $100,000 for the movie rights to *For Whom the Bell Tolls* shortly thereafter; this was a record amount at the time. The lead role of Robert Jordan was played by Gary Cooper, who became a lifelong friend of Hemingway and Lloyd Arnold. The beautiful, young Maria, who embodies many of the characteristics of Hemingway's new wife, Martha Gellhorn, the woman he brought to Sun Valley after his divorce from his second wife, Pauline Pfeiffer, was played by Ingrid Bergman. In the falls of 1939 and 1940, Hemingway went to Sun Valley to "hole up" and work on a big novel on the Spanish Civil War. He was focused on the task at hand, fell in love with Martha, and fell in love with the Sun Valley area.

Asked to speak to a group of boys at the Catholic church in Hailey, Idaho, in 1940, Hemingway agreed with great hesitation. Many do not know that "Hemingway was a nonfluent speaker…this includes persons with a slight hesitancy in their speech…one hallmark of the problem is for the persons to be precise and perfectionist in their habits, and very often are compulsive in their desire to be controlling."[21] While Hemingway was uncomfortable giving speeches (he did not give his Nobel Prize in Literature acceptance speech), he became obsessed about the things he could control: writing well and hunting well.

Spending his entire mornings writing well in the falls of 1939-40 in suite 206 of the Sun Valley Lodge, Hemingway was also encouraged by shooting well during his hunting adventures through south central Idaho. But as biographer Jeffery Meyers notes, "(Hemingway) insisted (on) discipline, for he could not give himself up to pleasure if he had not completed his daily work."[22] Later in life, Hemingway famously counted the number of words he wrote each day; he needed to feel a sense of professional accomplishment before he could commit to recreation with a good conscience. After completing the task of writing or editing well, Hemingway enjoyed the hunting adventures on Silver Creek, on the Little Wood River near Carey, in the fields of farms in Dietrich and Shoshone, in the Middle Fork of the Salmon, and in the Pahsimeroi Valley. Hemingway's early days in Idaho contained moments of great pleasure, of completing tasks well, and moments in which people failed to do so.

Some early hunting adventures provided moments when hunting companions did not complete tasks well. On one afternoon hunt on Silver Creek, Ernest went hunting with John and Anna Boettiger (Anna was President Franklin D. Roosevelt's daughter) and the Sun Valley resort's black Lab, "Bullet." John did not put the safety on his shotgun when he placed it in the canoe, and when he picked up the gun, he accidentally shot the hind leg of Bullet—"one of the fine Arden Labradors given to Sun Valley (Resort) by Averell Harriman."[23]

HEMINGWAY HUNTING NEAR SILVER CREEK WITH SUN VALLEY RESORT LAB, "BULLET." *Ernest Hemingway Collection. John F. Kennedy Presidential Library and Museum, Boston.*

Hemingway was furious and disgusted by the event and how easily it could have been avoided. Dorice Taylor recalls, "As always, Hemingway was enraged when a gun was handled carelessly, and the two men had to be taken back to (Sun Valley) lodge in separate cars."[24] John Boettiger failed to complete the unspoken hunting code principle of always putting the safety on an idle gun and always unloading a gun before traveling in a moving craft. Disgusted from being witness to such codeless behavior, Hemingway

> *retired to…suite (206) but Marty (Gellhorn) was having a drink on the terrace…when two shots rang out. "Good God," said Marty, "Papa has shot John Boettiger." Actually two wild geese, one badly hurt with a leg trailing, flew past the French doors (of Room 206). Hemingway had grabbed a gun and shot the cripple from inside the room.*[25]

4

Hemingway completed the task of another unknown hunter and put the goose out of its misery. Hemingway ended a regrettable hunting day by hunting well, by ending the pain of a wounded goose. Like Pedro Romero, who "wipes away" losing a fight to the insufferable Robert Cohn in *The Sun Also Rises* by wearing down a bull with grace and honor, Hemingway hoped to wipe away being witness to the unethical hunting behavior of others. He conveyed the code by his actions.

While Hemingway was to become one of the famous faces associated with Sun Valley Resort and many photos show him hunting with Gary Cooper and dining with Ingrid Bergman and Marlene Dietrich, he preferred to spend his time with real Idahoans. Local hunting guides Bud Purdy, Taylor Williams, and Lloyd Arnold were his favorite companions on his hunting adventures, for beyond enjoying their company, he admired their hunting skills, their knowledge of where the good hunting was, and their ability to live by an unspoken hunting code. In many of Hemingway's stories and novels, his characters surround themselves with mentors, with others who embody and exhibit the other principles of the code, but especially with those who have experiential knowledge, self-assess, and complete tasks well. And many characters in the stories and novels do not suffer fools well and detest being witness to codeless behavior. Valuing the brotherhood of coded companions in war, on a hunt, and in life emerges as a central principle in the Hemingway code.

Local hunting guide Taylor Williams became a lifelong friend of Hemingway, and they shared many hunts together at Silver Creek and in the Frank Church Wilderness, which was labeled a primitive area in the 1940s when Hemingway hunted there. In addition, Hemingway invited Taylor Williams to fish for marlin in Key West and Cuba from the *Pilar*—Hemingway's fishing boat named after his brave and feisty female character in *For Whom the Bell Tolls*. Loyal to his hunting guide and close friend, Hemingway defended Taylor Williams when he came under criticism as a hunting and fishing guide who demanded his clients complete tasks well. On one guided fishing trip with Colonel Robert Guggenheim, the colonel wasn't catching trout. Taylor Williams said, "Look how much line you have out...if you would pay attention to what

I tell you and not frighten the fish away with all that sloppy casting, you might get something."[26] This did not sit with well with the colonel. He turned to his wife, Polly, and asked her to give it a try. A novice fisherman, she listened to Williams's advice, kept a short amount of line out, made tight, taut loops with her fly casting, and caught "a sizeable trout on her first try. Taylor did not say another word" but "the story made the rounds of Sun Valley and delighted everyone."[27] Hemingway loved this story and, moreover, respected Taylor Williams for demanding that his clients learn the code of how to fish well.

But Taylor Williams's unrelenting drive to teach his clients how to behave in the outdoors came under fire by Union Pacific President George Ashby. Dorice Taylor recounts, "Union Pacific President Ashby, no sportsman, had several run-ins with Taylor Williams and demoted him from chief guide (at the Sun Valley Resort)."[28] On one hunt, "Ashby was caught riding on the fenders of a car and shooting doves on the go, strictly illegal…Taylor tried to speak to Ashby about it…but it did not go down with the little president." In *Sun Valley Stories*, Dorice Taylor continues:

> *Taylor (Williams) was assigned to take Ashby and a group of business executives pheasant shooting. The men got out of the car and started off in all directions. Taylor got back in the car and rolled up all the windows. Ashby, enraged, came back and asked what was up. Taylor replied that unless the party let him place them properly, he wasn't going to get out and risk his neck in that crossfire. That did it.*[29]

Hemingway resented Taylor Williams's demotion for following the proper way of conducting a dove hunt and a pheasant hunt. "From then on, Hemingway always stayed in Ketchum…and any news release had to be datelined Ketchum, and not Sun Valley."[30] Unwilling to share his name with Sun Valley Resort after its mistreatment of Taylor Williams for completing tasks well as a hunting guide, Hemingway made an interesting distinction between Sun Valley Resort and Ketchum, Idaho. This distinction still exists today. Locals still refer to their hometown as

Ketchum, while Sun Valley is associated with tourists and second homeowners, broadly speaking. But to hail from Ketchum, as Hemingway ensured that his correspondence indicated, is to claim a kinship with locals, with those who know where the hunting and fishing are good and how to conduct themselves on an outdoor adventure.

On October 28, 1939 (one month into Hemingway's first visit to Sun Valley), Gene Van Guilder (publicist of Sun Valley Resort), Lloyd Arnold (local hunting guide and photographer), and a young Sun Valley staff member, Dave Benner, went hunting in a canoe on the Snake River. Hemingway once told Lloyd Arnold about hunting with a canoe, "If you know what you are doing, (it is the best)…so open and handy."[31] Hemingway did not participate in this hunt, but the tragic events haunted him. With Van Guilder seated in the bow of the canoe, the apprentice guide, Dave Benner, in the middle, and Lloyd Arnold in the stern, Van Guilder noticed some small ducks working near the water. They swooped and careened off the sunlit Snake River to disappear over a patch of tulles. Van Guilder thought they were teal—a fast-moving, small-size duck, prized for both its beauty and its taste. They suddenly reappeared from behind the tulles, and they proved to be buffleheads—diver ducks about the same size of teal but far from the same taste. Van Guilder stood up in the bow of the canoe to take a shot. Bang. Buffleheads fall to the water. When Van Guilder recoiled from his shot, he crouched to grab the right gunwale. This rocked the canoe, and Van Guilder's sudden movement to steady himself on the gunwale surprised the young Sun Valley staffer, who was seated in the middle of the canoe. Bang. "Six birds down, but two were winged only and under they went," writes Lloyd Arnold in *Hemingway: High on the Wild*.[32] Dave Benner, who was seated in the middle of the canoe, had the fast-moving ducks lined up before Gene's recovery movement from rocking the canoe. The staffer's shot pierced Van Guilder in the back below the right shoulder blade, went through his right lung, and exited from the front part of his chest. Lloyd Arnold quickly paddled to the shores of the Snake River and closed the entry and exit wounds on Van Guilder's chest and back, but Gene Van Guilder died in half an hour. Sun Valley

FROM LEFT TO RIGHT, TOM GOODING, ERNEST HEMINGWAY, GENE VAN GUILDER, AND TAYLOR WILLIAMS AFTER A PHEASANT HUNT NEAR DIETRICH, IDAHO. *The Community Library, Ketchum, Idaho.*

Resort's publicist and quick friend of Ernest Hemingway, Gene Van Guilder was thirty-four years old.

Hemingway was devastated by the news. Hemingway had seen many unnecessary deaths caused by codeless behavior in World War I while covering the Greco-Turkish War in 1922 as a journalist and during the Spanish Civil War in the mid to late 1930s, and Gene's easily preventable, unnecessary death deeply disturbed him.

Both Gene Van Guilder's and the young Sun Valley staffer's inability to follow the unspoken code of hunting ethics and inability to complete tasks well led to the unnecessary and tragic death of the man who brought Ernest Hemingway to Sun Valley. As Lloyd Arnold puts it, "There's an old unspoken rule about shooting from a boat: Unless in a solidly anchored and specialized craft, it's a one man show—period. Weapons other than his are put aside."[33] These unspoken code principles are learned from experience. Those who follow the unwritten code add to the value of the hunting experience; those who do not ruin it.

However, most moments with "the family" of hunting companions were full of success from completing tasks well. In the fall of 1941, Hemingway enjoyed one of his finest moments while hunting in Idaho. In the Pahsimeroi Mountains, near Challis, Idaho, Hemingway and Sun Valley hunting guides Lloyd Arnold and Taylor Williams as well as Hemingway's three sons, Jack, Patrick, and Gregory, were tracking pronghorn. Lloyd Arnold was hoping to capture some photos of the hunt, but "after Arnold's metal lens cast a reflection of the sun, the pronghorn ran. Arnold motioned for Hemingway to make his move and he did, cursing as he passed Arnold some 20 yards, before halting, raising his rifle and firing a single shot cleanly into the shoulder of a large buck. Hemingway stood proudly and then asked Arnold how far away he was when he shot. Arnold measured the distance at 275 yards. According to Arnold, Hemingway said, 'I've made fair shots in my time but this (out) ranks them all.'"[34] This remarkable hunting feat manifested in the only story Hemingway published about Idaho; he called it "The Shot," and it was published in *True* magazine in 1951. "He always prided himself on being a very good rifle shot," Patrick Hemingway said. Completing tasks well with a group of like-minded, coded individuals proved edifying to Hemingway, and this is reflected in *For Whom the Bell Tolls* in which the protagonist Robert Jordan has one shot at blowing the bridge to delay the advance of Franco's troops. With diminished detonation capability (for Pablo stole and dumped some of the dynamite and detonators in the ravine), Robert Jordan successfully blows the bridge but not without the loss of his mentor and code follower Anselmo. The reflection of Lloyd Arnold's camera lens that made the pronghorn spook made "the shot" more difficult on the Pahsimeroi mountain side and also made the success of the shot all the more gratifying. Overcoming adversity, completing the task as well as one can, and surrounding oneself with a conclave of coded people who appreciate the difficulty of the task at hand made this hunt memorable.

NOVELS AND SHORT STORIES: COMPLETING TASKS WELL

As Hemingway wrote in "Big Two-Hearted River," the final story in *In Our Time*, "unless they are of your party," fishing rivers with others can ruin the experience. In that short story, he was referring to the memory of seeing dead trout that were handled by fishermen who did not wet their hands and, thereby, unknowingly removed the trout's protective layer that wards off disease.

Although "Big Two-Hearted River" is often anthologized and taught to students as a stand-alone short story, it is best understood in the context in which it was originally written. Clearly his most innovative and stylistically radical text, *In Our Time* depicts pre-WWI codeless behavior, codeless behavior during the war, and post-WWI codeless behavior. This is why the moments in "Big Two-Hearted River" in which Nick commits himself to a self-imposed way of fishing are so important to understanding Nick at the end of the short story collection. It is Nick's method of imposing order on a chaotic, seemingly amoral world. Nick Adams witnessed codeless behavior in his Uncle George and his father before the war, in the horrific, excessive, merciless violence Nick witnessed toward others and experienced himself during W.W.I., and in the unspeakable atrocities Nick witnessed in the Greco-Turkish War after W.W.I. and in post war America. Suffice it to say that Nick, who is easily viewed as a young Hemingway, hoped to control what he could control in his own immediate world after the war. In the short story "Big Two Two-Hearted River," this means that Nick Adams has an opportunity to strengthen his sense of self by fishing well, causing no unnecessary harm to the trout, and gaining an appreciation for the positive affirmations that stem from living by an unspoken commitment to completing tasks well.

After getting off the train in northern Michigan, a place young Hemingway fished both in his life and wrote about in the opening story, "Indian Camp," of *In Our Time*, Nick Adams sees that the land has been burned out by a fire that has spread from the town of Seney. Dismayed by the influence of this man-made fire (and the realization that the codelessness of man prevails at home after the war), he sets out to backpack, camp, and fish. After enjoying being occupied by hiking, making his camp, cooking his dinner, and losing himself in the process of completing tasks well, the river presents itself, as nature often does in the works of Ernest Hemingway, as an arena upon which he can project his own self-imposed moral code. The trout strikes his skewered grasshopper, and then in the process of landing the trout, Nick Adams wets his hand in the current before he handles the trout to release it. Hemingway writes, "The rod under his right arm, Nick stopped, dipping his right hand into the current. He held the trout, never still, with his moist right hand, while he unhooked the barb from his mouth, then dropped him back into the stream"[35] For readers unfamiliar with the "catch and release" that is so pervasive in the modern fly-fisher (and practiced religiously by Hemingway's first son, Jack "Bumby" Hemingway, who lived and fly-fished in Ketchum, Idaho), the idea of releasing trout back into the river may seem pointless or contradictory to the goal of fishing. While Nick does keep a few trout for dinner in the story, it is helpful to remember that Nick has seen excessive violence during the war and has committed himself to causing no unneeded harm to innocents. The "dipping (of) his right hand into the current" allows Nick to keep the protective mucus membrane of the trout intact, a membrane that wards off disease. Psychologically damaged from the war, Nick Adams respects the need to keep oneself intact and admires that trout have a protective layer to keep disease at bay. He honors the trout by releasing them with the protective layer of mucus intact and is encouraged by the idea that the trout will be able to ward off disease in the future.

In another story in *In Our Time*, Hemingway leaves the protagonist Nick Adams and tells us a story about Krebs—a soldier who has returned from World War I and who also suffers from PTSD. Unable to enter into relationships with women, pray, or even love anything at all, including his mother, Krebs spends most days on the porch of his family's home pouring over maps from the war. When asked to tell his stories about the war, he finds that they fall flat because they were not courageous enough. He loathes himself for lying about the war and inventing stories just to please others. (Hemingway also did this in his hometown of Oak Park, Illinois, after he returned from the war.) Recalling moments at war when "he had been able to make himself feel cool and clear inside himself…the times so long back when he had done the one thing for a man to do, easily and naturally, when he might have done something else," Krebs feels "all the old feeling."[36] But this is a memory, and the story connected to the moment in which he behaved well at war and "had done the one thing for a man to do, easily and naturally," does not impress others and he stops telling it. As Nick's mind is diffused into the consciousness of Krebs, the reader of *In Our Time* concludes "that many must have" felt the same way. For Krebs and Nick, it is important to the development of the self to be able to complete tasks well and "make (themselves) feel cool and clear inside." While Krebs wallows in despair and is unable to renew this feeling, Nick is able to fish well and do the things he needs to do in order to recapture his positive sense of self.

In the fascinating short story "The Short Happy Life of Francis Macomber," first published in *Cosmopolitan* magazine in 1936 (three years prior to Hemingway's first visit to Sun Valley), Francis is an uncoded hunter who does not complete tasks well. Hemingway's fictional account of a codeless hunter was prescient. Hunting a lion with the guide Wilson, Francis takes a bad shot and wounds the lion in its belly. Francis was unable to hit the lion in the head and kill it promptly and properly. Hemingway writes:

> *Macomber stepped out of the curved opening at the side of the front seat, onto the step and down onto the ground. The lion still stood looking majestically and coolly toward this object that his eyes only showed in silhouette, bulking like some super rhino. There was no man smell carried toward his and he watched the object, moving his great head a little from side to side. Then watching the object, not afraid, but hesitating before going down the bank to drink with such a thing opposite him, he saw a man figure detach itself from it and he turned his heavy head and swung away toward the cover for the trees as he heard a cracking crash and felt the slam of a .30-06*

220-grain solid bullet that bit his flank and ripped in sudden hot scalding nausea through his stomach. He trotted, heavy, big-footed, swinging wounded full-bellied, through the trees toward the tall grass and cover, and the crash came again to go past him ripping the air apart. Then it crashed again and he felt the blow as it hit his lower ribs and ripped on through, blood sudden hot and frothy in his mouth, and he galloped toward the high grass where he could crouch and not be seen and make them bring the crashing thing close enough so he could make a rush and get the man that held it.

Macomber had not thought how the lion felt as he got out of the car…He raised the rifle, sighted on the junction of the lion's head and shoulders and pulled the trigger. Nothing happened though he pulled until he thought his finger would break. Then he knew he had the safety on and as he lowered the rifle to move the safety… Macomber fired, he heard a whunk that meant that the bullet was home; but the lion kept on going. Macomber shot again and everyone saw the bullet throw a spout of dirt beyond the trotting lion.

"I hit him," Macomber said. "I hit him twice."

"You gut-shot him and you hit him somewhere forward," Wilson said without enthusiasm. The gun-bearers looked very grave. They were silent now.[37]

(my italics)

As Hemingway cringed at the sight of John Boettiger shooting the leg off the Sun Valley Resort Lab "Bullet" on Silver Creek, Hemingway imagines Wilson and the gun bearers cringing at Francis's poor shooting of the lion and the prospect of having to go in and shoot the lion in the bush. "Macomber had not thought how the lion felt as he got out of the car," Hemingway writes. An inability to complete tasks well in this moment stemmed from an inability to empathize with one's prey. As the story continues, hunting guide Wilson has to finish off the lion for Francis who not only does not hunt well; he does not handle his marriage well either. For readers of Hemingway, Francis Macomber is a man without a code for most of his life. He is too insecure to break off his relationship with his wife after their love has faded. She is unfaithful to him, and he is a poor hunter who does not possess the skill to kill the lion instantly and respect his prey enough to kill it after he shoots it in the gut. Francis only lives well *for a moment* by completing the task of hunting water buffalo that are charging him at the end of the story. In this moment, Francis does not cower but stands in the charging lane of the buffalo and shoots one successfully in the head. However, his wife, Margot Macomber, has no faith that her husband will shoot the buffalo successfully and aims her gun at the charging buffalo. She misfires and hits her husband in the back of the head and kills him instantly. Or, as some critics have it, she kills him intentionally for Francis is now asserting himself and will likely leave her. Francis only lived well in this brief moment of shooting the buffalo, and this was his "short life." Francis's codeless shooting and Margot's "accidental" shooting of Francis predates the tragic, accidental death of Gene Van Guilder. Three months into his first visit to Sun Valley, Hemingway must have recalled his short story "The Short Happy Life of Francis Macomber" in the moments after hearing of Gene's tragic death on the Snake River.

In one of the greatest fishing stories of all time *The Old Man and the Sea*, Ernest Hemingway creates the quintessential Hemingway coded character in Santiago. Having gone eighty-four days without a marlin, Santiago resolves to fish again way out beyond sight of the coast of Cuba. Without going into the negative outcomes of "going out too far" alone, it is helpful to our purposes to look to how Santiago fishes his lines well at the "exact depth" to induce a successful take. An aficionado of expert marlin fishing and expert marlin fisherman himself, Hemingway writes:

> *Each line, as thick around as a big pencil, was looped onto a green-sapped stick so that any pull or touch on the bait would make the stick*

> *dip and each line had two forty-fathom coils which could be made fast to the other spare coils so that, if it were necessary, a fish could take out over three hundred fathoms of line. Now the man watched the dip of the three sticks over the side of the skiff and rowed gently to keep the lines straight up and down and at their proper depths...He looked down into the water and watched the lines that went straight down into the dark of the water. He kept them straighter than anyone did, so that at each level in the darkness of the stream there would be a bait waiting exactly where he wished it to be for any fish that swam there. Others let them drift with the current and sometimes they were at sixty fathoms when the fishermen thought they were at a hundred. But, he thought, I keep them with precision. Only I have no luck any more. But who knows? Maybe today. Every day is a new day. It is better to be lucky. But I would rather be exact. Then when luck comes you are ready.*[38]

It is fortuitous to be randomly lucky, but being exact allows one to be ready when luck comes and allows one to take some pride in the purposeful luck or "pluck." It is the care with which Santiago takes in completing the task of setting his baited lines well that allows him to transcend luck into pluck. That is, by being precise in the depths with which he fished, he perseveres beyond his unlucky eighty-four days and prepares well so that "when luck comes (he is) ready." His skillful fishing is rewarded, and unlike the codeless Francis Macomber in the first lion hunt and the uncoded fly fishermen in "Big Two-Hearted River," Santiago empathizes with the marlin he so skillfully hooks and lands. Santiago wants a successful and honorable taking of this marlin—a fish he identifies with as his brother.

But it is important to separate the fictionalized coded heroes from the life of Ernest Hemingway. It is interesting that the man who created common code principles that his fictionalized heroes follow fell short of following them in his own life. In particular, while Santiago is exact in his placement of the bait, calm in his setting of the hook, and tireless in his beating of the sharks when they devour the marlin strapped to the skiff, Hemingway did not follow Santiago's lead in his own fishing for tuna and marlin. While Hemingway was a phenomenally talented deep-sea fisherman, he did not humbly and futilely attempt to ward off sharks as Santiago does when they attack: he instead machine guns them. Author John Dos Passos recounts a tuna- and marlin-fishing excursion with Hemingway:

> *The fish are huge—a thousand pound tuna and 800 pound sharks…we had the tuna on the line for eight hours—Ernest finally brought him up…five sharks rushed at once…shearing off thirty pounds at a bite…Ernest shoots them with a machine gun… the bullets ripping through them…the sharks thrashing the blood and foam.*[39]

A stark contrast from Santiago warding off the sharks with a piece of wood. No acceptance of the loss of the tuna. No calm, methodical resistance to the sharks—a predator species that is merely attacking what appears to be a wounded fish. No victory in defeat by maintaining one's dignity in the process of resistance. Just the orgasmic "rrrrrr" of the machine gun ripping through the sandpaper skin of the sharks. But this is why fiction is helpful: it can create better versions of ourselves so that we have models for how to improve.

In *The Sun Also Rises*—a novel full of codeless behavior—Pedro Romero, a young version of Santiago, emerges as a coded hero in both relationships and bullfighting. Pedro has an admirable ability to complete tasks well in both arenas. Jake Barnes, the protagonist of *The Sun Also Rises*, is an "aficionado" of bullfighting, and when he takes Brett Ashley to a bullfight, he wants her to appreciate the artistry in the matador Pedro Romero. To be an aficionado, one must be able to discern the actions of experts from those of amateurs, or worse, of posers. Directing Brett to admire the expertise of Romero (a future lover of Brett's), Hemingway writes:

I sat beside Brett and explained to Brett what it was all about. I told her about watching the bull, not the horse, when the bulls charged the picadors, and got her to watching the picador place the point of his pic so that she saw what it was all about, so that it became more something that was going on with a definite end, and less of a spectacle with unexplained horrors. I had her watch how Romero took the bull away from a fallen horse with his cape, and how he held him with the cape and turned him, smoothly and suavely, never wasting the bull. She saw how Romero avoided every brusque movement and saved his bulls for the last when he wanted them, not winded and discomposed but smoothly worn down. She saw how close Romero always worked to the bull, and I pointed out to her the tricks the other bull-fighters used to make it look as though they were working closely. She saw why she liked Romero's cape-work and why she did not like the others. Romero never made any contortions, always it was straight and pure and natural in line. The others twisted themselves like corkscrews, their elbows raised, and leaned against the flanks of the bull after his horns had passed, to give a faked look of danger. Afterward, all that was faked turned bad and gave an unpleasant feeling. Romero's bullfighting gave real emotion, because he kept the absolute purity of line in his movements and always quietly and calmly let the horns pass him close each time. He did not have to emphasize their closeness. Brett saw how something that was beautiful done close to the bull was ridiculous if it were done a little way off…Romero had the old thing, the holding of his purity of line through the maximum of exposure, while he dominated the bull by making him realize he was unattainable, while he prepared him for the killing.[40]

Unlike Francis Macomber, who could not empathize with how the lion felt, Pedro does not want to "waste the bull" and does not cause it to be "winded and discomposed." Pedro wants to dominate the bull with the bull's capacities and honor and dignity intact. This completing of the task of killing the bull well strengthens Pedro after he is beaten up by

Robert Cohn over the love triangle between Cohn, Pedro, and Lady Brett Ashley. Moreover, Jake Barnes helps Brett appreciate the "maximum of exposure" and "purity of line" Pedro inhabits when entering "into the terrain of the bull" during the fight. There is grave risk to Pedro's life in doing so, and he honors the life and death endeavor of bullfighting by completing the task well. To do less would dishonor the bull and the art of bullfighting. With Jake as her guide, Brett perceives and comprehends this task completed well by Pedro and values it.

While there are more moments of codeless bullfighting than coded ones in the vignette "chapters" of Hemingway's innovative short story collection *In Our Time* (1925), Hemingway did share a moment in which a matador becomes one with the bull in the final moment of the bull's demise. It is important to recall that the bullfighting vignettes occur at the end of this short story collection after the protagonist Nick Adams has been shot in the spine and watched his friend Rinaldi take his last breath in a battle with the Austrians. Readers can presume that Nick is bumming around Europe and going to bullfights in Spain after his injury and release from his duties assisting the Italians in WWI. You will recall that seventeen-year-old Hemingway received hundreds of pieces of shrapnel in his leg while assisting the Italians as an ambulance driver and handing out chocolates and cigarettes to wounded Italian soldiers in WWI. Hemingway also delayed his return to the States after the war. The many vignettes of bullfighting in which the matador is too drunk to stick the bull well or lacks the skill to defeat the bull with honor ask the reader to ponder what Nick must be thinking about the unnecessary violence during the bullfights as the crowd cheers the "bad sticking." Like the dead trout in the river in Upper Michigan from the codeless fisherman and the poor hunting of Francis Macomber, the mistreatment of the bulls reminds Nick of the unnecessary, pointless, unheroic violence he witnessed during the war. However, there is a moment of exemplary bullfighting akin to Pedro Romero's in the final vignettes in *In Our Time*. In Chapter XII, Hemingway writes:

When he started to kill it was all in the same rush. The bull looking at him straight in front, hating. He drew out the sword from the folds of the muleta and sighted with the same movement and called to the bull, Toro! Toro! and the bull charged and Villalta charged and just for a moment they became one. Villalta became one with the bull and then it was over. Villalta standing straight and the red hilt of the sword sticking out dully between the bull's shoulders. Villalta, his hand up at the crowd and the bull roaring blood, looking straight at Villalta and his legs caving.[41]

Like Brett who learns to be an aficionado of Pedro's matador skills, Nick admires this matador's ability to kill this bull humanely and perfectly, becoming one with and matching the bull's intensity. As Hemingway biographer Jeffery Meyers notes, Hemingway was "drawn to the ritual that emphasized strict rules, extreme compression, skillful technique, pagan drama, and high courage."[42] The final moment in which the matador approaches the wounded bull and finishes the bull off by penetrating the sword between the shoulders and into the bull's heart is a "ritual" of "Pagan drama" that requires efficient, "compressed" movements and "high courage" and "skill."

When Bud Purdy watched Hemingway flush three mallards on the Little Wood River in Central Idaho, swing the shotgun through the flared ducks, and "bang, bang, bang," hit each duck with the three pulls of his gun, Bud was an aficionado of Hemingway's expert shooting. As Brett and Jake admire the expertise of Pedro Romero's "purity of line through the maximum of exposure, while (Pedro) dominated the bull by making him realize he was unattainable, while he prepared him for the killing," both Bud and Hemingway were strengthened by their appreciation of a jump shoot well done after Hemingway had a morning of productive writing of *For Whom the Bell Tolls*. In the early years of Hemingway's autumn stays in Sun Valley, he combined writing well, shooting well, and loving well. He felt "unattainable" in those early years in Sun Valley and returned throughout his life to central Idaho to recapture these feelings of "dominance."

While Hemingway was coming off of a failed marriage to his second wife, Pauline, in 1939 during his first visit to Sun Valley, Pedro Romero in *The Sun Also Rises* was coming off his failure to defeat Robert Cohn—one of Brett's many lovers—before he fought a bull that afternoon. While Cohn poses no threat to Romero's relationship with Brett Ashley, Cohn does prove a threat to Romero physically, for Cohn was a championship boxer in his undergraduate days at Princeton University. After discovering that Romero was sleeping with Brett, Cohn challenges Romero to a fight and pummels Romero. That afternoon, Brett and Jake watch Romero regain his strength and sense of self by brilliantly wearing down a bull. After witnessing Romero complete the task of wearing down the bull well, Brett remarks, "He's wiped out that damned Cohn."[43] In his first trips to Sun Valley, Hemingway wiped out the ugliness of the ongoing divorce to Pauline by disciplining himself in his writing of *For Whom the Bell Tolls*, gaining financial independence in the publishing of this novel, dedicating himself to Martha Gellhorn, and hunting well with local guides. Similarly, Romero restored his sense of self, his self-confidence, and his pride by committing himself to the task at hand with great attention and skill. Lifelong friend and Sun Valley local Tillie Arnold recalled that Hemingway's "primary interest in coming to Sun Valley was to hole up and work on his book without interruptions. His top priority was writing."[44] Referring to the Sun Valley Lodge room 206, a room he was given in exchange for Sun Valley Resort's right to use Hemingway's image in publications and advertisements for the resort, Hemingway remarked, "This is a pretty fancy wigwam, don't you think?...I've never had it so good in the West, but don't tell anyone I'm flat-ass broke."[45] Hemingway needed to write a good book and needed to be disciplined about writing it. His commitment to complete the task of writing well in Sun Valley strengthened him and "wiped out" the bad feelings associated with losing Pauline, losing access to her wealth, and the bad reviews of *Death in the Afternoon*, *To Have and to Have Not*, and *Green Hills of Africa* published in the 1930s.

In *A Farewell to Arms*, we encounter "an initiate" in Frederic's closest friend, Rinaldi—an accomplished surgeon who loses himself in his work yet still is uninitiated about finding faith in love since he spends his nights after surgery in the Villa Rosa brothel. Rinaldi has "the discipline of his profession"; this "discipline seems to be…technical, the style of the artist or the form of the athlete or the bullfighter."[46] "I am only happy when I am working," remarks Rinaldi in a phrase Hemingway himself would repeat about the discipline of writing. There is an edifying feeling in completing tasks well that runs an order through the chaos of life and keeps the randomness of violence, loss, and the consequent despair at bay. But Rinaldi is an incomplete code hero because he does not find faith in love. One swallow does not make a summer, as Aristotle informs us when he expresses that happiness can only be achieved by committing to many virtues over a lifetime. In Hemingway's fiction and life, one code principle does not mean one is a hero. The code principles are mutually enhancing and must be followed consistently over time.

In the best-selling novel *For Whom the Bell Tolls*, Hemingway creates Robert Jordan, a University of Montana professor of Spanish who joins a group of Republican guerilla fighters in the mountains of northern Spain in their resistance to Franco's troops and the Nazis. He joins the Republicans, who fight for democracy, religious freedom, separation of church and state, and individual liberty. Like Santiago, Pedro, Rinaldi, and Frederic, Robert Jordan is strengthened by completing tasks well as he assists the Republican effort in its, of course, failed attempt to in the war. It is the process of blowing the bridge to prevent the enemy from advancing that focuses Cohn's attention, and it is the doing of it well that allows him to embrace the present and not think of the future successes or failures of the overall resistance. In preparation for the task of blowing the bridge, Robert Jordan meets Pilar, a half gypsy, and she anticipates Robert's imminent death in a palm reading. Hemingway writes:

> "What did you see in it?" Robert Jordan asked her. "I don't believe in it. You won't scare me."
>
> "Nothing," she told him. "I saw nothing in it."

"Yes you did. I am only curious. I do not believe in such things."

"In what do you believe?"

"In many things but not in that."

"In what?"

"In my work."[47]

You will recall that Hemingway wrote chapters of this novel in Sun Valley; the code principle of completing tasks well was certainly on his mind and informed this work. Jordan believes in his work of blowing the bridge and helping the Spanish defend the liberties so cherished in the US. Exhibiting the Hemingway concept of "negation of apprehension"—the ability to ignore the future consequences to oneself—so necessary for soldiers and bullfighters to complete their tasks well, Robert Jordan ruminates, "What if they were killed tomorrow? What did it matter as long as they did the bridge properly? That was all they had to do tomorrow."[48] Giving readers an insight into Robert Jordan's mind during the preparation of dynamiting the bridge, Hemingway writes, "Now as he worked, placing, bracing, wedging, lashing tight with wire, thinking only of demolition, working fast and skillfully as a surgeon works…Finishing wiring the grenades down, he no longer heard the firing from up the road. Suddenly he was working only with the noise of the stream."[49] Robert Jordan works quickly and skillfully to complete his job well and ignores the firing up the road and its potential future consequences. After the successful bridge blowing, Jordan reflects, "You did the thing there was to do and knew that you were right. You learned the dry-mouthed, fear-purged, purging ecstasy of battle and you fought that summer and that fall for all the poor in the world, against all tyranny, for all the things that you believed and for the new world you had been educated into."[50] He takes great risk to his own life because he is committed to the Republican cause and his self-imposed code of completing tasks well. In doing so, he knows there is still use left in him.

Even at the end of the novel when Robert Jordan is left behind with his broken leg from the horse that falls on him and is hunted down by the ruthless and codeless Lieutenant (Lt.) Berrendo, Jordan believes he can still complete the task of resistance well and die with himself still intact. Lying on the ground in immense pain and steeling himself for the task of shooting the oncoming enemy, Robert Jordan thinks, "…there is something you can do yet. As long as you know what it is you have to do it…*And if you wait and hold them up even a little while or just get the officer that may make all the difference. One thing done well can make—*"[51] (my italics). One thing done well can make all the difference—all the difference in one's sense of self, in one's ability to live up to the unspoken code of conduct in life. In this moment, Robert Jordan realizes that, even though he will undoubtedly die, if he shoots the officers when they come, he can still assist the cause and help his friends and his lover, Maria, escape. Readers are left to fill in the action at the end of the novel, but we can infer that he resists the onslaught well and dies a coded man. Pedro, Santiago, Nick, and Robert Jordan are all strengthened by committing to the task at hand, embodying the principle of "negation of apprehension" of the future, and serve as our coded heroes for their actions. Chapters of Hemingway's *For Whom the Bell Tolls*—a novel that develops all of the mutually enhancing code principles in Robert Jordan (the only character to exhibit nearly all of the code principles)—were completed well in the mountains of Idaho when Hemingway so desperately needed to do so.

2
Value Mentors and Community

Learn from and maintain faith in others who embody and exhibit the other principles of the code.

Sun Valley Stories: Valuing Mentors and Community

To develop any skill, to develop experiential knowledge, to attain a level of expertise worthy of being appreciated by aficionados, Ernest Hemingway knew the value of surrounding himself with mentors and a community of like-minded individuals. Our second code principle—"value mentors and community"—is best defined as developing and maintaining faith in others who embody and exhibit principles of the code. And it is best exhibited by "the family" of hunting guides and friends he developed during his time in central Idaho.

Hemingway had literary mentors: *Kansas City Star* reporters and their style guide; Stephen Crane and Joseph Conrad (through his readings); and Ezra Pound, F. Scott Fitzgerald, and Gertrude Stein (through literary relationships). He found a literary mentor in Stephen Crane, who depicted the American Civil War without having witnessed a single battle. Similarly, while Hemingway did experience WWI as an ambulance driver for the Italian Red Cross, he did not witness the retreat from Caporetto that he so accurately captures in *A Farewell to Arms*.

He had mentors in every endeavor in which he became an expert. He learned to be an aficionado of war from his grandfather who was shot in the leg during the American Civil War, of "woodcraft, trout fishing, and wing shooting from his father, of journalism from Kansas City Star staff, of editing from (Ezra) Pound," of bullfighting from matador

Carmen Ordonez, and of big game hunting from African hunting guide Philip Percival.

But in his early years growing up in Oak Park, IL, Hemingway was surrounded by four sisters and was forced to wear dresses by his mother until he was 12.[52] While this was common in late nineteenth century and early twentieth century, some have argued that this forced wearing of dresses sparked his lifelong obsession with masculinity and his desire for strong male mentors. Hemingway biographer Jeffery Meyer also notes that "Hemingway taught his friends, wives and children to fish and shoot; Jack became a superb fly fisherman, Patrick a big game hunter in Africa, and Gregory a champion wing shot."[53] Hemingway valued mentors and became one to his sons and others.

ERNEST IN OAK PARK, ILLINOIS, CIRCA 1901. *Ernest Hemingway Collection. John F. Kennedy Presidential Library and Museum, Boston.*

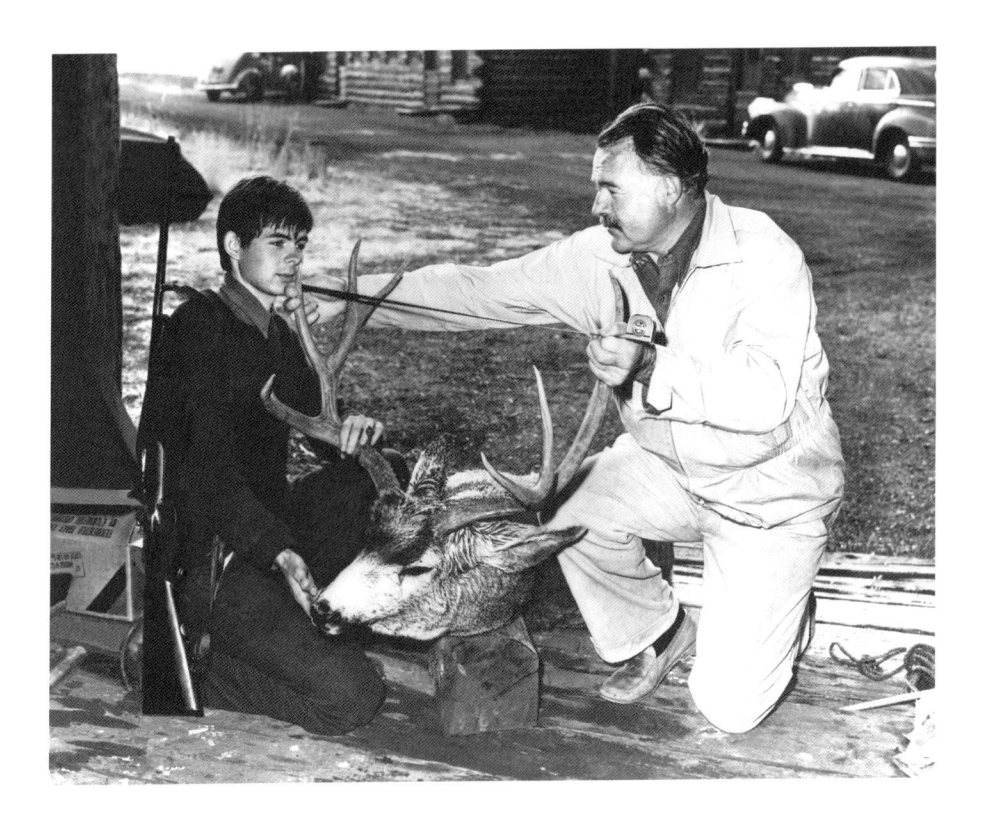

HEMINGWAY AND SON PATRICK WITH PATRICK'S DEER HARVESTED IN THE WOOD RIVER VALLEY. *The Community Library, Ketchum, Idaho.*

Hemingway also created imaginative mentors in his fiction: Manolin's mentor is Santiago in *The Old Man and the Sea*, Robert Jordan's mentor is Anselmo in *For Whom the Bell Tolls*, Frederic Henry's mentors are Count Greffi and the priest in *A Farewell to Arms*, and Francis Macomber's mentor is Robert Wilson in "The Short Happy Life of Francis Macomber." And Hemingway had hunting and fishing mentors in central Idaho—Bud Purdy, Lloyd Arnold, and Taylor Williams— and "his family" of friends in the community of Sun Valley. Whether it was writing, war, love, or hunting/fishing, Hemingway valued the influence and advice of experts.

During all of his visits to Sun Valley, Hemingway appreciated the influence of the local hunting guides on his hunting and knowledge of the wildlife in the Wood River Valley, Pahsimeroi Valley, and Middle Fork of the Salmon River. In the foreword to Lloyd Arnold's *Hemingway: High on the Wild*, Jack Hemingway (Ernest Hemingway's first son) writes on March 21, 1968, "(Lloyd Arnold) was a good and true friend of Papa's over the span of 22 years…and was permanently a part of Hemingway's life in Idaho…he has a well-founded understanding of the elements which go to make a sportsman as well as a deep love and appreciation for a sportsman's country."[54] Jack continued his reflection on the community of mentors his Dad experienced in central Idaho by writing, "I am convinced that one of the principal charms of Sun Valley, Idaho that kept my father returning at every opportunity was the warmth of the welcome and the wonderful coterie of kindred spirits he found there."[55] Robert Frost famously stated in a "talk" that all he was ever looking for in his life and in readers of his poems were "kindred spirits." (Frost referred to his poetry readings as "talks" because he rarely read from his poems but recited them from memory and interspersed his "saying of the poems" with off-the-cuff commentary.) The "kindred spirits" Hemingway found in the hunting guides, their wives, and locals in Sun Valley were always referred to as "the family." First son Jack Hemingway continues, "A lot of things appealed to my Dad about Idaho. He liked westerners because no one treated him like a celebrity. Westerners don't kiss ass…He liked it because he could work all morning, yet get out into the field and hunt…It was also a family thing with him…When he wrote letters to me, he referred to his friends like they were family members."[56] Famous from his successful novels and film adaptations of *A Farewell to Arms* and *The Sun Also Rises*, Hemingway was a celebrity and a known iconic image in 1939, and this was precisely the reason Sun Valley Resort's Steve Hannagan and Gene Van Guilder recruited Hemingway to stay for free at the resort in exchange for using images of Hemingway hunting and fishing on the resort's promotional posters and brochures. Today, Sun Valley continues the tradition of attracting celebrities with Tom Hanks, Arnold Schwarzenegger, Bruce Willis, and Demi Moore as homeowners who appreciate that the locals let them enjoy all of the amenities of the mountain resort without being mobbed by fans.

In the falls of 1939 and 1940, Hemingway cherished the loving, supportive feeling of friends and hunting companions in Idaho, because he rarely felt this during his upbringing in Oak Park and because he had recently fragmented his family during the divorce with first wife, Hadley, and second wife, Pauline. Sons Jack, George, and Patrick were caught in the crossfire of these divorces. During Hemingway's first visits to Idaho, Pauline remained in Key West, and Jack was at boarding school in New York. Hemingway arrived at Sun Valley Resort nineteen days after Hitler invaded Poland. WWII was on the horizon, and he needed to finish his book on the Spanish Civil War—a proxy war in which the Nazis flexed their military muscles.

During the five summer/fall visits of 1939 and the 1940s, Hemingway had time to write and space to be himself. Hunting guides and lifelong friends, Taylor Williams, Lloyd Arnold, and Bud Purdy enjoyed Hemingway's company and were not men in awe of celebrity. As Tillie Arnold—wife of hunting guide Lloyd Arnold—writes in her book *The Hemingway Idaho*, "Hemingway liked real men-men who had guts and pride and were good at what they do. Lloyd Arnold was a man like that. Gene Van Guilder was a man like that. And so were Chuck Atkinson and Bud Purdy and Forrest (Duke) MacMullen and George Saviers and all the other Idaho men who would become his friend over the years."[57]

In a fascinating 1948 introduction to *A Farewell to Arms*, Hemingway rejects the leaders who make war but praises the soldiers for "wars are fought by the finest people there are…the closer to the fighting, the finer people you'll meet."[58] But he also takes the opportunity to reject the wealthy, idle rich who visit Sun Valley Resort by writing "When this year started in Sun Valley, Idaho with champagne others paid for and people playing, seriously, some kind of game where they had to crawl under a stretch cord without touching their over-inflated bellies…I was sitting in a corner…with Miss Ingrid Bergman and I said to her…this is going to be the worst year we have ever seen. Miss Bergman asked me why…I told her…the sight of the wealthy crawling on their backs under this stretched cord did nothing to reassure me" that this year would be anything but the worst year yet."[59] Here, we have Hemingway's skepticism of both the leadership removed from the realities of war and the idle rich who are only expert at their idleness. Hemingway, we can presume, spent the next morning writing about the atrocities of the Spanish Civil War and the afternoon hunting with Bud, Lloyd, and Taylor.

Dr. John Moritz counters the infamous biographical descriptions of Hemingway as an irascible, confrontational, egoist by stating, "My best assessment of Ernest Hemingway is to judge him by the company he kept. Take all of those people who were like family to him: Lloyd and Tillie Arnold, Bud and Ruth Purdy, MacMullen, George Saviers, Taylor Williams…they were all very intelligent; they had a common quality of humility; they were competent and not self effacing…(Hemingway's) built in bull shit detector…made him intolerant of phony people."[60] Hemingway's family of friends in Sun Valley was full of genuine, candid, and authentic individuals. Both Hemingway and his new family of friends measured people by their current actions, not their reputation from past accomplishments. They passed Hemingway's famous "bullshit detector," and he passed theirs. Never close to his family members in Oak Park, Illinois, and having lost his father to suicide when Hemingway was twenty-nine years old, Hemingway longed for the familial feeling of solidarity and found it in Sun Valley—the place of the only house Hemingway ever purchased in America. (Pauline, his second wife, purchased the Key West house.) Hemingway found more than a house in Ketchum; he found a new home. All of his Idaho friends remained "the family" through his final days here.

HEMINGWAY WITH "THE FAMILY" OF WOOD RIVER VALLEY
HUNTERS. *The Community Library, Ketchum, Idaho.*

Beyond finding mentors in the guides and friends in Sun Valley, Hemingway respected the community beyond the Wood River Valley as well. In Penney Brons's 1983 interview with Neil Regan, the Sun Valley publicist who replaced Gene Van Guilder after Gene's tragic death in 1939, Neil recalled hunting for rabbits with Hemingway near the farms in Shoshone and Dietrich, towns about an hour drive south of Sun Valley Resort.

"He always asked permission at the farmhouse," remarked Neil, and within days of a hunt, he would "return with an armful of groceries and often stay for dinner."[61] Hemingway respected the ranch owners and the camaraderie and friendships he developed with these people after thanking them for allowing him to hunt on their property. He would even hunt with them to rid their farms of the uncontrolled growth of crop ruining rabbits. Beyond "the family" of hunting guides and their wives, Hemingway also valued the open and supportive community of ranch owners south of the Wood River Valley. He was grateful for their hospitality and their local knowledge of where the hunting is good.

Contrary to his macho, misogynistic reputation, Hemingway was also known to relish becoming a mentor to others, teaching Sun Valley locals, especially the wives of hunting companions, how to hunt. He turned up at hunting guide Bud Purdy's house located near Silver Creek, and while Bud prepared the guns and the decoys, Hemingway asked why Bud's wife, Ruth, was in dress slacks and not ready to hunt. Ruth quickly changed and joined Bud and Hemingway on the hunt. In Wendy Warren's interview with Anita Gray in 2000, Anita recalled getting up the courage to talk with Hemingway about his time in northern Michigan, a place she knew from her early years. Anita remarked that "Hemingway liked to have women out hunting." While jump shooting on Silver Creek with Hemingway, Anita recalled that "Papa got a double (or a triple) and brought a big mallard to me and said, 'This is yours...this is the one you shot.' I never knew if I was the one who shot it...He was very fond of all in the group. His family was all of us: Bud Purdy, George Saviers, Taylor Williams."[62] Hemingway not only took great pleasure in teaching women how to hunt, he also wanted all in the group to feel good about their hunting. He wanted Anita Gray to believe she shot one of the mallards so she would keep hunting and develop an appreciation for nature through the predator-prey relationship. He found a group of like-minded individuals in Sun Valley and felt comfortable in a community of local people who loved the adventure of a hunt.

The family of hunting enthusiasts—both men and women of the Wood River Valley—would gather for what became the annual magpie shoot on Bud Purdy's ranch on Silver Creek. Bud would trap the magpies on a ranch because they are known to eat the eggs of ducks, geese, and songbirds and exacerbate the sores on cattle by pecking at them. Instead of poisoning them, Hemingway held an annual "magpie shoot."

Phil Huss

HEMINGWAY AT THE "MAGPIE SHOOT" ON BUD PURDY'S PROPERTY NEAR SILVER CREEK, 1958. *The Community Library, Ketchum, Idaho.*

Hemingway even went so far as to create a cup for whoever shoots the most magpies. Anita Gray fondly recalls these gatherings with "Bud and Ruth Purdy, George Saviers, Don Anderson, the Arnolds, the Spiegels, and Taylor Williams." Clara Spiegel, a friend of Hemingway since the Paris years and Wood River Valley resident, recalled that "it was just a group of friends, no fanfare" and the "shooting parties only consisted of the family." The magpie shoots were an excuse to bring the family together, and "his family was all of us," recalled Anita Gray.[63] Hemingway valued his mentors in the Wood River Valley and loved the genuine sense of community of like-minded individuals he found. When you visit the Hemingway grave, you will see that he is still surrounded by both his biological family and "the family" of friends.

NOVELS AND SHORT STORIES: VALUE MENTORS AND COMMUNITY

In *The Sun Also Rises* (1926), Hemingway depicts with ruthless candor characters who are adrift without mentors and without the discipline to follow the principles of the code. The protagonist, Jake Barnes, falls short of upholding many of the code principles, particularly valuing love by failing to recognize what is *not* love. However, Jake does value mentors and a community of like-minded individuals who possess admirable attributes. Clearly, this community of individuals is not composed of Robert Cohn, Lady Brett Ashley, and Mike Campbell. Jake finds acceptance and mentorship at the Hotel Montoya in Pamplona. Hotel owner Montoya knows that Jake is an aficionado of bullfighting and values that Jake knows the difference between skillful matadors, unskilled matadors, and seemingly skilled matadors. In a conversation between Jake and Montoya, Montoya asks Jake:

> *"Your friend, is he aficionado, too?"*
>
> *"Yes. He came all the way from New York to see the San Fermin."*
>
> *"Yes?"* Montoya politely disbelieved. *"But he's not aficionado like you."*
>
> *He put his hand on my shoulder again embarrassedly.*
>
> *"Yes," I said. "He's a real aficionado."*
>
> *"But he's not aficionado like you are."*
>
> *Aficion means passion. An aficionado is one who is passionate about the bullfights. All the good bullfighters stayed at Montoya's hotel; that is, those with aficion stayed there. The commercial bullfighters stayed once, perhaps, and then did not come back. The good ones came each year...Those who were aficionados could always*

> get rooms even when the hotel was full. Montoya introduced me to some of them. They were always very polite at first, and it amused them very much that I should be an American. Somehow it was taken for granted that an American could not have *aficion*. He might simulate it or confuse it with excitement, but he could not really have it. When they saw that I had *aficion*, and there was no password, no set questions that could bring it out, rather it was a sort of oral spiritual examination with the questions always a little on the defensive and never apparent, there was this same embarrassed putting the hand on the shoulder, or a "buen hombre." But nearly always there was the actual touching. It seemed as though they wanted to touch you to make it certain.
>
> Montoya could forgive anything of a bullfighter who had *aficion*. He could forgive attacks of nerves, panic, bad unexplainable actions, and all sorts of lapses. For one who had *aficion* he could forgive anything. At once he forgave me all my friends. Without his ever saying anything they were simply a little something shameful between us, like the spilling open of the horses in bullfighting.[64]

Embarrassed by the codeless behavior of his amoral, drunk "friends" (one evening in the hotel ends in Jake's friends getting into an inebriated brawl over Brett), Jake finds a sort of redemption in being accepted by a community of matadors and aficionados of bullfighting at the Hotel Montoya. When Jake receives the hand on his shoulder and the approving comment "buen hombre," he knows he is being celebrated as one who has aficion or passion. A spectator at a bullfight or any performance is one who sees a performance without appreciating the skillful mastery and adherence to a strict, self-imposed code of behaving. But an aficionado is one who not only appreciates the skillful mastery and adherence to a strict, self-imposed code, but is also one who possesses the passion to be coded himself. Jake's drunk and amoral friends and Jake himself are shameful in the way that the gored horses are shameful in a bullfight: we all must endure shortcomings and regrettable actions.

But the difference that Montoya as a mentor and the community of matadors and aficionados of bullfighting see in Jake is that Jake's appreciation of skill, passion, and discipline in matadors must mean that he possesses the potential to develop skill, passion, and discipline in his life. The comment from Hemingway's doctor, John Moritz, about Hemingway's community of friends in Sun Valley comes to mind. Dr. Moritz did not judge Hemingway by his failed marriages or shortcomings as a father or posthumously by the biographical reports of his temper, fights, and ruthless competitiveness with contemporary authors and literary critics who rejected Hemingway's work; he judged Hemingway by Hemingway's passion for adventure and for his dedication to "the company he kept." Readers of *The Sun Also Rises* are relieved when Jake rejects the company of Robert Cohn, Lady Brett Ashley, and Mike Campbell. Readers are especially relieved by Jake's rejection of Brett at the end of the novel when he says sardonically to Lady Brett "isn't it *pretty* to think" we could be good together as a couple. (my italics) There is a passion to respect himself in his relations with others that emerges in Jake, but he needs to find a community of like-minded individuals beyond the matador aficionados at the Hotel Montoya. Hemingway found a community of like-minded individuals and mentors in "the family" of Sun Valley.

In *For Whom the Bell Tolls*, Hemingway develops the coded Anselmo, the most enduring and celebrated mentor in all of Hemingway's fiction, but Hemingway also depicts Robert Jordan's grandfather as a mentor as well. In his mental preparation for the task of blowing the bridge, Jordan reflects, "I wish my grandfather were here."[65] Jordan wishes to ask his grandfather for advice since his grandfather saw combat in the American Civil War. With fascinating passages about Robert Jordan's rejection of his father due to his father's suicide and revealing commentary about Jordan's celebration of his grandfather as a man of courage, self-discipline, and passion, *For Whom the Bell Tolls* reveals Hemingway's view of his father and grandfather. In a photograph on the Fourth of July, a young Hemingway is shown with his grandfather who wore his Civil War uniform for the occasion.

HEMINGWAY AS A BOY, THIRD FROM THE LEFT, AND GRANDFATHER IN HIS CIVIL WAR UNIFORM, 1907. *Ernest Hemingway Collection. John F. Kennedy Presidential Library and Museum, Boston.*

As was noted, Hemingway lost his own father to suicide and presumably admired his grandfather's service in the Civil War since Hemingway himself was involved in WWI, the Spanish Civil War, and WWII. In *For Whom the Bell Tolls*, Robert Jordan recalls saying goodbye to his father before heading off to war. Rejecting both his father's religiosity and open display of emotions, Hemingway writes:

> *Robert Jordan had not felt this young since he had taken the train at Red Lodge to go down to Billings to get the train there to go away to school for the first time. He had been afraid to go and he did not want anyone to know it and, at the station, just before the conductor picked up the box he would step up on to reach the steps of the day coach, his father had kissed him good-by and said, "May the Lord watch between thee and me while we are absent the one from the other." His father had been a very religious man and he*

had said it simply and sincerely. But his moustache had been moist and his eyes were damp with emotion and Robert Jordan had been so embarrassed by all of it, the damp religious sound of the prayer, and by his father kissing him goodbye, that he had felt suddenly so much older than his father and sorry for him that he could hardly bear it.[66]

In this moment in *For Whom the Bell Tolls*, Hemingway establishes Jordan's father as falling short of being a mentor both in his untested faith in God's providence and in the open emotional display. Hemingway had deeply religious parents, even though Hemingway's father was a doctor. Hemingway attended church each Sunday and became an altar boy in his high school years in Oak Park, Illinois. Readers can find examples of Hemingway's struggle with his faith through numerous characters and stories, but suffice it to say that the horrors of war led Hemingway to question the existence of a benevolent, providential God. Hemingway was not religious after his Oak Park days until his second wife, Pauline Pfeiffer, asked Hemingway to convert to Catholicism. After their divorce, Hemingway was an irregular churchgoer at best and then not at all in his later years.

In contrast to Jordan's departure with his father in which Jordan "felt suddenly so much older than his father and sorry for him," Hemingway juxtaposes this moment with the parting of Jordan and Anselmo, an elderly guerilla fighter for the Republican cause. It is instructive to notice how Anselmo and Jordan depart by ensuring that they are prepared to complete the task well—our first code principle. Hemingway writes:

"When thou firest," Robert Jordan said, "take a rest and make very sure. Do not think of it as a man but as a target, de acuerdo? Do not shoot at the whole man but at a point. Shoot for the exact center of the belly—if he faces thee. At the middle of the back, if he is looking away. Listen, old one. When I fire if the man is sitting down he will stand up before he runs or crouches. Shoot then.

If he is still sitting down shoot. Do not wait. But make sure. Get to within fifty yards. Thou art a hunter. Thou hast no problem."

"*I will do as thou orderest,*" Anselmo said.

"*Yes. I order it thus,*" Robert Jordan said.

I'm glad I remembered to make it an order, he thought. That helps him out. That takes some of the curse off. I hope it does, anyway. Some of it. I had forgotten about what he told me that first day about the killing.

"*It is thus I have ordered,*" he said. "*Now go.*"

[…]

He remembered his father in the railway station and the wetness of that farewell and he did not say Salud nor good-by nor good luck nor anything like that.

"*Hast wiped the oil from the bore of thy gun, old one?*" he whispered. "*So it will not throw wild?*"

"*In the cave,*" Anselmo said. "*I cleaned them all with the pull through.*"

"*Then until soon,*" Robert Jordan said.[67]

There is no need for wishing luck; there is only the need to complete tasks well. For as was established with Santiago setting the marlin-baited lines at exact depths, for those who complete tasks well, one knows that "when luck comes, one will be ready." There is no teary-eyed goodbye nor religious platitudes about God and divine providence; there is only Jordan's ordering of the killing and the check-in that Anselmo's gun preparation has been completed well. Anselmo is Jordan's mentor with respect to Anselmo's disgust with the killing that must occur in war (thus the desire for the order), Anselmo's preparation for the killing, and Anselmo's faith that they will see each other again if they complete tasks well.

Before the blowing of the bridge, Jordan also responds to the "religious feeling" of being a part of a community of individuals who are all committed to the same task and in defense of principles in which they all believe. "War groups the maximum of material and speeds up the action and brings out all sorts of stuff that normally you have to wait a whole lifetime to get," writes Hemingway to F. Scott Fitzgerald in a letter.[68] Like his group of friends and hunting guides in Sun Valley who were all committed to the unspoken code of hunting ethics and valued a community of like-minded individuals, Jordan finds the self-disciplined ways of the Spanish guerilla fighters to be edifying. Hemingway writes:

> *You felt, in spite of all bureaucracy and inefficiency and party strife, something that was like the feeling you expected to have and did not have when you made your first communion. It was a feeling of consecration to a duty toward all of the oppressed of the world which would be as difficult and embarrassing to speak about as religious experience and yet it was authentic as the feeling you had when you heard Bach, or stood in Chartres Cathedral or the Cathedral at Leon and saw the light coming through the great windows; or when you saw Mantegna and Greco and Brueghel in the Prado. It gave you a part in something that you could believe in wholly and completely and in which you felt an absolute brotherhood with the others who were engaged in it. It was something that you had never known before but that you had experienced now and you gave such importance to it and the reasons for it that your own death seemed of complete unimportance; only a thing to be avoided because it would interfere with the performance of your duty.*[69]

(my italics)

Harkening back to his rejection of religion in the farewell to his father, Jordan finds a spiritual feeling not in becoming a member of the church as a youth during his first communion, but in being part of a community of coded individuals who all believe in defending democracy, religious freedom, and individual liberty. The "absolute brotherhood" with others who share the same values was replicated in Sun Valley and sustained Hemingway's lifelong love affair with Idaho.

Anselmo is also a mentor for Robert Jordan because Anselmo reflects on the need for redemption through future positive action after all of the killings during the war. In the following passage, Jordan reflects on the little difference between the Nationalist guards on the bridge and their Republican group. Jordan thinks, "I have watched them all day and they are the same men that we are. I believe that I could walk up to the mill and knock on the door and I would be welcome except that they have orders to challenge all travelers and ask to see their papers. It is only orders that come between us. Those men are not fascists. I call them so, but they are not. They are poor men as we are. They should never be fighting against us and I do not like to think of the killing."[70] Jordan has orders from Russian General Golz, and Anselmo has orders from Jordan to kill these guards, but both Jordan and Anselmo know they must atone for the killing of men caught up in the machine of war as they have been. Unlike *In Our Time*'s Nick Adams, who returns to America without a desire to be a husband or father and without a community of mentors to guide him through the healing from the atrocities of war, and unlike *A Farewell to Arms*'s Frederic Henry, who is left alone in Europe to heal from the tragedy of losing his love and child and witnessing the atrocities of war, Robert Jordan has a mentor in Anselmo, who helps guide Jordan toward healing after the war. Anselmo shares with Jordan, "I think that after the war there will have to be some great penance done for the killing. If we no longer have religion after the war then I think there must be some form of civic penance organized that all may be cleansed from the killing or else we will never have a true and human basis for living. The killing is necessary, I know, but still the doing of it is very bad for a man and I think that, after all this is over and we have won the war, there must be a penance of some kind for the cleansing of us all."[71] The importance of living a coded life, of surrounding oneself with a community of coded people, of contributing positively to this community manifested in Hemingway's time in Sun Valley. While Hemingway was creating Anselmo as a mentor in his new novel, Hemingway found models for how to cleanse the self in his "family" of peers. After his failed marriage to Piper (Pauline Pfeiffer), Hemingway found love in Marty Gellhorn. After witnessing the atrocities of WWI so vividly depicted in *In Our Time* and after witnessing the barbaric violence during the Spanish Civil War, Hemingway had a deep-seated need to contribute positively to and benefit positively from a community of individuals who valued love, completed tasks well, and valued their community of like-minded individuals. He felt an "absolute brotherhood" with Sun Valley's hunting guides, their families, and friends. In the Sun Valley area, Hemingway "felt apart of something" he could "believe in wholly."

3

VALUE NATURE AS AN ETHICAL ARENA

Develop an appreciation of nature as therapeutic. View the natural world as an arena upon which to project ethical behavior.

Ernest Hemingway was not a Romantic pantheist, for he did not find a spiritual presence manifesting in the natural world. He was also not an environmentalist, as the term is defined today, for he did not act upon the preservation of wild places much beyond his desire to be able to visit intact ecosystems in which to hunt or fish. However, Hemingway had a deep appreciation for the natural world and was a keen observer of nature. He valued nature by developing an appreciation of nature's beauty, intricacy, and wholeness as therapeutic. He also valued nature as an arena upon which to project one's ethical code. The characters in his stories and novels either demonstrated that they could or could not follow unspoken hunting and fishing codes of conduct.

The pure perception of natural objects is a pleasure in much of Hemingway's works. Whether it is Robert Jordan relishing the calm of the false dawn of the morning before blowing the bridge in *For Whom the Bell Tolls* or "looking at the thick bush we passed in the dark, feeling the cool wind of the night and smelling the good smell of Africa, I was altogether happy" in *Green Hills of Africa*.[72] Looking at the dark African landscape replete with predators on the hunt, drinking in the natural scene at night, smelling the "good smell of Africa," Hemingway, as the narrator of the nonfiction work *Green Hills of Africa*, never goes beyond the surface sensations. There is no Emersonian transparent eyeball moment in which "the currents of the Universal Being circulate through" him; there is no Thoreauvian oneness with nature in which "the whole body is one sense, and imbibes delight through every pore." But there is the pleasant perception of "looking" and "smelling" (an intoxicating drinking in of the scene) that leads to happiness. There is "a pure perceptual pleasure," as modernist critic Frank Lentricchia puts it, in perceiving the natural world. Both Hemingway's characters and Hemingway himself value nature by developing an appreciation of nature's beauty, intricacy, and wholeness as therapeutic. No divine transcendence, no genuflecting toward a supreme being behind the material forms of nature or within man. Just the "relish of sensation" in perceiving nature, for its own sake on its own terms.

Hemingway sought out frontiers and had a deep appreciation for the wildness that a frontier existence provided. Whether it was marlin fishing off of Key West and his beloved Cuba in the vast wilderness of the sea, or backcountry skiing in the mountain wilderness of the European Alps, or big game hunting in the wilds of Africa, or bird, pronghorn, and deer hunting in the wilderness of central Idaho, Hemingway loved the awe-inspiring feeling of *participating* in the intact ecosystems of wild places. His skill as a keen observer of nature as a naturalist and expertise as a hunter and fisherman informed his views of nature. Hemingway's experiences in the Sun Valley area and his natural descriptions in his pantheon of fiction and journalism underscore his deep appreciation of nature. Moreover, his evolving views of and practices in nature throughout his lifetime and writings reflect his reactions to man's outsize detrimental impact upon nature.

Sun Valley Stories: Valuing Nature as an Ethical Arena

You may recall from the introduction that when Hemingway was looking back at the Idaho Sawtooth Mountains (now a wilderness area) and the headwaters of the Salmon River from atop Galena Summit, he told a hunting companion, "You'd have to come from a test tube and think like a machine to not engrave all of this in your head so that you never lose it."[73] This comment was unknowingly prescient. A machine—the electroshock treatment machine used to treat Hemingway's depression at the Mayo Clinic—would rob Hemingway of his ability to recall, to think, and, consequently, to write in his final years at Sun Valley. Nonetheless, atop Galena Summit in 1940 with the full powers of his mind, Hemingway remarked that he wants to "engrave" in his head the vast landscape of the immense, jagged peaks of the Sawtooth mountains and the longest salmon run in the world at the headwaters of the Salmon River so he "will never lose it."

HEMINGWAY'S BUST AT THE TRAIL CREEK MEMORIAL ON SUN VALLEY ROAD NEAR THE SUN VALLEY LODGE.
The Community Library, Ketchum, Idaho.

After the tragic death of Gene Van Guilder by gunshot in a canoe on the Snake River on October 28, 1939 (one month into Hemingway's stay in Sun Valley), Ernest wrote Gene's eulogy and ended it with, "Best of all he loved the fall, the leaves yellow on the cottonwoods, leaves floating on the trout streams, and above the hills the high blue windless skies… now he will be a part of them forever." And while these words were written by Hemingway to memorialize Gene Van Guilder, they can be easily be applied to Hemingway and his love for Idaho's rivers, streams, wilderness, and wildlife. Hemingway's bust currently resides on the banks of Trail Creek just north of the Sun Valley Lodge. His bust faces the cottonwoods and the trout stream and looks out admiringly at the intact ecosystem that produces trout-filled rivers.

Hemingway found central Idaho to be a place of phenomenal hunting and fishing unparalleled in the American West. In the falls of 1939 and 1940, Hemingway often followed his morning ritual of writing *For Whom the Bell Tolls* in his room at Sun Valley Resort with lunch with friends and a hunting adventure at Silver Creek. In the 2000 Wendy Warren interview with Anita Gray, a friend and hunting companion of Hemingway's in Sun Valley, Anita remembered a duck hunt with Hemingway on Silver Creek, a beautiful trophy trout spring creek where Hemingway hunted and fished. As they were walking along the gin-clear, trout-packed, thin ribbon that was a tributary to Silver Creek, Hemingway noticed bobcat tracks. "He showed me the larger (bobcat) tracks and the smaller (bobcat tracks) and then pheasant tracks," recalled Anita. "He said, 'she taught the cub how to kill a bird.' He could read it all in the tracks."[74] Hemingway's respect for how nature works and the mentoring of the young cub is evident here and is often lost in the iconic images of Hemingway with his trophy kills during the African safaris. Hemingway scholar Susan Beegel notes, "(Hemingway) had a Darwinian view of animals in competition, but little understanding of cooperative relationships among species (the application of ecological science to preserve species and their habitat was not prominent)"[75] While ecology had yet to be a science frequently applied to habitat restoration, wilderness preservation, and species protection in his lifetime, Hemingway shows in this moment near Silver Creek that while he had a Darwinian understanding of species in competition and viewed himself as a hunter able to enter into this competition, he also had a deep appreciation for natural processes, particularly the mentorship of this mother bobcat in training her cub to hunt.

In the same interview with Anita Gray, Anita recalled the wounded owl Hemingway nursed back to health in the Heise House in Ketchum. He loved that owl and kept it around the house and fed it until it was able to heal its wing and fend for itself. He loved to show the owl to guests. Appreciative of the predator-prey relationship in hunters and fishermen

HEMINGWAY WITH THE INJURED OWL HE NURSED BACK TO HEALTH. *The Community Library, Ketchum, Idaho.*

and their prey and in the bobcat and the pheasant and the owl and mice, Hemingway valued all those who hunted well.

In a recent talk I attended at the Hemingway Festival in Ketchum in September of 2017, Ketchum resident Jed Gray recalled his teenage years when he was able to hunt with Ernest Hemingway. Jed told us a tender story about Hemingway slipping out of a dinner party to come read *The Old Man and the Sea* to Jed who was in bed. And Jed told us about how Hemingway loved being around kids and created impromptu contests for who can kick a can higher. But it was the hunting instruction that Jed remembers most. Hemingway always allowed Jed to get the first and best shot at approaching ducks. Hemingway wanted to instill good hunting technique into the young man and have him respect the predator-prey relationship that hunting created for the hunter.

Hemingway wanted young Jed to emerge as a participant in the ecosystem and not a mere observer; this changes one's understanding of habitat, of where animals thrive, and of what is needed for these animals to exist in significant number.

But as is often the case when Hemingway's code principles are applied to his life, there are moments when both Hemingway's peers and Hemingway himself failed to act ethically in nature. You will recall the story when Hemingway was hunting on Silver Creek with John Boettiger and John failed to unload his gun and put the safety on his gun while traveling in the canoe. John went to grab his gun and pulled the trigger and shot the Sun Valley Resort black Lab in the leg. Even more tragic was the failure of Lloyd Arnold, Sun Valley photographer and hunting guide, to tell a young apprentice guide not to shoot while traveling in a canoe. You remember that Gene Van Guilder was in the bow and Dave Benner, the young apprentice guide, was in the middle and Lloyd Arnold was in the stern of the canoe when Benner swung his gun and shot Gene right in the back. Gene died within half an hour.

While Hemingway's peers failed to act ethically in nature, Hemingway also fell short on some hunts in the Wood River Valley. A few years ago, I invited Bud Purdy to my classroom at the Sun Valley Community School to share stories about guiding Ernest Hemingway. Bud was twenty-two years old when he first guided Hemingway in 1939, and Bud was ninety-four years old when he stood at the front of my classroom and delivered story after story with remarkable clarity about hunting with Hemingway. It was as if the hunts happened a week ago. One story required Bud to explain to my students the different mindset of hunters in 1940 compared to that of hunters today. Bud explained Hemingway's "magpie shoot" mentioned earlier. Bud explained to my students that magpies are a nuisance on his Silver Creek ranch because they eat the eggs of songbirds, ducks, and geese, pick at cuts and sores on livestock, and pick at the eyes of newborn calves. So Bud trapped them and disposed of them. At the time, there was a bounty for magpies: eleven cents per magpie. When Hemingway learned of this, he asked Bud if they could have a "magpie shoot" by releasing the magpies and having a slew of hunters have at them. The winner was the one who killed the most magpies. This seems less than sporting and out of step with fair-chase hunting principles. But Hemingway loved how the annual magpie shoot brought the family of hunting companions together; he even created a "trophy cup" for the annual winner of the magpie shoot.

In addition, as you know, Hemingway was more than happy to visit the farms in Shoshone, Dietrich, and Gooding (all farming towns south of the Wood River Valley) and assist farmers in addressing the overpopulation of rabbits that were devastating their crops. Without limits on rabbits, the hunters could make a serious dent on the rabbit population. Clay Stewart, a hunting and fishing guide for the Sun Valley Resort in the early 1940s, remarked that Hemingway was a "man's man, a real macho guy; he was rough and tough," but then he went on to state that "from a hunting standpoint, I didn't like him" because he loved to "kill, kill, kill, kill, and kill."[76] Stewart is referring to the rabbit hunts and the magpie shoots during which "nuisance species" were harvested in great number. Also, as Andy Beck—a neighbor of Hemingway's for two years—recalled, Hemingway and others would often take the "rabbit carcasses and hang them in trees" to attract magpies and crows, so they could return and shoot them.[77]

While numerous biographies reveal Hemingway's unwillingness to pass up the chance to kill coyotes (even, reportedly, from the air) in the Wood River Valley, hyenas while on safari, sharks with machine guns from his boat *Pilar* in the waters off Key West or Cuba, rabbits on a farm, and even magpies trapped in a net, there is still the Hemingway who has a great respect for the natural world. Hemingway especially valued the predator-prey relationship in an ecosystem and the opportunity hunting affords for man to enter into the predator-prey relationship in an ecosystem. And Hemingway had the greatest respect for nature's ability to provide moments in which he and others could exercise their knowledge of where the animals would be and their skill in shooting them well so their deaths were instant. This is best captured in Hemingway's hunt with Bud Purdy near the Little Wood River in central Idaho. They knew the small ribbon of a tributary was great mallard habitat and when they flushed the ducks, Hemingway got three drake (male) mallards with three pulls of his gun. He knew which ones to shoot and how to kill them humanely. As Bud put it, "You could have given (Hemingway) a million dollars and he would not have been any happier."[78]

HEMINGWAY WITH A STRINGER OF MALLARDS AFTER A JUMP SHOOT ON THE LITTLE WOOD RIVER. *Magnum Photos*.

Novels and Short Stories: Value Nature as an Ethical Arena

The respect for the predator-prey relationship in nature manifested in Nick Adams's fly-fishing for trout in northern Michigan after the war in *In Our Time*, in the vignettes on bullfighting in *In Our Time*, in his celebration of bullfighting in *Death in the Afternoon*, in his hunting expeditions in Africa in *Green Hills of Africa*, and in Santiago's struggles with the giant marlin in *The Old Man and the Sea*. In some of the most famous moments from the texts, Hemingway's characters value nature as an arena upon which to project the unspoken but understood code of ethics in hunting and fishing and how to care for the animal after it has been taken. Recall Santiago's desperate struggle to defend his marlin from the predatory sharks in *The Old Man and the Sea*. And recall hunting guide Wilson's resolve to put the lion out of its misery after Francis Macomber gutshoots the lion in "The Short Happy Life of Francis Macomber." Developing Francis as an unethical hunter during this African hunting safari, Hemingway allows Francis to ask Wilson:

> "Why not just leave him?"
>
> "You mean pretend to ourselves he hasn't been hit?" responded Wilson…
>
> "Why not?"
>
> "For one thing, he's certain to be suffering. For another, someone else might run onto him…I'll go ahead when we go in."[79]

Disgusted both by Macomber's poor skill as a hunter and his lack of empathy for the lion's suffering, Wilson cannot tolerate a hunter who disrespects his prey. But this moment also brings out the moral dilemma of all big-game trophy hunting. Rarely can a lion or water buffalo be brought down with one shot. A hunter must be willing to pursue the blood trail and finish off the apex predator and risk life and limb in doing so. This is to say nothing of the moral dilemma over shooting animals for sport and trophies and not for food. Nonetheless, a hunter must be able to empathize with its prey, as Francis proved in the above passage that he is unable to do. To show that Francis does not value the lion nor care for its suffering, Hemingway's narrator describes the experience of being shot from the perspective of the lion.

Hemingway writes, "There was no man smell carried toward his and he watched the object, moving his great head a little from side to side. Then watching the object, not afraid, but hesitating before going down the bank to drink with such a thing opposite him, he saw a man figure . . . he heard a cracking crash and felt the slam of a .30-06 220-grain solid bullet that bit his flank and ripped in sudden hot scalding nausea through his stomach . . . it crashed again and he felt the blow as it hit his lower ribs and ripped on through, blood sudden hot and frothy in his mouth."[80]

Unlike Francis, Hemingway asks the reader to empathize with the lion by forcing the reader to view the wounding of the lion from the lion's perspective. The bullet wound caused the lion a shocking "hot scalding nausea" that "ripped through his stomach" and sent "blood sudden hot and frothy in his mouth." Hemingway ends the passage by stating that "Macomber had not thought about how the lion felt as he got out of the car." Francis does not complete the task of shooting well, does not hunt humanely, and suggests that they not go finish off the lion. The situation leaves the other members of the group "looking very grave" and feeling extremely disturbed by the ineffective shooting of the lion. Francis does not value nature because he does not have the experience or the desire to shoot the lion well enough to kill him immediately. He lets the lion suffer enormously before gaining the courage to look for the wounded animal. It is obvious through his actions that Francis doesn't value the lion's life nor lament its suffering.

Hemingway's view of nature was significantly shaped by his readings of Teddy Roosevelt's accounts of his big game hunting in Africa. As Ron Berman notes, in Roosevelt's *African Game Trails* (1910), Roosevelt admits that "his group routinely miss their shots, kill the wrong animal, leave wounded beasts in the brush, use the wrong caliber guns, and even end up shooting, 'mysteriously, a domestic house cat.'"[81] Teddy Roosevelt was the quintessential image of a macho adventurer, hunter, public intellectual, and president. And Ernest Hemingway was one of the first macho adventurer, hunter, fiction writers. Roosevelt's adventurous accounts and gruff, macho persona had an outsize effect on Hemingway's pursuit of adventures and development of a macho persona. In one infamous Roosevelt bear hunt in Mississippi in 1902, a young, mangy bear was lassoed, clubbed, and tied to a tree in order to be then killed by Teddy Roosevelt. Roosevelt refused and was disgusted by the situation as an affront to hunting ethics. Interestingly, Teddy Roosevelt's famous "Teddy Bear" was created from this moment of moral crisis in which Teddy refuses to shoot a bear tied to a tree in the fall of 1902. A political cartoon at the time depicted Roosevelt refusing to kill the bear tied to the tree.

Then, toy manufacturers created a stuffed animal bear from the cartoon and named it "Teddy's Bear." This story of the iconic "Teddy Bear" is a harbinger of the changing views of nature that Americans were undergoing. Bear, wolves, and coyotes were being systematically exterminated by the hand of the federal government as anathema to the advancement of civilization. The nation's fascination over the "Teddy Bear"—a stuffed animal that captured the innocence of the bear—showed that American views of the bear as a threat to life, limb and livestock were undergoing a sea change. But this story of President Roosevelt refusing to take the bear in a way that violated its dignity and his honor as a sportsman is well captured in Hemingway's "The Short Happy Life of Francis Macomber." Hunting guide Wilson refuses to leave the lion in the bush to bleed out; Wilson refuses to violate the dignity of the lion and his honor as a sportsman.

Moreover, Hemingway's early depiction of the catch-and-release ethic in "Big Two-Hearted River" (1925), refusal in the 1950s to big game hunt in *True at First Light* and his support for policy as vice president of the International Game Fish Association (IGFA) for catch-and-release marlin fishing and a closed season for marlin when they are spawning capture the transition that Roosevelt conservationists made in the early to mid-twentieth century. As Susan Beegel notes in *Ernest Hemingway in Context*, "Hemingway practiced catch and release of marlin and called for a closed season during spawning time...he became Vice President of the International Game Fish Association that promoted sportsmanlike fishing practices and conservation efforts on behalf of species in decline."[82]

Hemingway's readings of Roosevelt's and others' African safari hunts and his experiences on these hunts allowed Hemingway to conclude that hunting ethics are compromised often in these big-game trophy hunts. Hemingway is able to capture these compromises both in Francis Macomber's misfires, cowardice, and unempathetic view of the lion's suffering. It is interesting to note that Hemingway published "A Short Happy Life of Francis Macomber" in 1936, three years prior to his first arrival in Sun Valley and the formation of his hunting circles he called "the family" in the Wood River Valley.

You will recall that when John Boettiger fails to put the safety on his gun in a canoe on Silver Creek and accidentally shoots the leg of Sun Valley Resort's hunting Lab, "Bullet," Hemingway is so disgusted he leaves to return to the resort in a separate car. You also recall that when Hemingway hears of the unnecessary and tragic death of Sun Valley publicist Gene Van Guilder because a young Sun Valley staff member shoots from the middle position in a three person unanchored canoe, Hemingway admonished Lloyd Arnold for knowing better than to allow two individuals to shoot from an untethered canoe. Of course, there were many successful hunts on Silver Creek, in the farm fields of Shoshone, and in the Frank Church Wilderness (it was not designated wilderness at the time of Hemingway's hunt, but it was unspoiled land replete with big game and still is). The moments in which people failed to follow the unspoken code of hunting ethics placed the successful hunts in relief. As a result, Hemingway valued the local Sun Valley "family" members who knew how to behave well on a hunt all the more. Moreover, the fact that Hemingway was writing *For Whom the Bell Tolls* at the time of these hunts in Sun Valley provides us a great context in which to judge the moral failings of characters in this text. In room 206 of the Sun Valley Lodge, Hemingway depicts Pablo as a traitor and uncoded soldier during the Spanish Civil War and develops how Pablo's moral failings provide the relief in which to value the noble actions of both Robert Jordan and Anselmo as coded soldiers at war.

Later in "The Short Happy Life of Francis Macomber," Wilson provides Francis with another moment to prove himself to be a skilled and ethical hunter. Describing the safari car chase toward the water buffalo, Hemingway writes, "The car was going a wild forty-five miles an hour across the open and as Macomber watched, the buffalo got bigger and bigger…and he was raising his rifle, when Wilson shouted, 'Not from the car, you fool!'"[83] Wilson's admonition to Francis to get out of the car before shooting the water buffalo underscores the unspoken ethic of fair chase, while the reader is left, as is often the case in Hemingway's works, to infer that Wilson's chasing of the water buffalo in cars is ethically suspect as well. Hemingway is not immune to criticism as a hunter (the machine-gunning of sharks, the magpie shoot, the slaughter of rabbits), but this adds to the intrigue of allowing the reader to conclude that the hero of the story—Wilson—is an imperfect hunter. Recall the Bud Purdy-Hemingway magpie-shoot story. Purdy and Hemingway loathed the notion that the magpies were eating duck and goose eggs and, thereby, potentially decreasing the numbers of ducks and geese to hunt. When Bud told Hemingway the magpies were to be poisoned, Hemingway scoffed at that and told Bud, "Let's let him loose and have us a shoot." As you know, this became an annual tradition for Hemingway, Bud, and friends, but it reveals what Susan Beegel refers to as Hemingway's Teddy Roosevelt conservationist mindset. She writes that Hemingway was "steeped in the conservation values of the hunter-naturalist…his conservation values were attuned to saving resources for future exploitation rather than to preservation for its own sake."[84]

During the Teddy Roosevelt era (1901–1909) there was a great debate over American perspectives on nature and policies toward protecting nature. In 1906, San Francisco suffered a catastrophic earthquake that caused a great portion of the city to burn down. They ran out of water in their attempts to put out the fires caused in part by the earthquake.

There was an immediate call for a more reliable water source for the city. Administrators looked to the Sierras and, in particular, the newly minted Yosemite National Park. This national park—the second in the nation's history—was created October 1, 1890. Adjacent to Yosemite Valley in the national park was an equally stunning valley called Hetch Hetchy within the park. San Francisco city administrators called for the damming of Hetch Hetchy Valley for a reliable water source and future hydropower generation. The issue of what can and cannot be done in a national park became a national crisis. Roosevelt's newly created secretary of the interior, Gifford Pinchot, embodied the Hemingway-Roosevelt hunter-naturalist conservation approach to natural resource management and advocated for the damming of Hetch Hetchy Valley. Gifford Pinchot argued:

> *The first great fact about conservation is that it stands for development. There has been a fundamental misconception that conservation means nothing but the husbanding of resources for future generations. There could be no more serious mistake. Conservation does mean provision for the future, but it means also and first of all the recognition of the right of the present generation to the fullest necessary use of all the resources with which this country is so abundantly blessed...The first principle of conservation is development, the use of the natural resources now existing on this continent for the benefit of the people who live here now. There may be just as much waste in neglecting the development and use of certain natural resources as there is in their destruction.*[85]

This passage from Gifford Pinchot captures the Progressive era's conservationist, as opposed to preservationist mindset. There is an implied acceptance of human interests superseding the interests of the ecosystem, notwithstanding the privileging of the current generation's needs over future generations' needs. This is the conservationist mindset accepted and practiced by Hemingway for most of his life.

Wilderness preservationist, pantheist, adventurer, and nature writer, John Muir vehemently opposed the damming of Hetch Hetchy Valley. Muir, who explored extensively both the Yosemite and Hetch Hetchy valleys, made it the end of his life's work to oppose the damming of Yosemite National Park. In a Sierra Club bulletin in 1908, Muir passionately wrote, "Hetch Hetchy water is the purest, wholly unpolluted, and forever unpollutable…These temple destroyers, devotees of ravaging commercialism, seem to have a perfect contempt for Nature, and, instead of lifting their eyes to the mountains, lift them to dams and town skyscrapers. Dam Hetch-Hetchy! As well dam for water-tanks the people's cathedrals and churches, for no holier temple has ever been consecrated by the heart of man."[86]

John Muir lost the battle for protecting Hetch Hetchy Valley for President Roosevelt favored Pinchot's proposal to build the dam in Yosemite National Park. President Wilson gave final approval for the dam construction in 1913. Hetch Hetchy Reservoir still remains today. This is all to say that Hemingway was very much in the Roosevelt-Pinchot conservationist camp that viewed nature anthropocentrically, as a resource to be used for the benefit of man.

However, as was noted, Hemingway's views of policies affecting nature evolved over his lifetime and, interestingly, were enacted in both policy and action by Hemingway's first son, Jack Hemingway, who considered Sun Valley his home until his death in 2000. Foregoing big-game trophy hunting on an African safari in 1953, Ernest Hemingway "pledged to only hunt what he could eat and only hunted nuisance animals."[87] Hemingway had witnessed man's and his own outsize influence on the predator-prey relationship in the natural world. In his innovative short story collection *In Our Time* (1925), Nick Adams fly-fishes in "Big Two-Hearted River I and II" for trout on a solo journey to return to the former innocence he once had fly-fishing with his dad and Uncle George before he experienced the horrors of WWI. It is important to note that the town of Seney, Michigan, and the surrounding forest are burned down in this final story of the collection *In Our Time*. Hemingway reflected upon his early fishing and hunting adventures with his dad on the shores of Lake Walloon near Petoskey, Michigan, a refuge from the expanding sprawl of Hemingway's hometown in Oak Park, Illinois. It is important to note that the Hemingways' cottage on Lake Walloon embodied the early twentieth century fascination with returning to nature that was also revealed in the creation at the time of the Boy Scouts (1910), Camp Fire Girls (1910), and the expansion of the Sierra Club (1892) as an organization that organized backpacking trips and served as an advocate for preservation. Reflecting on his youthful rambles in the woods, lakes, and streams near Lake Walloon, Hemingway notes, "Michigan I loved when I lived in it. Country of forests, lakes, streams, and pastures, always with a background of woods."[88] He *loved* Michigan when he lived in it, but there is an implication that the area had been ruined by development, timber harvest, and industrial expansion after Hemingway's return from WWI. In "Big Two-Hearted River," the town of Seney and forest had been burned down by unregulated clear-cutting practices and the burning of the remaining "stumpage and slash left behind." By 1907, "more than 10.7 million acres of the state had been clear cut," and "the state was periodically swept by devastating fires."[89] Not only is there no returning to the innocence of Nick Adams's youth after witnessing the unethical slaughters of WWI, there is no returning to the unaxed woods and unpolluted streams of his youth.

When Nick climbs through the burned out forest near Seney in "Big Two-Hearted River," he notices that the grasshoppers have turned black from immersing themselves in the soot and ash after the fire. Nick hopes to collect some of these hoppers and skewer them to his hook at the end of the line of his fly rod. As Nick picks up one of the blackened hoppers, the omniscient narrator of "Big Two-Hearted River" notes:

> *The grasshopper was black…They were all black…He realized that they had all turned black from living in the burned-over land. He realized that the fire must have come the year before, but the grasshoppers were all black now…'Go on, hopper,' Nick said. 'Fly away somewhere.' He tossed the grasshopper up into the air and watched him sail away to a charcoal stump across the road.*[90]

This moment depicts the Hemingway "tip of the iceberg" concept of writing perfectly. Heavily influenced by American modern poets' insistence that poems convey meaning in images alone, Hemingway theorized about his elliptical writing style. Literary mentor and editor of Hemingway's work Ezra Pound (who was born in Hailey, Idaho,) published an essay titled "A Few Don'ts by an Imagiste" (1913). In this tremendously influential essay, Pound argues that "it is better to present one image in a lifetime than to produce voluminous works" and a great writer must "use no superfluous word, no adjective, which does not reveal something," for "an 'image' is that which presents an intellectual and emotional complex in an instant of time…Go in fear of abstractions."[91] Hemingway brought this focus upon imagery as capturing an "intellectual and emotional complex" to his short story and fiction writing. In Hemingway's theorizing, he referred to the idea of allowing the reader to provide the emotion and the thought to a well-presented image as "tip of the iceberg." Hemingway writes, "I always try to write on the principle of the iceberg. There is 7/8ths of it underwater for every part that shows. Anything you know you can eliminate and it only strengthens your iceberg. It is the part that doesn't show," and as stated in *Death in the Afternoon*, "If a writer of prose knows enough of what he is writing about he may omit things that he knows and the reader, if the writer is writing truly enough, will have a feeling of those things as strongly as though the writer had stated them. The dignity of movement of an iceberg is due to only one-eighth of it being above water."[92] The "part that does not show" in the tip of iceberg description of the blackened grasshopper is the idea that Nick is wondering whether his disturbed mind would ever recover from witnessing the atrocities of war. While PTSD was not a clinical term available to Hemingway nor his doctors during his composition of *In Our Time* (1925) nor during his visits to the Mayo Clinic in the late 1950s and early 1960s, Hemingway's *In Our Time* captures the formation of a debilitated consciousness from witnessing horrors. Nick's witnessing of the firing squad that killed the incapacitated soldier, the memory of the scared and drunk battalion members near the Western Front, and his recollection of his friend Rinaldi taking his last breath as Nick lies incapacitated by a bullet wound shaped Nick's PTSD. His mind is burned over as the Seney forest is burned over. Nick turns the grasshopper over to see if the belly of the hopper is black as well. It is. This conveys the idea that his whole mind has been adversely affected by the war. Nick's desire to have the hopper "fly away" depicts his wish that the hopper will find a place in the forest unaffected by the clear-cut fire, by man's reckless degradation of nature. But Nick watches the hopper "sail away to a charcoal stump across the road." There is no place to go where the hopper will escape being shaped by past atrocities. The reader "reveals" the seven-eighths of the iceberg under the water and participates in Nick's concern that he, like the hopper, may never be untarnished by the past.

By allowing the reader to confer meaning onto the image of the blackened hopper unable to escape the ash and soot from the fire, Hemingway resists telling the reader what Nick is feeling, and this makes Nick's despair all the more strongly felt. Nature in Hemingway was not depicted with "superfluous words" nor "abstractions," nor through the pathetic fallacy, but rather in images "which present an intellectual and emotional complex in an instant of time."

It is also important to note the influence of Hemingway's time as a reporter for the *Kansas City Star* and its now famous *The Star Copy Style Guide*. Hemingway was a reporter for the Kansas City Star from 1917-18. "Hemingway later remarked to a reporter that the admonitions in this stylesheet were 'the best rules I ever learned in the business of writing.'"[93] In this guide, the reporters demand that journalists "use short sentences. Use short first paragraphs. Use vigorous English...Eliminate every superfluous word...Try to preserve the atmosphere of the speech...Watch out for trite phrases."[94] Moreover, the famous style guide for a few generations E. B. White's and William Strunk's *The Elements of Style* (first published in 1918) urged writers to follow the following writing principles: "Write with nouns and verbs." "Omit needless words." "Use definite, specific, concrete language." "Use the active voice." Ezra Pound, *The Star Copy Style Guide*, and White and Strunk's *The Elements of Style* had a profound impact of Hemingway's terse, elliptical, declarative sentences and stark presentation of natural images; Hemingway was confident that good readers could supply the emotions and ideas inherent in these images.

After Nick Adams collects a few of the blackened grasshoppers in "Big Two-Hearted River," he catches a few trout that he keeps for dinner and catches and releases a trout. Both the moments of killing and cleaning the trout for dinner and the releasing of the trout provide an interesting insight into Hemingway's relationship with nature and prove to be prescient for his evolving views on man's interaction with the natural world. Describing the moment of killing and cleaning the trout, Hemingway writes:

> *He took out his knife, opened it and stuck it in the log. Then he pulled up the sack, reached into it and brought out one of the trout. Holding him near the tail, hard to hold, alive, in his hand, he whacked him against the log. The trout quivered, rigid. Nick laid him on the log in the shade and broke the neck of the other fish the same way. He laid them side by side on the log. They were fine trout. Nick cleaned them, slitting them from the vent to the tip of the jaw. All the insides and the gills and tongue came out in one piece. They were both males; long grey-white strips of milt, smooth and clean. All the insides clean and compact, coming out all together. Nick tossed the offal ashore for the minks to find.*[95]

Nick completes his task of both killing the trout humanely and cleaning the trout well and finishes an often messy task quickly and effortlessly. There is an unspoken code of how to take an animal's life humanely. The "whacking" of the trout's head and "breaking of its neck" against the log kills the trout instantly, for the "trout quivered" and then went instantly "rigid." The uninitiated without experiential knowledge might leave the trout to die by suffocation. Moreover, the tossing of the trout's entrails—the "offal"—to the shore "for the minks to find" reflects Nick's concern that all of the trout be eaten and that other unseen members of the ecosystem benefit from his taking. This is the beginning of Nick's transformation from a PTSD-suffering veteran to one who is able to control his actions according to a code and heal himself through his actions. As Nick begins to commit himself to completing more and more tasks well within the arena of nature, he is healing and becoming mentally and emotionally whole again.

Nick positively influences his surroundings—a river and forest that have been adversely affected by man's reckless, shortsighted, unsustainable practices of clear-cutting and burning of stumps and slash. Nick values nature, and this is shown when he catches and releases a trout while fly-fishing. Knowing that he has enough trout for his dinner, Nick takes precautions in order to avoid unneeded harm and death to the trout he will not eat. In the process of Nick landing of a rainbow trout in the fast-moving riffles of the river, Hemingway writes:

> *Nick stooped, dipping his right hand into the current. He held the trout, never still, with his moist right hand, while he unhooked the barb from his mouth, then dropped him back into the stream. He had wet his hand before he touched the trout, so he would not disturb the delicate mucus that covered him. If a trout was touched with a dry hand, a white fungus attacked the unprotected spot. Years before when he had fished crowded streams, with fly fishermen ahead of him and behind him, Nick had again and again come on dead trout, furry with white fungus, drifted against a rock, or floating belly up in some pool. Nick did not like to fish with other men on the river. Unless they were of your party, they spoiled it.*[96]

As noted in the "Complete tasks well" chapter, by wetting his hand, Nick does not ruin the protective mucus layer of the trout. In the context of Nick's dejected state of mind after the war, it should not go unnoticed that Nick admires any creature that has a protective barrier to ward off disease—physical or psychological. He does not want to contribute to any unnecessary harm in the world and, particularly, in the once-pristine woods and rivers of his youth. The "other" fishermen on previous fishing trips who do not follow the unspoken code of how to catch and release properly violate the fishing code and cause unnecessary death—something Nick has seen too much of at war.

Nick Adams also values nature as an ethical arena in "Big Two-Hearted River" by not acting, by not fishing the swamp, and by not hooking trout he knows he cannot land. A swamp is extremely difficult to fish: the trout are easy to lose because the fishing line can get caught in the branches and roots of the fallen trees beneath the surface. As opposed to fishing the active riffles and eddy lines of the fast-moving water in the river, fishing in the swamp is slow, and this could allow Nick's mind to wander back to the horrors he experienced in WWI. Deciding not to fish the swamp due to his inability to focus and successfully land the trout, Nick Adams states, "Beyond that the river went into the swamp. He did not want to go in there now. He felt a reaction against deep wading with water deepening up under his armpits, to hook big trout in places impossible to land them."[97] Nick goes on to state that fishing the swamp "would be tragic." Many critics interpret this as an indication that Nick's post-traumatic stress disorder would emerge in the slow fishing in the swamp and that the emotional weight of the war is manifest in the heavy water threatening to spill over into his waders and send him to the muck at the bottom. These critics are right to focus on Nick's postwar, fragile emotional state, but for our purposes, Nick will not enter into a fishing experience without confidence that he can complete the task well. In Sun Valley, Hemingway favored hunting with those who knew how to complete tasks well and could decide how and when to shoot, how to handle a gun, and how to care for the birds, deer, or pronghorn after a successful hunt. Those who could not do this "were (not) of your party, (and) they spoiled it." The codeless behavior that led to shooting the Sun Valley Lab Bullet's leg and the codeless behavior that allowed two men to shoot from a moving canoe and caused the death of Sun Valley Resort's publicist Gene Van Guilder deeply bothered Hemingway.

At the outset of the story "Big Two-Hearted River," Nick admires the trout and their ability to hold themselves in the current. He admires how perfectly adapted trout's sleek bodies are in facing into the current, how this allows the trout to see the flowing buffet of aquatic and terrestrial insects on the surface, and how trout hold themselves in the current with the least flickering of their tails. Hemingway writes:

> *Nick looked at the burned-over stretch of hillside, where he had expected to find the scattered houses of the town and then walked down the railroad to the bridge over the river. The river was there. It swirled against the log piles of the bridge. Nick looked down into the clear, brown water, colored from the pebbly bottom, and watched the trout keeping themselves steady in the current with wavering fins. As he watched them they changed their positions by quick angles, only to hold steady in the fast water again. Nick watched them for a long time.*[98]

The burned-out hillside. The loss of houses from the manmade clearcut forest fire. But the bridge was still there, Nick and the reader come to discover. "The river was there," Hemingway writes as only he could. Readers are left to fill in the emotion of relief that the river still flows as it once did. And then we discover, along with Nick, that the river is still healthy enough in water quality after all of the ash and soot has passed through to sustain a healthy population of trout. *Not all is lost* by man's mistreatment of the forest and unsustainable clearcutting and slash burning, and by implication and inference, not all is lost for Nick Adams after witnessing the horrors of war. Nick "watches for a long time" how the trout hold themselves effortlessly in the current. Readers are left to unearth the seven-eighths of the iceberg underneath this image; we are left to infer that Nick is heartened by the sustenance of water quality in the river. And we are left to supply the emotional satisfaction Nick experiences as he witnesses a creature associated with his youthful innocence that has survived mistreatment by man. We are also left to supply the emotional longing Nick has to emulate the trout who are able to hold in the flux of things, who are able to resist being swept away by the current, who are able to adapt to a ruined environment and flourish.

On his journey toward the river, Nick Adams finds some heather and is reminded of its medicinal qualities and its palliative fragrance. He crushes it and enjoys its smell as he backpacks toward his camp. Hemingway writes:

> *Nick kept his direction by the sun. He knew where he wanted to strike the river and he kept on through the pine plain, mounting small rises to see other rises ahead of him and sometimes from the top of a rise a great solid island of pines off to his right or left. He broke off some sprigs of the heathery sweet fern, and put them under his pack straps. The chafing crushed it and he smelled it as he walked.*[99]

Nick's fishing trip is a journey toward healing himself: we see that as Nick begins to make the intrinsic journey to a coded state of being; he begins to value nature and its beauty and crushes the heather beneath his pack for the sweet, therapeutic smell. The smell of crushed heather has long been associated with healing, and it is this valuing of nature that is beginning to heal Nick. Heather has long been an ancient remedy to ailments ranging from stomach pain to arthritis to insomnia. It is the cure for insomnia that is instructive for Nick Adams, for Nick fears "the flywheel of his thoughts" before sleep. So readers can assume Nick keeps the heather as a mild sedative or sleep aid. While we do not know if Nick drinks heather-infused tea at camp, we do see Nick enjoy the healing fragrance of heather as he backpacks, and we will see the fear of insomnia and nightmares from the war that plague Nick's sleep in the tent. Nick is hoping to begin the process of healing during this solo trout fishing trip in the region of his youth. The heather, completing tasks well, and valuing nature as an ethical arena aid Nick in his journey toward psychological recovery.

In Hemingway's *For Whom the Bell Tolls*, Hemingway returns to the medical properties of heather when describing a stroll in the mountains of northern Spain during the Spanish Civil War. As he and Maria walk through the mountains, he is overcome by the beauty of their surroundings and his love for her and is able to completely let go for a time of the impending task of blowing the bridge and focus solely on the healing power of the mountains and his love for Maria. Hemingway writes:

> *Then there was the smell of heather crushed and the roughness of the bent stalks under her head and the sun bright on her closed eyes and all his life he would remember the curve of her throat with her head pushed back into the heather roots and her lips that moved smally and by themselves and the fluttering of the lashes on the eyes tight closed against the sun and against everything, and for her everything was red, orange, gold-red from the sun on the closed eyes, and it all was that color, all of it, the filling, possessing, the having, all of that color, all in a blindness of that color.*[100]

The smell of "crushed heather," like the crushed heather under Nick Adams's backpack straps, cues the reader to the healing properties in nature. Robert Jordan later contemplates the bittersweet irony of meeting Maria, the love of his life, and only having three days to spend with her before he must blow the bridge and risk his life that he loses in the retreat after the bridge. It is the simplistic and calming nature of his surroundings and the healing fragrance of the heather that allow him to be more present and enjoy every moment he has with her and, in doing so, put aside both his worries about the future and his potentially fatal task of blowing the bridge.

Being immersed in the task of doing something well has the capacity to heal throughout Hemingway's stories: Francis Macomber and the water buffalo hunt, Santiago and the long, arduous task of bringing a nine-hundred-pound marlin to the skiff, Nick Adams and his expert hooking, landing, and releasing of the trout. But just being immersed *in nature* and fully present in mind and body in the moment in the natural world also has healing properties for many Hemingway characters. You will recall the famous eulogy Hemingway wrote for Sun Valley publicist Gene Van Guilder, who shared Hemingway's love for completing tasks well in nature. Gene was an expert horseman, fly fisherman, and hunter, and his life was cut too short by a young Sun Valley staff member who violated the code of hunting ethics by shooting from behind Gene in a moving canoe. What is left out from the famous excerpt on the Trail Creek Memorial bust and pedestal from Hemingway's heartfelt eulogy for Gene is the line "(Gene) loved the hills in the winter when the snow comes." Of course, Hemingway learned to love the cold, dry, sunny winters of Sun Valley. After Sun Valley Resort reopened in December 21, 1946 (it served as a naval retreat during WWII), Hemingway spent a few winters with "the family" in Sun Valley and his new wife, Mary. Known for his telemark skiing in the Alps after WWI, Hemingway was more than competent at "backcountry skiing"— the act of climbing a mountain on your skis by the use of adhesive skins and then descending down with the skins removed.

HEMINGWAY BACKCOUNTRY SKIING IN THE ALPS IN GSTAAD,
SWITZERLAND. FEBRUARY 1927. *Ernest Hemingway Collection.
John F. Kennedy Presidential Library and Museum, Boston.*

Describing his backcountry ski experiences in the Alps, Hemingway writes, "Finally there was the great glacier run, smooth and straight, forever straight if your legs could hold it, your ankles locked, you running so low, leaning into the speed, dropping forever and forever in the silent hiss of the crisp powder. It was better than any flying or anything else, and you built the ability to do it and to have it with the long climbs, carrying the heavy rucksacks. You could not buy it nor take a ticket to the top. It was the end we worked all winter for, and all the winter built to make it possible."[101] Here is a moment in nature when the observer and the observed become one, when the participant in nature becomes a part of nature. In *A Moveable Feast*, a memoir he worked on in 1957 in Sun Valley and that was published posthumously in 1964, Hemingway laments, "Nobody climbs on skis now." With Sun Valley Resort sending skiers up on chairlifts (in 1936 Sun Valley Resort had the first ski lift service in America), Hemingway lamented the loss of climbing mountains on skis.

He would be pleased to know that Sun Valley currently has a healthy community of backcountry skiers. Hemingway loved the adventure of backcountry skiing, the fortitude and determination it takes to climb a mountain on skis, and the all-day adventure of climbing and descending through mountain glades that were earned by sheer effort. While Hemingway did not ski in Sun Valley (Mary bought him snowshoes to keep him active in his later years), he loved the atmosphere of high-elevation mountain towns and the cold, clean, crisp air associated with them.

Interestingly, in the short story "Cross-Country Snow," a story in the collection *In Our Time* (1925), Hemingway reflects on skiing in the American West but says the mountains are too far away and too hard to access. Developing a conversation that occurs post-WWI between Nick Adams and George, who are traveling Europe before returning to the United States after the war, Hemingway writes:

> *"Will you ever go skiing together in the States?"*
>
> *"I don't know," said Nick.*
>
> *"The mountains aren't much," George said.*
>
> *"No," said Nick. "They're too rocky. There's too much timber and they're too far away."*
>
> *"Yes," said George, "that's the way it is in California."*
>
> *"Yes," Nick said, "that's the way it is everywhere I've ever been."*[102]

At the writing of this story (published in 1925), Sun Valley Resort did not yet exist. But Averell Harriman and his Union Pacific Railroad connected major cities to Sun Valley through a spur line in the 1930s, and the interstate highway system allowed Hemingway to change his tune on accessing Sun Valley, but as a destination resort that still involves long drives by car or multiple changeovers in planes, Sun Valley still retains a remote, isolated feeling. In the same conversation in "Cross-Country Snow," Nick and George reflect on their climb to the inn at which they are eating and the long descent they have ahead of them: "'There's nothing really can touch skiing, is there?' Nick said. 'The way it feels when you first drop off on a long run.' 'Huh,' said George. 'It's too swell to talk about.'"[103] Here, Hemingway finds the adventure of being fully immersed in the untouched powder of the mountains and the act of linking multiple turns in complete solitude to be "too swell" to capture in words.

It is also informative to recall that Frederic Henry in *A Farewell to Arms* longs for not only the awe-inspiring feeling of being in a mountain town at the height of winter, but also the community of coded people that inhabit mountain towns. Frederic admires mountain people's sincere appreciation of the mountains, ability to move through them safely, and respect for those who share their sense of adventure. In speaking with the priest about where he hopes to go on leave, Frederic learns about the priest's town of Abruzzi—a high mountain town in the mountains of Italy with the tallest peak Gran Sasso d'Italia reaching 9,560 feet. The Italian priest attempts to persuade Frederic to go to his hometown of Abruzzi. The priest describes Abruzzi as "full of good hunting. You would like the people though it is cold, clear and dry."[104] When Frederic comes back from leave having spent his time not in Abruzzi but in the cafés and whorehouses of Milan, Frederic ruminates:

> *I had wanted to go to Abruzzi. I had gone to no place where the roads were frozen and hard as iron, where it was clear cold and dry and the snow was dry and powdery and hare-tracks in the snow and the peasants took off their hats and called you Lord and there*

> *was good hunting. I had gone to no such place but to the smoke of cafes and nights when the room whirled and you needed to look at the wall to make it stop, nights in bed, drunk, when you knew that that was all there was, and the strange excitement of waking and not knowing who it was with you, and the world all unreal in the dark and so exciting that you must resume again unknowing and not caring in the night, sure that this was all and all and all and not caring...sometimes (there was) a dispute about the cost.*[105]

This description of Abruzzi could easily be a description of Sun Valley, save the peasants calling you "Lord." In the winters of Sun Valley, Hemingway loved to walk the "roads...frozen and hard as iron, where it was clear cold and dry and the snow was dry and powdery and haretracks in the snow." But in this passage, Frederic Henry does not find renewal in the "clear cold and dry" winter landscape of Abruzzi; he numbs himself with alcohol and prostitutes.

Certainly, Hemingway discovered "there was good hunting" in the Wood River Valley. Abruzzi, where the inhabitants all live by a shared, yet unspoken, ethical code founded in respect for their environment and each other, is immune to the war due its remoteness and due to the snow. From the Italian front in the rain-soaked valley, Frederick sees the sucking mud churned by thousands of feet and vehicles, the stumps of trees cut or blown down, farm animals shot dead in their abandoned pastures, but always, he sees the "*mountains beyond*," white-capped with snow. Even though the advancing Austrian army captures one mountain after the other, there are always more remote snow-filled mountains that remain unconquerable. Frederick has an appreciation for the mountains, and he is drawn toward them. But Frederic does not go to Abruzzi and becomes disgusted with himself for whoring around and drinking too much to make his actions more tolerable. Frederic cleanses himself from the war, literally cleansing himself in the Tagliamento River as he escapes being executed by the military police during the retreat from Caporetto. Frederic then commits to going to the mountain town of Montreux with his love Catherine Barkley to await the birth of their child. He and Catherine lived in "a brown wooden house in the pine trees on the side of a mountain":

> *Outside, in front of the chalet a road went up the mountain. The wheel ruts and ridges were iron hard with the frost, and the road climbed steadily through the forest and up and around the mountain to where there were meadows, and barns and cabins in the meadows at the edge of the woods looking across the valley. The valley was deep and there was a stream at the bottom that flowed down into the lake and when the wind blew across the valley you could hear the stream in the rocks.*[106]

This is the country Frederic wanted to find: he loved the roads "iron hard with the frost" and "the cabins" and "the meadows" and the "stream at the bottom." And he loved the innkeeper of Montreux, and the people of Montreux treated him and themselves with respect and dignity.

This is the Sun Valley Hemingway found: coded people, frozen roads, cabins, winter meadows, and the Big Wood River at the bottom of the valley. Hemingway imaginatively created the mountain town he was seeking in 1929 in *A Farewell to Arms*, and this became a self-fulfilled prophecy that was realized with "the family" of friends he created in Sun Valley between 1939 and 1961.

Frederic and Catherine's life, like the lives of Ernest and his fourth wife, Mary, whom he met in London during WWII, changes dramatically once they have been encompassed by the soothing, peaceful calmness of mountain life. Hemingway writes, "The

HEMINGWAY AND BUMBY, SKIING.
Ernest Hemingway Collection. John F. Kennedy Presidential Library and Museum, Boston.

snow lay all over the country down almost to Montreux…It was a fine country"[107] For Frederick, the mountains represent a place that remains uncorrupted by the war and by the uncoded behavior of the soldiers. Frederic respects the snow and the mountain weather because it has the power to "purify" the land and stop the fighting of the war. Frederick values nature, in particular mountainous environments not only as a therapeutic presence but also as an arena to project his own morality, for in Montreux he completely commits to his love for Catherine.

As Nick Adams loves the feeling of carving a telemark turn in deep powder, Jake Barnes, in *The Sun Also Rises*, loves how water has the capacity to make him feel buoyant when fully immersed in it. But it is a long process for Jake to get to the point in both body and mind to feel cleansed and buoyant by the elastic and baptismal properties of water. In *A Farewell to Arms*, Frederic Henry escapes the war and its atrocities by swimming across and being fully immersed in the Tagliamento River; Frederic reflects upon the experience, "Anger washed away in the river along with any obligation."[108] Similar to Frederic Henry, who dives into the Tagliamento River to escape being shot during the Italian Retreat from Caporetto and emerges cleansed and born again on the other side and committed to forego war for his love for Catherine, Jake Barnes must ultimately address and reject a false love with Brett Ashley before he can feel the healing properties of being fully immersed in the sea at the end of the novel. In a poignant scene of *The Sun Also Rises*, Jake enters into a church with Brett and leaves after dipping his hand in the holy water at the church's exit. Describing Jake's desire for a religious feeling in the church but falling short, Hemingway writes:

> *At the end of the street I saw the cathedral and walked up toward it. The first time I ever saw it I thought the facade was ugly but I liked it now. I went inside. It was dim and dark and the pillars went high up, and there were people praying, and it smelt of incense, and there were some wonderful big windows. I knelt and started to pray and prayed for everybody I thought of, Brett and Mike and Bill and Robert Cohn and myself, and all the bullfighters, separately for*

the ones I liked, and lumping all the rest, then I prayed for myself again, and while I was praying for myself I found I was getting sleepy, so I prayed that the bull-fights would be good, and that it would be a fine fiesta, and that we would get some fishing. I wondered if there was anything else I might pray for and I thought I would like to have some money, so I prayed that I would make a lot of money...thinking of myself as praying, I was a little ashamed, and regretted that I was such a rotten Catholic, but realized there was nothing I could do about it, at least for a while, and maybe never, but that anyway it was a grand religion, and I only wished I felt religious and maybe I would the next time; and then I was out in the hot sun on the steps of the cathedral, and the forefingers and the thumb of my right hand were still damp, and I felt them dry in the sun.[109]

Akin to the moment in Mark Twain's *The Adventures of Huckleberry Finn* in which Huck prays for some fishing line and hooks but finds it does not work and gives up on prayer and religion, Frederic also performs a very shallow and narcissistic prayer. Remember that Ernest Hemingway said that "all modern American literature comes from one book by Mark Twain called *Huckleberry Finn*. American writing comes from that. There was nothing before. There has been nothing as good since."[110] Hemingway may have had Huck's shallow prayer in mind when writing Jake's shallow prayer. Nonetheless, without Hemingway providing the act of dipping his fingers in the holy water, the reader supplies the action and thinks of Jake giving the holy water a go but finding no religious healing in the process. His forefingers and thumb quickly dry in the sun. His prayer and half-hearted crossing of himself quickly evaporate as ineffectual.

It is not until Jake escapes the love "square" between Brett Ashley, Jake Barnes, Robert Cohn, and Mike Campbell and their empty, alcohol-induced uncoded behavior by traveling to the mountains of northern Spain with his friend from New York Bill Gorton that Jake discovers the healing properties of water. Surrounded by the noble and pure wilderness of the Irati River, Jake is able to appreciate the river's beauty and the water's healing powers. Hemingway writes, "I sat on one of the squared timbers and watched the smooth apron of water before the river tumbled into the falls. In the white water at the foot of the dam it was deep...It was hot enough so that it felt good to wade in a cold stream, and *the sun dried you* when you came out and sat on the bank. We found a stream with a pool deep enough to swim in."[111] (my italics) Jake's full body is immersed in the water and like the holy water of the church that dries on his fingers in the hot sun, his body dries in the sun. But Jake is more immersed in the healing powers of river water than in a holy water bowl. The water of the Irati is cleansing in a way that the holy water failed to be. Bill and Jake share a positive, restorative experience fishing for trout and swimming the Irati River. Bill tells Jake, "Listen. You're a hell of a good guy, and I'm fonder of you than anyone on earth."[112] Jake needed to hear that. He needed the restorative experience of being fully immersed in a pure river and the uninterrupted time with a friend who is "fond of him" before they go to the festival in Pamplona and reengage with the now codeless love "pentagon" of Brett, Robert, Mike, Jake, and Pedro—the young matador.

Later in the novel, Jake, again, finds himself separated from the influence of the codeless behavior of his "friends" and removed from the hurt of witnessing his one-time lover Brett fall in love with Pedro Romero. Surrounded by the water in the bay off the coast of San Sebastian, Spain, Jake swims out past the whitewater of the breakers and rolls over fully buoyed by the water. In this state, he can only see the blue sky above him and feel the movement of the water below him. This sense of isolation was also induced by Jake's experience fishing on and swimming in the Irati River. When he reaches the dock that floats out, he observes the town. Jake states:

> *The water was cold. As a roller came, I swam out under the water and came to the surface with all the chill gone. I swam out to the raft...I lay on the raft until I was dry...and then swam ashore. I*

lay on the beach until I was dry. I looked around at the bay, the old town, the casino, the line of trees along the promenade, and the big hotels with their white porches and gold-lettered names...The raft rocked with the motion of the water.[113]

(my italics)

Jake Barnes is fully immersed in the cold, cleansing ocean water and as with the holy water and the river water, he dries in the hot sun. Hemingway juxtaposes Jake's observation of the old town and the casinos and his new point of view coming from his solitary floating on pure ocean waters. Floating on the water, Jake is free from his troubles with Brett and his acquaintances who are all hoping to be with Brett. This comparison of the town and the ocean as completely separate arenas distances Jake from the life he leads in society and puts his own position into perspective. This juxtaposition helps Jake begin his eventual shift toward leading a coded life as a respectable man, as a man who respects himself enough to recognize that his love for Brett Ashley is not reciprocated. Like Pedro Romero, who is lifted by the crowd and strengthened by completing his task well after his successful bullfight, Jake is lifted up by the water after his successful release from his troubles. Jake finally found the healing and holy properties of water that he longed for and did not find in the church. Jake is ready for the task of breaking off his relationship with Brett. Once again, nature calms and heals.

At the end of *For Whom the Bell Tolls*, Robert Jordan finds his ability to be immersed in nature and fully aware of its calm, self-sustaining processes to be edifying in his preparation for blowing the bridge to thwart the Nationalist progress against the Republicans in Spain. As Jordan waits for the planes to arrive to signal his need to blow the bridge, he feels attuned with nature, and this calms him. Hemingway writes, "Robert Jordan lay behind the trunk of a pine tree on the slope of the hill above the road and the bridge and watched it become daylight. He loved this hour of the day always and now he watched it; feeling it gray within him as though he were a part of the slow lightening that comes before the rising of the sun."[114] When Robert Jordan is alone in the woods and "feeling (the sunlight) gray within him as though he were a part of the slow lightening that comes before the rising of the sun," he feels connected to the reassuring processes in nature that commit unconsciously to sustaining life. Like Jake Barnes in the stream and on the raft in the ocean, Jordan is buoyed by this immersion in the half light of dawn and is able to commit to his task with confidence.

Like Jake Barnes and Robert Jordan, Nick Adams of "Big Two-Hearted River" also finds nature to be a reassuring presence and an arena upon which to project his morality. At the end of one of his most famous stories about the healing properties of water "Big Two-Hearted River I and II," a two-part story that is interrupted by a "chapter" vignette about the hanging of Sam Cardinella, Nick refuses to fish the swamp that is one of the two swamps or "hearts" of the river. The reader's and Nick's time on the river is interrupted by this horrifying vignette that describes a hanging. At the end of the "Big Two-Hearted River I," we leave Nick falling to sleep in his tent and pleased that the "flywheel" of the mind did not get started and that he was able to "choke" his mind with sleep. Readers presume that Nick recollects the hanging and the disproportionate number of African Americans on this death row (three of the waiting five men to be hung are African American) as he "waits for sleep." This is "the stuff that (nightmares) are made on." Hoping to go to sleep quickly to hold back horrifying memories is hardly an excellent defense mechanism against PTSD. Nick will need more to hold off a permanently debilitated mind. He will need to conduct himself well, and once again, nature (and water) provide the arena upon which Nick can heal himself. Knowing when and how to take a shot at a duck that will kill it instantly, knowing how to shoot a deer (or lion) to minimize its suffering, and knowing where to fish so that the landing of the trout is possible constitute the unspoken code of fishing and hunting. This knowledge can only be gained by experience. If he is to practice catch and release, Nick does not want to "hook big trout in places impossible to land them." The roots and downed trees and their branches provide excellent refuge for a hooked trout and there is a strong likelihood of breaking the hook off in the mouth of the trout. This would make the fishing "tragic." He does not want to unnecessarily harm the very trout he so admires for their perseverance through man's mistreatment of their environment, through the clear-cutting and burning of the remaining downed trees. If he is to practice catch and release, he wants to do so properly.

Hemingway would be pleased to know that most of Sun Valley's Big Wood River and Silver Creek are now "catch and release, fly-fishing only" streams that are closed to fishing in the months of April and May when trout are spawning. As one of the first literary writers to depict catch-and-release fishing and as an older man who advocated and practiced catch-and-release marlin fishing and argued for a closed season on marlin fishing during the spawning season, Hemingway would be encouraged to know that these practices took hold in the wild country he so loved in Sun Valley.

Hemingway's first son, Jack, picked up his dad's lead and, like his father who was vice president of the International Game Fish Association (IGFA), Jack became Idaho's Fish and Game Commissioner in the 1970s. In this role, Jack was integral to the Nature Conservancy's purchasing of Silver Creek preserve and the easements established with local ranch owners whose land borders Silver Creek. Jack was also an advocate of the catch-and-release fly-fishing only policies that govern Silver Creek preserve. While Ernest Hemingway was shaped by the Roosevelt-Pinchot conservationist mindset captured in Gifford Pinchot's claim "the first principle of conservation is development, the use of the natural resources now existing on this continent for the benefit of the people who live here now," Ernest Hemingway began to arrive in thought and practice that nature and its inhabitants have an intrinsic right to exist and that current and future generations of flora, fauna, and humans have an equal right to be able to flourish in intact ecosystems.

In *Green Hills of Africa*, Hemingway explicitly acknowledges the celerity with which modern man can destroy an intact ecosystem. Constantly seeking out the frontiers of the Gulf Stream, the wilderness of Idaho, the immense plains of Africa, Hemingway became conscious of the devastating impact of modern men in contradistinction with native peoples and their native intelligence that leads to a sustainable relationship with the land. Reflecting on the impact of the "foreigner" upon native ecosystems, Hemingway writes:

> *A continent ages quickly once we come. The natives live in harmony with it. But the foreigner destroys, cuts down trees, drains the water, so that the water supply is altered and in short time the soil... starts to blow away as it has blown away in every old country. The earth gets tired of being exploited. A country wears out quickly...A country was made to be as we found it. We are the intruders and after we are dead we may have ruined it but it will still be there.*[115]

In language that anticipates the best rants of Edward Abbey in *Desert Solitaire* or Gary Snyder in *The Practice of the Wild*, Hemingway articulates *his* awareness of modern man's unconscious destruction of the sustainability of an ecosystem. But he states this in a nonfiction account of big game hunting safaris that were very much of the Gifford Pinchot and Teddy Roosevelt Progressive era conservationist mindset. Hemingway was of his era in his interactions with nature for much of his life but also beyond his era in anticipating a more preservationist mindset that valued intact ecosystems as an intrinsic good.

It took the actions of his first son, Jack Hemingway, to realize his father's nascent environmentally conscious practices. Jack also followed his father's lead to war as well and even jumped out of airplanes during WWII into conflict areas with a fly rod as well as a gun. The Hemingway Silver Creek Legacy memorial is a rock that bears the epigraph to *The Sun Also Rises* excerpted from Ecclesiastes:

THE HEMINGWAY LEGACY
ONE GENERATION PASSES AWAY, AND ANOTHER GENERATION COMES; BUT THE EARTH ABIDES FOREVER. THE SUN ALSO RISES, AND THE SUN GOES DOWN, AND HASTENS TO ITS PLACE WHERE IT AROSE.

HEMINGWAY SILVER CREEK MEMORIAL. *Author's collection.*

The next "generation" after Ernest's death in 1961 in Ketchum, Idaho, was inhabited by Jack Hemingway and afforded him the opportunity through the burgeoning environmental movement to ensure not only that the earth abides forever but also that the remarkable wildlife diversity of Silver Creek remains intact for this and future generations of moose, ducks, deer, elk, trout, and people. This is one of the many Hemingway legacies.

Hemingway's second son, Patrick, whom he had with his second wife, Pauline Pfeiffer, said Papa taught his sons how to shoot and hunt. Being a "social hunter," Papa liked having his kids and friends around, but also liked his hunts to be well organized. Those formative years hunting for duck, dove, pheasants, rabbit, pronghorn, and deer in Idaho made a deep impression on Patrick who followed his father's lead by becoming involved in wildlife management in East Africa. "Patrick retired to Montana in 1975 after careers as a safari outfitter and wildlife management instructor in East Africa. He said his father was very much at home in the Idaho mountains from 1939 to 1947, when Papa spent five fall seasons in Sun Valley and Ketchum."[116] Patrick recalls, "(Papa) was very fond of that area. He had a lot of good friends in Ketchum." The legacy of acting upon powerful, formative experiences in nature by committing to manage wildlands lives on in both Jack and Patrick Hemingway long after Ernest's passing.

In addition, Ernest Hemingway would also be pleased to know that the wild but unregulated country of central Idaho has been protected in perpetuity by the federal designation of three wilderness areas in a state that now has the second most federally designated wilderness in the lower forty-eight states. In 1964, the Wilderness Act decreed:

> *A wilderness, in contrast with those areas where man and his own works dominate the landscape, is hereby recognized as an area where the earth and its community of life are untrammeled by man, where man himself is a visitor who does not remain...land retain(s) its primeval character and influence, without permanent improvements or human habitation, which is protected and managed so as to preserve its natural conditions and which generally appears to have been affected primarily by the forces of nature, with the imprint of man's work substantially unnoticeable (and) has outstanding opportunities for solitude or a primitive and unconfined type of recreation*[117]

The Sawtooth Mountains Ernest Hemingway so admired from Galena summit became a wilderness area in 1972, the Middle Fork of the Salmon area that Hemingway hunted became the Frank Church River of No Return Wilderness area in 1980, and the Boulder White Cloud mountains, the peaks Ernest could see from the trap-shooting deck of his Ketchum, Idaho, home, became three wilderness areas in 2015.

Moreover, Ernest would smile at knowing that one of the three wilderness areas that comprise the Boulder White Cloud Wilderness bears the name "Hemingway Boulders Wilderness."

Since son Jack was so heavily involved in the preservation of Silver Creek Preserve with the Nature Conservancy, Mary Hemingway bequeathed the Hemingway House in Warm Springs, just outside of Ketchum, to the Nature Conservancy. (The Hemingway House is now under the supervision of The Community Library in Ketchum). Since the house and fourteen and one-half acres of riverfront property have been largely untouched since Mary's passing in 1986, the property will forever preserve this section of the Big Wood River riparian area. The Hemingway legacy of love for wild places lives on.

4

FIND FAITH IN LOVE

Take risks in love as an antidote to despair in order to find that love is a "religious feeling."

SUN VALLEY STORIES: FIND FAITH IN LOVE

Ernest Hemingway was always in love. Just not always with the same woman. Always married from his twenty-second year until his death, Hemingway had four wives: Hadley Richardson (1921–1927), Pauline "Piper" Pfeiffer (1927–1939), Martha Gellhorn (1940–1946), and Mary Welsh (1946–1961). What did Hemingway value about being in love? He valued love as salvation from faithlessness in the world, in world leaders, in war, and in God. He valued love's ability to become "a religious feeling" in the sense that those in love possess a desire to serve and honor the other and sacrifice for the other. It may be too easy and be too much of an oversimplification to state that Hemingway valued being in love so much that when love ended or waned, he moved on, but this is certainly the case in many of his relationships. And in many of his stories and novels, characters end relationships when couples stop loving, and those who do not honor love hang on to a failed love, much to their regret. While deeply self-critical of moving on from his love for his first wife, Hadley, and deeply affected by each failed marriage, Hemingway honored the ideal of love by moving on when love waned.

It is important to separate Hemingway's personal relationships from the relationships he depicts so vividly in his texts, but we need only list a few of the famous relationships in his texts to grasp Hemingway's criticism of characters who hang on when the love is gone. Think of the unnecessarily prolonged relationship of Francis and Margot Macomber in "The Short Happy Life of Francis Macomber"; the American and Jig in "Hills Like White Elephants"; Harry and his wife in "The Snows of Kilimanjaro"; Mr. and Mrs. Elliot in "Mr. and Mrs. Elliot"; the couple in "Out of Season"; and the couple in "Cat in the Rain." And in stark contrast, think of the intensity of the love between Frederic and Catherine in *A Farewell to Arms* and between Robert and Maria in *For Whom the Bell Tolls*.

Hemingway's first significant love was Agnes Von Kurowsky, a British nurse who helped Ernest recover from the leg wound that he incurred while handing out chocolates and cigarettes to wounded Italian soldiers in World War I. (Ernest volunteered for the Italian Red Cross Ambulance Service after he believed he would be unable to enlist in the US Army for his poor eyesight.) Agnes became the inspiration for Catherine Barkley in *A Farewell to Arms*, as Marty Gellhorn became the inspiration for Maria in *For Whom the Bell Tolls*. Interestingly, both fictional relationships, unlike their real-life inspirations, sustained a passionate love that is only interrupted by death: Catherine dies in childbirth in *A Farewell to Arms*, and Robert Jordan dies, we presume, while defending Maria and others as they escape an attack in the Spanish Civil War novel *For Whom the Bell Tolls*. During WWI, British nurse Von Kurowsky left Hemingway for an Italian officer when Hemingway returned to the States after the war. However, in an autobiographical WWI short story understatedly titled "A Very Short Story" (it is a page and a half long) in *In Our Time*, Hemingway creates a nurse who leaves the soldier and depicts the male narrator as heartbroken and despairing over whether he will love again. In contrast, Hemingway creates a fictional WWI relationship with nurse Catherine Barkley in *A Farewell to Arms*, and this love is sustained up until the moment of Catherine's tragic death in childbirth. Here in *A Farewell to Arms*, readers experience Hemingway's use of "the freedom of fiction" to create a better version of events, a better version of characters involved than reality provided.

Hemingway's first wife, Hadley Richardson (eight years older than Ernest), looked like Agnes Von Kurowsky. Ernest and Hadley were married in 1921 after Hemingway's return from WWI and then lived in Paris on her trust fund and earnings from Hemingway's journalistic pieces.

Ernest and Hadley had Jack Hemingway who became a longtime Sun Valley resident. While raising Jack "Bumby" Hemingway in Paris, Hemingway met Pauline Pfeiffer, a wealthy, chic, cosmopolitan model who befriended Hadley as a foray to seduce Ernest. After suspecting and confirming her suspicion about the affair, Hadley forced Hemingway to sign a document that stated that he would agree to avoid seeing Pauline for one hundred days. Hadley stated in this "contract," that if after the one hundred days, Hemingway still loved Pauline, then she would file for divorce. Well, Hemingway signed this contract and sealed his fate in the signing, for a few weeks into the one hundred days, Hadley filed for divorce.

Hemingway married Pauline Pfeiffer (four years older than Ernest) in 1927, and they lived in the house she purchased in Key West. They had two sons, Patrick and Gregory. "Ernest felt he had made a mistake leaving his first wife Hadley, to marry his current wife Pauline...Ernest still loved Hadley many years after they had both remarried," writes Tillie Arnold in *The Idaho Hemingway*.[118] Hemingway never completely let go of Hadley.

Tired of domestic life in Key West and after a few critically disfavored books, *Death in the Afternoon* (1932), *Green Hills of Africa* (1935), and *To Have and Have Not* (1937), Hemingway was restless. He had an affair with Jane Mason in Key West and Cuba, but she attempted suicide and broke her back by falling from a balcony. Callously, Hemingway once described Jane as "the girl who fell for me...literally."[119]

During this restless period, Hemingway became immediately smitten after seeing Marty Gellhorn at Sloppy Joe's Bar in Key West. Ernest fell in love with Marty (nine years younger than Hemingway) during his marriage to Pauline Pfieffer. Marty was a war correspondent and joined Hemingway in covering the Spanish Civil War. After his second visit to Sun Valley with Marty, Hemingway married her in Cheyenne, Wyoming, in 1940 during a drive from Sun Valley. This intense, fiery love between two independent souls with equal passion for adventure and writing only lasted until 1946.

While in Sun Valley, Ernest took Marty on his hunting adventures, which she tolerated with feigned enthusiasm. Marty was smart, independent, adventurous, and fearless. Ernest was deeply in love with her during his early visits to Sun Valley, and it was an intense passion that would find expression in the intense three-day love affair between Robert Jordan and Maria in *For Whom the Bell Tolls*—a text he worked on while staying in room 206 of the Sun Valley Lodge. With Marty as immediate inspiration, Hemingway paints Maria in these words, "Her teeth were white in her brown face and her skin and eyes were the same golden tawny brown…He did not believe there would be any such thing as a long time anymore but if there ever was such a thing he would like to spend it with her…Why not marry her? Sure, he thought. I will marry her. Then we will be Mr. and Mrs. Robert Jordan of Sun Valley, Idaho."[120] Hemingway associated Maria and Marty with the earth, with golden brown hair that flows as a field of grain flows in a gentle wind. The young, vital muse of the author and journalist, Marty Gellhorn inspired this image of fertility, of youth, of vitality in Maria in the fall of 1939 in Sun Valley. Well, indeed, Ernest and Marty became Mr. and Mrs. Ernest Hemingway of Sun Valley, Idaho but spent most of their time at the home—the Finca Vigia—that Marty purchased in Cuba.

Beyond learning dove, duck, partridge, pronghorn, deer, and elk hunting from Sun Valley resort hunting guide and photographer Lloyd Arnold, Hemingway also admired Lloyd's deep love for his wife, Tillie Arnold. In a telegram from Cheyenne, Wyoming, after marrying Marty Gellhorn on November 21, 1940, Hemingway wrote to Lloyd and Tillie Arnold, "We hope we can live up to our wedding pictures and also to be as good a pair as you two."[121] Lloyd Arnold took the photos of Hemingway and Marty looking off into the Sun Valley hills before they

HEMINGWAY AND HIS THIRD WIFE, MARTHA GELLHORN.
The Community Library, Ketchum, Idaho.

left to get married on their trip to their new house in Cuba. While the Hemingway-Gellhorn marriage did not last as long as the Arnolds' marriage, Hemingway deeply admired the love between Lloyd and Tillie. Hemingway valued Lloyd as a mentor for his knowledge and appreciation of good hunting country as well as his knowledge and appreciation of a good woman.

Hemingway's traditional, Congregationalist Oak Park, Illinois, upbringing, while rejected on many fronts by Hemingway in his life and in the characters of Santiago, Nick Adams, Robert Jordan, and countless others in his fiction, influenced Hemingway's respect for the tradition of marriage (despite the three divorces) for Hemingway always committed to marrying the women he loved. In fact, Frederic Henry of *A Farewell to Arms* openly struggled with the idea of having a child with Catherine Barkley out of wedlock and repeatedly urges them to get married despite Catherine's insistence that they are "married" in her mind. Robert Jordan also promises Maria that they will get married after the war, even though Maria claims that the traditions of a religiously approved marriage did not matter to her, since the Loyalists had claimed Catholicism. Hemingway's love for Marty Gellhorn was on full display during the early fall visits of 1939 and 1940. Young, fearless, adventurous, intelligent, passionate, independent, and beautiful, Marty was a welcome contrast to the domesticated family life of raising his two boys Patrick and Gregory with Pauline "Piper" Pfeiffer in Key West Florida in the 1930s. His failed marriage to the religiously devout Piper did not sway Hemingway's commitment to the tradition of marriage. Within a year of his divorce from Pauline, Hemingway married Marty in 1940. As rival modernist fiction writer William Faulkner put it, "Hemingway's mistake was that he thought he had to marry all of them."[122]

Hemingway's final marriage to Mary Welsh lasted for fifteen years, his longest marriage. Like Marty, Mary was also an independent woman and accomplished writer whom he met during his time as a journalist during WWII. Their marriage returned Hemingway to Sun Valley where they purchased a house together. Hemingway's multiple marriages and the fact that he was never not married stem from his "instinctive self protection…he guarded himself against betrayal and loneliness by conducting a liaison with a future wife during the current marriage; when he had ensured his own emotional security, he (often) abandoned his wife before she could leave him… When the current love was over, he secured the next one to sustain both his *faith in love* and his deep fear of being a man without a woman, of being without someone to love. This all stems from his first loss of Agnes and his trepidation of feeling that emotionally vulnerable again.[123] (my italics)

HEMINGWAY AND MARY, HIS FOURTH WIFE, ON A CHUKAR HUNT. *The Community Library, Ketchum, Idaho.*

In his final days in Ketchum, Hemingway lost his capacity for love. A man always interested in love as both his life and his works attest, Hemingway, unfortunately, believed he had outlived his ability to value being in love in the end.

NOVELS AND SHORT STORIES: FIND FAITH IN LOVE

Known for being a fine writer of action in war, bullfighting, fishing, and hunting, Hemingway is often overlooked for his keen ability to capture accurately both the tension and deep contentment between those in love. In the early collection of short stories in *In Our Time*, Hemingway depicts, through the protagonist Nick Adams and others, an early lost love and the anxieties of being unable to love again after witnessing the horrors of WWI.

We all first learn the definition of love by witnessing the relationship of our parents. Resentful of, in his view, his father's inability to stand up to his domineering and deeply religious and traditional mother (whom Hemingway referred to as "an All American bitch"), Hemingway depicts the chasm between Nick's mother and father in the short story "The Doctor and the Doctor's Wife" in *In Our Time*. It is interesting to note that the wife (Nick's mother) is not given a name but is depicted as the "doctor's wife" in the title. Signaling the now rejected traditional view of marriage that the wife should subordinate her interests and property rights to those of the husband, "the doctor's wife" (like the title Mr. and Mrs. Robert Jordan of Sun Valley, Idaho), Hemingway hints at the expectation that the husband should be supported by his wife who should suppress her views to support her husband's.

This does not occur in the story. After a near physical altercation between Nick's father and Native American laborer "Dick Boulton" over Dick's accusation that Nick's father was stealing the logs washed ashore, Nick's father comes home angry. Capturing the tension between Nick's mother, who is a Christian Scientist who questions the use of medicine to impede God's will with the sick and Nick's father, who is a doctor, Hemingway writes:

> *"Was anything the matter?"*

> *"I had a row with Dick Boulton."*

"Remember that he who ruleth his spirit is greater than he who taketh the city…"

Her husband did not answer.

[…]

"Tell me, Henry…what was the trouble about?"

"Well, Dick owes me money from pulling his squaw through pneumonia and I guess he wanted a row so he would not have to take it out in work."

His wife was silent.

[…]

"Dear…I really don't think anyone would do a thing like that."

"No?"

[…]

The doctor went out on the porch. The screen door slammed behind him.

He heard his wife catch her breath when the door slammed.

"Sorry," he said, outside her window with the blinds drawn.

"It's all right, dear," she said.[124]

Silences are important in Hemingway's fiction. The husband silently rejects his wife's religious platitude. The wife silently rejects her husband's racist account of Dick Boulton. The doctor lies to his wife about the fight, and she espouses her religious platitude that one who controls anger surpasses one who does not. Speaking past each other and rejecting each other in silence, the husband and wife exhibit the tension in their relationship. As we must in reading Hemingway, readers can assume that Nick internalizes their dysfunctional relationship, if not in overhearing this conversation, then in overhearing others of the same ilk. Hemingway's "tip of the iceberg" theory of writing is exhibited in this dialogue. On the surface of this moment, the scene seems fairly unspectacular, but underneath, a more potent source of tension exists between the couple. When the husband apologizes from "outside her window with the blinds drawn," this implies that the wife doesn't want to see his aggression and that they live in different worlds. The husband was resistant to explain to his wife why he was in an argument, and when he does, he lies, seemingly because he doesn't expect her to understand the reasoning behind, in his belief, a man's need to be tenacious and aggressive toward other men when honor is questioned, even when he knows that he is in the wrong. Nick's father apologizes to Nick's mother for slamming the door, but this is far from resolving the tension between them. Nick's mother asks her husband to have Nick return to the house. When Nick's father finds Nick, Nick rejects his mother's request and joins his dad in a hunt for black squirrels. Nick identifies with his father's masculinity and aggressiveness. The relationship of the doctor and the doctor's wife may have irresolvable tensions, and Nick and the reader know that, at times, men and women live in different worlds. Worlds that may not be bridged once love has come to an end.

In the next story of *In Our Time*, "The End of Something," Nick exhibits this knowledge of the communication gap between men and women and breaks off his relationship with his high school sweetheart Marjorie (similar to Marty / Martha and Maria—women who occupy both Hemingway's real and imagined worlds later in life). Not only is it the end of the relationship between Nick and Marjorie, it is also the end of lumber mill town of Horton's Bay (the "second growth" of trees is just emerging), and it is the end of America's and American soldiers' innocence as WWI begins. But it is interesting how Hemingway depicts both Nick's and Marjorie's emotional states through actions and silences, as he did in "The Doctor and the Doctor's Wife." Nick and Marjorie are trolling for trout in Horton's Bay. No fish are biting, and Marjorie points out "they are feeding," and Nick responds "but they won't strike" in a subtle reference to Nick's desire to leave Marjorie before questions of marriage arise.[125]

After a day of no luck with the fish, Nick and Marjorie light a fire and lay out a blanket on a beach on the lake. They do not touch each other. Marjorie has been suspecting that something is bothering Nick. However, he is reluctant to tell her. Hemingway writes:

> *They sat on the blanket without touching each other and watched the moon rise.*
>
> *"What's really the matter?" Marjorie said.*
>
> *"I don't know."*
>
> *"Of course you know."*
>
> *"No I don't."*
>
> *"Go on and say it."*
>
> *Nick looked on at the moon, coming up over the hills.*
>
> *"It isn't fun any more"*
>
> *He was afraid to look at Marjorie. Then he looked at her.*

She sat there with her back toward him. He looked at her back.

"It isn't fun anymore. Not any of it."

"Isn't love any fun?"

"No," Nick said

"I'm going to take the boat," Marjorie called to him.

[…]

"I'll push the boat off for you."

"You don't need to," she said. *Marjorie was afloat in the boat on the water with moonlight on it.*[126]

Unable to express how he really feels, how their love has lost its allure, how he fears that Horton's Bay has no future for him, how he longs for an adventure at war, or how marriage scares him, Nick talks past Marjorie by hinting that the trout refuse to strike. Marjorie conveys her independence and lack of desire to wait for Nick to mature and love and marry her by setting out on the boat by herself without help from Nick. While Hemingway often created characters who were not true to love by hanging onto a relationship long after the love had dissipated (see the Macombers in "The Short Happy Life of Francis Macomber" and Jake and Brett, Mike and Brett, and Robert Cohn and Brett in *The Sun Also Rises*), this depiction of a young man recognizing the end of a love shows a respect for love. This is not to say that Nick does not later regret his decision and wish to return to Marjorie in "Three Day Blow," but this only underscores the difficult but necessary transition out of a love that has no future.

As Nick listens in front of a fire in "Three Day Blow" to his friend Bill celebrate Nick's break up with Marjorie, Nick naively believes he may be able to return to Marjorie and their love. Bill tells Nick, "Once a man is married he is absolutely bitched…done for…they get this sort of fat married look."[127] Hemingway conveys meaning in silences again and writes, "Nick said nothing." Readers must supply the "seven-eighths" below this iceberg and infer that Nick disagrees and longs for his lost love. Nick holds onto the hope that he can go to town Saturday night and get Marjorie back, but this never occurs. Nick goes hunting with Bill and looks for Nick's dad, who is hunting in the swamp.

Hemingway creates many recurring images in the tightly unified short story cycle of *In Our Time* and unifies them by the images that carry over from story to story and even story to chapter. Fire. Silences. Folded legs. Readers presume that Nick recalls the fire on the beach with Marjorie while Nick is sitting in front of the fire with Bill. Nick knows his father's silences spoke volumes about his father's disagreements with his wife, as Nick silently disagrees with Bill.

And Nick once again chooses the masculine over the feminine by joining Bill to go hunt in the swamp and look for Nick's dad. It is telling that the next chapter vignette (Chapter V) in *In Our Time* depicts a firing squad during WWI, and then the next story shows Nick punched off a train, as he travels to Chicago to enlist in WWI. Reading Hemingway, we learn that there is a respect for love in breaking off a love with no future, but also that there are also consequences to men without the tempering, calming influence of women.

As the short story collection evolves, many chapters and stories depict violence at war, but one, "A Very Short Story," reveals a quick war romance that ends badly. Nearly autobiographical, Hemingway's "A Very Short Story" conveys Hemingway's love for nurse Agnes Von Kurowsky, who tended to Hemingway's wounds in his leg after he was shot working in an Italian Medical unit. After Hemingway returns to the United States, her "Dear John" letter breaks nineteen-year-old Hemingway's heart. On March 7, 1919, Agnes wrote Hemingway the following letter:

Ernie, dear boy,

I am writing this late at night after a long think by myself, and I am afraid it is going to hurt you, but, I'm sure it won't harm you permanently.

For quite awhile before you left, I was trying to convince myself it was a real love-affair, because, we always seemed to disagree, and then arguments always wore me out so that I finally gave in to keep you from doing something desperate.

Now, after a couple of months away from you, I know that I am still very fond of you, but, it is more as a mother than as a sweetheart. It's alright to say I'm a Kid, but, I'm not, and I'm getting less and less so every day.

So, Kid (still Kid to me, and always will be) can you forgive me some day for unwittingly deceiving you? You know I'm not really bad, and don't mean to do wrong, and now I realize it was my fault in the beginning that you cared for me, and regret it from the bottom of my heart. But, I am now and always will be too old, and that's the truth, and I can't get away from the fact that you're just a boy—a kid.

I somehow feel that someday I'll have reason to be proud of you, but, dear boy, I can't wait for that day, and it was wrong to hurry a career.

I tried hard to make you understand a bit of what I was thinking on that trip from Padua to Milan, but, you acted like a spoiled child, and I couldn't keep on hurting you. Now, I only have the courage because I'm far away.

Then—and believe me when I say this is sudden for me, too—I expect to be married soon. And I hope and pray that after you thought things out, you'll be able to forgive me and start a wonderful career and show what a man you really are.

Ever admiringly & fondly,

Your friend,

Aggie[128]

Aggie sees no future for them and values love by letting Hemingway know that their love affair has no future. It is interesting to note how Hemingway captures this heartbreak in his imagination in "A Very Short Story." Waiting for surgery, the soldier (an anonymous "he" who could be Nick, any veteran, and, of course, Hemingway) "went under the anesthetic holding tight to himself so he would not blab about anything during the silly, talky time."[129] This desire for silence is linked to a desire to not let out all of the horrors he has seen at war and, thereby, appear emotionally and psychologically weak.

The soldier's potential PTSD is exacerbated after he falls in love with the nurse Luz and his heart is broken when she expresses in a letter to him that their love was "only a boy and girl love"—a line that smacks of Agnes's derisive comment in her letter that "you're just a boy—a kid." Hemingway ends the story with Luz rejected by her fiancé and with the American soldier "contracting gonorrhea from a sales girl…while riding in the back of a taxi cab."[130] In Hemingway's fictional and actual worlds, men without women to love behave badly. As Hemingway stated in a letter to Howell Jenkins in June of 1919, "I loved (Agnes) once and then she gypped me. And I don't blame her. But I set out to cauterize her memory and I burnt it out with a course of booze and other women and now it's gone."[131] But as we know in *A Farewell to Arms*, Hemingway wrote an entire novel on what a sustained love with a WWI nurse *would* have been like. While Hemingway shows Nick breaking off a love without a future in "The End of Something," he shows us what it feels like to be on the receiving end of this in "A Very Short Story." But neither relationships' end devalues love, for neither Nick and Marjorie nor the soldier and Luz (nor Hemingway and Agnes) were in relationships in which love could be sustained. Hemingway's stories show a deep respect for love because when love faded in these relationships, all involved moved on.

Hemingway's innovative approach in the short story collection *In Our Time* includes unchronological narration, chapters that are one paragraph vignettes, short stories that blend fiction and journalism, recurring images to unify the stories, and the diffusion of the protagonist Nick Adams's consciousness into the consciousnesses of other characters seemingly unrelated to Nick. Let's examine what the stories with other characters reveal about how Hemingway and Nick Adams valued love. In the famous and often anthologized short story "Soldier's Home," Harold Krebs is a WWI veteran who returns to his home in Kansas City and who likely suffers, as Nick suffers, with PTSD—although this mental diagnosis did not exist at the time of writing the story. During a conversation between Krebs and his mother about what he will do with himself now that he is returned from the war, Krebs says that he has no desire to get a job, marry, and settle down. He fears the emotional consequences of opening up to a woman. Krebs's mother expresses her despair for her son and her fear for his future. Developing a conversation between them, Hemingway writes:

> *"God has some work for everyone to do. There can be no idle hands in His Kingdom."*
>
> *"I'm not in His Kingdom,"* Krebs said.
>
> *[...]*
>
> *"I pray for you all day long, Harold."*
>
> Krebs looked at the bacon fat hardening on his plate.
>
> *"You father is worried…He thinks you have lost your ambition…"*

Krebs said nothing.

"Don't you love your mother, dear boy?"

"No," Krebs said.

His mother looked at him from across the table. Her eyes were shiny. She started crying.

"I don't love anybody," Krebs said.[132]

Recalling the religious platitudes of Nick's mother in "The Doctor and the Doctor's Wife," Hemingway shows how Krebs, like Nick's father, also rejects easy, unquestioned faith. And the silences recur in this story. After hearing that God has work for him and that his father thinks he has lost his ambition, Krebs says nothing. Like Nick, who disagrees in silence with Bill in "Three Day Blow," and like Nick's dad, who disagrees with his wife in silence in "The Doctor and the Doctor's Wife," Krebs chooses to reject both faith and his father's despair about him in silence.

When Krebs's mother asks him about loving her, Krebs breaks his silence and says he does not love anybody and longs for his previous silence. How can he explain to his mother that after the war, after the atrocities, after bearing witness to his own failure to behave well, he is having difficulty loving himself, his country, others, and God? Krebs's mother then asks him to pray with her. Krebs tells her he cannot pray, but the scariest part of all of this is Krebs's emotional numbness. "None of it had touched him."[133] After telling his mother that he does not love anybody and does not believe in God or live in his kingdom, Krebs was not emotionally distraught. Not being able to respond emotionally to a heart-wrenching moment is more disturbing than feeling the full emotional weight of the moment.

In his most truthful moment so far, Krebs admits to his mother that he doesn't have the capability to love anyone anymore (especially himself). To love requires an emotional balance, which the reader can see that Krebs does not have after his worldview completely changed through the war. But Krebs's mother cannot understand this because she has no means to identify with his experiences. In this quote, Hemingway uses short, monosyllabic words in sentences to add more to the piece by subtracting from it. This writing style also shows Krebs's inability to articulate emotional complexity after his experiences at war. Krebs wants a simple life where he can be with girls without opening up, where he can understand his experiences without having to relive them, and where he can have faith without having to reconcile with himself. But Krebs realizes during his conversation with his mother that he doesn't want to keep pretending that everything can be fine and normal after what he has been through. Krebs's disconnect with women is also shown earlier in the chapter when he describes how "he wanted a girl but he did not want to have to work to get her," and he "did not want to get into the intrigue and politics," or "to tell any more lies" just to be with a woman. Most importantly, Krebs "did not want any consequences ever again"[134] The reader can see Krebs's inability to be in a real relationship because he is left without faith or hope after seeing such horror and violence, which most people are lucky enough to never experience. Hemingway uses the story "Soldier's Home" to demonstrate the ways in which the war stole faith from soldiers like Nick and Krebs, which furthermore served to create a deep disjointedness in their relationships with women afterward. Hemingway diffuses Nick's consciousness throughout these chapters and stories by showing his experience of war through multiple minds, and goes beyond Nick into Krebs and others who were affected by both witnessing and participating in atrocities at war. Again, men without women to love are dangerous to themselves and the world. The experience of war took away a capacity for love; this is the great tragedy of "Soldier's Home." Of course, Krebs's faithlessness in love after the war is Nick's and by further extension, at times, Hemingway's.

In the post-WWI stories that follow "Soldier's Home" in *In Our Time*, the reader is bombarded with failed relationships in which men do not have the capacity to love well and do not value love enough to move on when the relationship is over. Hemingway is honoring his definition of love by stating what love is not and disparaging those who hang on too long in a relationship after love has waned. Continuing to diffuse the consciousness of Nick Adams into other characters, Hemingway depicts post-WWI couples traveling around Europe on the cheap after the war without being in love and without a sense of a long-term commitment to the other and without a plan to end their relationships. The first couple we meet in the short story collection *In Our Time* is Mr. and Mrs. Elliot. They are not in love and may never have been in love. She mocks him for his naïveté and sincerity (Mr. Elliot had never kissed a woman before her). Mrs. Elliot feels so emotionally unsatisfied by the relationship that she invites her girlfriend to join them in Europe to live with them. Out of touch with his wife's emotional needs and out of touch with modern poetry's focus on brevity, Mr. Elliot slept alone in a separate bed after staying up late writing long poems. But neither the husband nor the wife escape Hemingway's implied criticism, for each does not value love enough to leave the other.

Still expanding Nick's life experience into another postwar couple, Hemingway connects the couple in "Cat in the Rain" specifically to WWI by having the woman look at the war memorial in the rain. So while Nick in "Big Two-Hearted River" is home gathering himself on the river and hoping to gain some self-confidence to honor his love for Helen and their impending child, Hemingway takes us to Italy after the war and into the lives of a couple that is no longer in love. It seems reasonable to conclude that the man in "Cat in the Rain" was a soldier and may be suffering from the feelings of despair and lack of capacity for faith shared by Nick. The wife in "Cat in the Rain" identifies with the cat out in the rain for both hate their current circumstances: the cat hates the rain, and the woman hates the slow deterioration of her relationship with her lover George.

She tells her lover George how badly she wants to save the cat from the rain, but he doesn't take any interest and continues reading his book. The wife goes out to get the cat but cannot find it. She comes back distraught and feeling extremely unhappy with her life. Depicting their failed love through a conversation back in the hotel room, Hemingway writes:

> "And I want to eat at a table with my own silver and I want candles. And want it to be spring and I want to brush my hair out in front of a mirror and I want a kitty and I want some new clothes."
>
> "Oh, shut up and get something to read," George said.[135]

The wife's rant reveals her feelings about her itinerant life and her waning relationship with George. Her demands for silver and a bedroom mirror are euphemisms for her desire to settle down in America and start a family in a house. She desires company and attention that her husband won't give her. George's response "to shut up and get something to read" solidifies both her unhappiness and his indifference to her unhappiness. He doesn't care about her or her needs, so when the concierge or "padrone" has his maid deliver the cat to the room, the reader concludes that the concierge cares more about the "American wife's" needs and desires than her husband does. George is happy to simply read his book. This relationship is tense and unloving: a common theme seen in Hemingway's post-WWI couples in *In Our Time*. Through this story we see what failed love looks like, and readers are disgusted that neither character will honor love enough to move on from this failed relationship.

After the reader travels through multiple post-WWI relationships, Hemingway returns us to the protagonist of *In Our Time* Nick Adams's feeling about returning to America and settling down with his wife, Helen, in the short story "Cross-Country Snow." Developing this backcountry ski trip with his friend George, Hemingway writes beautifully about the feeling of making a turn in untracked powder. Nick says, "There's nothing really can touch skiing, is there? [...] The way it feels when you first drop off on a long run. George concludes their post-ski gushing with the retort, "(It's) just too swell to talk about." Nick suggests that they continue on with the American male fantasy of irresponsibility and rejection of domesticity that marriage and child rearing entail; Nick tells George:

> *Mike, don't you wish we could just bum together? Take our skis and go on the train to where there was good running and then go on and put up at pubs and go right across the Oberland and up the Valais and all through the Engadine and just take repair kit and extra sweaters and pajamas in our rucksacks and not give a damn about school or anything.*[136]

With a baby on the way and a promise to marry Helen, Nick imagines a life of male bonding and skiing from ski hut to ski hut without the responsibility of caring for his child and nurturing a romantic relationship with Helen. Like Krebs, Nick fears the necessary emotional consequences of sustaining a romantic relationship with a woman and the requisite stability a father must provide a child and wife. He will have to "fish the emotional swamp" of the "Big Two-Hearted River" and open up to Helen about the atrocities he witnessed at war, and he has mixed feelings about how this will affect his relationship with Helen. As we know from recent research in treating post-traumatic stress disorder, sustaining loving relationships and purging one's fear and anguish by revisiting the very trauma that caused the deep emotional disturbance are necessary for PTSD patients to recover. But these are the very cures Nick resists.

Nick expresses his ambivalent feelings about revealing his emotional trauma to Helen by answering George's questions about marrying Helen with curt answers. Hemingway writes:

> *"Is Helen going to have a baby?" George said, coming down to the table from the wall.*
>
> *"Yes."*
>
> *"When?"*

"Late next summer."

"Are you glad?"

"Yes. Now."

"Will you go back to the States?"

"I guess so."

"Do you want to?"

"No."

"Does Helen?"

"No."

George sat silent. He looked at the empty bottle and the empty glasses.

"It's hell, isn't it?" he said.

"No. Not exactly," Nick said.

"Why not?"

"I don't know," Nick said.[137]

Revealing the limited expressive ability of two grown men speaking about love and the anxiety surrounding a deep, emotional relationship for veterans of a brutal war, Hemingway links the reader back to earlier silences in the short story collection. The reader recalls the terse, limited responses of Nick and Bill talking about Nick breaking up with his high school sweetheart Marjorie. In the story "Three Day Blow," Bill says that men must "not let women ruin you," for a married man is "absolutely bitched…hasn't got anything more. Nothing. Not a damn thing. He's done for. You've seen the guys that get married…You can tell them…They get this sort of fat married look. They're done for… Fall for them but don't let them ruin you."[138] Hemingway conveys Nick's disagreement with Bill's assessment of love and marriage with the line "Nick sat quiet." How much has the conversation evolved about love now that Nick is talking with George about love and marriage? Not very much. Nick says he is fine with keeping the baby and marrying Helen with the line "Yes. Now" in response to George's query about being a potential father and future husband.

When George looks at the empty bottles on the table, the reader can conclude that George is thinking of the empty feeling Nick must have about wanting to be in a loving relationship but fearing it. So George asks, "It's hell, isn't it?" and Nick responds, "No. Not exactly." This is not a ringing endorsement of the healing capacity of being in love. Nick cannot and does not let George into the fear he has for opening up emotionally to Helen about the war. He does not have the expressive capacity and may fear being vulnerable to his friend. But it can be argued that Nick knows he needs to find the courage to love and become vulnerable to exposing his post-traumatic stress to Helen. None of this is stated, and Hemingway ends the story with what men *can* do together: enjoy outdoor activity in silence. Hemingway concludes the story with "They took down their skis from where they leaned against the wall of the inn. Nick put on his gloves. George was already started up the road, his skis on his shoulder. Now they would have the run home together."[139] Outside the tense discussion of fearing the consequences of a romantic relationship and raising a child with the aftereffects of PTSD, the men, as boys do, go play together without talking.

To step out of the short story collection *In Our Time* for a moment, it is worth visiting the often anthologized story "Hills Like White Elephants" in which a post-WWI couple contemplates the merits of having a child together or having an abortion. Famously, Hemingway never calls "the simple operation" an abortion, but the tension in this short story captures the tension Nick is feeling with a pregnant lover in "Cross-Country Snow." As the couple waits for a train in "Hills Like White Elephants," they are at a junction in their journey and in their relationship. As the woman "Jig"—a method of fishing for marlin and other big game fish—looks out at the fertile valley and the barren hills of the Ebro River Delta, she sees the difference between fertility and infertility in nature. The man, the "American" (no real names are used), took the bait of the jig, so to speak, and she has conceived. They are traveling around Spain, one assumes post-WWI, and it is clear that the man wants to continue on traveling, "trying new drinks," and sleeping together in hotel rooms. Their suitcases, like the one in Hemingway's bedroom in the Ketchum house, is plastered with stickers from the hotels they have visited. As they sit in a café and order drinks, the initial small talk takes a turn to a serious conversation. The man addresses the uncomfortable tension that is felt between them. As he breaks the tension with Jig, Hemingway writes:

> *"It's really an awfully simple operation, Jig," the man said. "It's not really an operation at all."*
>
> *The girl looked at the ground the table legs rested on.*
>
> *"I know you wouldn't mind it, Jig. It's really not anything. It's just to let the air in."*
>
> *The girl did not say anything.*
>
> *"I'll go with you and I'll stay with you all the time. They just let the air in and then it's all perfectly natural."*
>
> *"Then what will we do afterward?"*
>
> *"We'll be fine afterward. Just like we were before."*

"What makes you think so?"

"That's the only thing that bothers us. It's the only thing that's made us unhappy."[140]

The American is frustrated with Jig, for he is frustrated with her seeming reluctance to get an abortion, but she is contemptuous of his comments about the simplicity of the operation and his lack of concern for their relationship and the child they have conceived. One can imagine that Nick Adams and Helen had a similar conversation about the possibility of an abortion. Of course, Nick tells George that he is fine "now" with the idea of having the child, getting married to Helen, and returning to America "where the good skiing is too far away." The "Cross-Country Snow" short story was published eleven years before Averell Harriman opened the Sun Valley Ski Resort and brought adventurers by his Union Pacific Railroad to the mountain resort. But to the point, Nick commits to being a husband and father after WWI with great trepidation. "Hills Like White Elephants" develops a post-WWI couple that gets pregnant, with the potential father urging the potential mother to abort the child. The "American" believes that Jig's pregnancy is the reason that their relationship isn't going well now, and he admits that he does not want anyone to come between them. Like Francis Macomber who "fails to think about how the lion felt" when Francis gutshoots the lion, the American fails to think of how Jig is feeling about being pregnant and her desire to settle down and raise a family. Jig refers to the drink absinthe as tasting "like licorice" as all things do, "especially the things you have waited so long for." Of course, Jig is referring to her long wait to become pregnant. Jig's reference to the barren sagebrush hills of Spain's Ebro Valley as "white elephants, but not really white elephants…it is just the coloring of their skin through the trees" is a not so oblique nor veiled reference to the skin of her developing fetus. Thinking of her fertility and the life inside her, Jig looks at the stark difference between the fertile cottonwoods on the riverbanks and the barren, sun-bleached white hillsides of Spain. White elephants evoke the image of a pregnant woman's belly, and an albino elephant is a rarity in nature, not unlike the rare event of becoming pregnant in a woman's lifetime. In addition, Jig is thinking of how she will be like the hills when the abortion is performed; she will be barren. Having enough of her references to the skin of the life inside of her and her references to waiting so long to be pregnant, the American goes to have a drink at the bar of the railroad station. Adverbs are as rare as white elephants in Hemingway's prose and often have great significance. Hemingway writes that the American notices that all of the passengers are "waiting reasonably for the train." Unlike Jig, who he thinks is being unreasonable about wanting to raise a child and get married, the American believes he has reasonably concluded that their itinerant lifestyle (like the couple in "Cat in the Rain") should not be interrupted by giving birth to and raising a child.

When the American returns to the outdoor table where Jig is drinking alone, he asks her how she feels. Jig responds, "There is nothing wrong *with me*. I feel fine." (my italics) Jig bitterly emphasizes "with me." Jig suggests in her contemptuous tone that he is unreasonable, for he does not value their relationship, does not value the human life inside of her, and is not mature enough nor responsible enough nor in love enough to commit to a sustained relationship involving marriage and child-rearing. Again, Hemingway is showing us through sparse description and mostly dialogue, a couple that is not in love. And he shows us what not finding faith in love looks like. The priest in *A Farewell to Arms* informs Frederic Henry that to be in love means to "sacrifice for, to want to serve, to do things for."[141] While the priest is referring both to love of God and love of another, Frederic hears this as a marker for determining if he is in love with Catherine Barkley. Later in *A Farewell to Arms*, Count Greffi—another mentor in addition to the priest—tells Frederic that while he has not developed a love for God, he has developed a love for his wife and for his life. The count goes on to say that "old men do not grow wise…they grow careful" about how they conduct their lives and how they love. At the end of the conversation between Frederic and the count, the count opines that he has loved his life and does not wish for more from this life, because, for him, "love is a religious feeling."

The American in "Hills Like White Elephants" is not in love; we know this because he does not want "to serve" Jig nor to "sacrifice for her." Nick Adams in *In Our Time* takes the other route with his similar momentous decision to be a husband and father. With fear of being inadequate in both roles, Nick commits to Helen and their child and we hope learns to manage his damaged mind from the war and become a good husband and father. In his tip-of-the-iceberg writing style, Hemingway leaves the reader to determine if Nick will learn to sacrifice for Helen, serve her, do things for her, and sustain a commitment to love.

In contrast to a reader's hope that Nick Adams finds a way to open up emotionally to Helen and be able to serve *her* emotional needs and sacrifice for her emotional well-being, readers of *The Sun Also Rises (1926)* suffer no delusions that the post-WWI couple of Lady Brett Ashley and Jake Barnes is defined by love. Interestingly, Hemingway makes Lady Brett Ashley more emotionally damaged from WWI than the men. While Jake Barnes suffers from an emasculating wound and has, we presume, witnessed the horrors of WWI akin to those witnessed by Nick Adams, it is Lady Brett Ashley's wartime emotional losses that make her give up on love after the war. Having lost her first lover to dysentery during the war and with a second lover that sleeps on the floor with a gun, Brett resolves to keep an emotional distance from lost love and does so by gratifying her sexual desires without any emotional attachment. In this way, she is like the young Frederic Henry who spent his leave in Milan drinking too much and not knowing who was in the bed when he woke up. But unlike Frederic who is educated out of that naive view of gratifying one's lust as "all in all" by falling in love with Catherine Barkley, Brett chooses to approach relationships as mere opportunities for sexual gratification because the death of her first lover at war and the loss of her second lover's mind have taught her the consequences of opening up emotionally in a relationship.

In a revealing description of Lady Brett's eyes early in *The Sun Also Rises*, Hemingway reveals the emotional impact the loss of love has had upon Brett. In post-WWI Paris, wounded veteran Jake Barnes and Lady

Brett embrace in the first two significant taxicab rides in the novel. The first cab ride interaction, described from Jake's perspective, unfolds as follows:

> "Don't you love me?"
>
> "Love you? I simply turn all to jelly when you touch me."
>
> "Isn't there anything we can do about it?"
>
> She was sitting up now. My arm was around her and she was leaning back against me, and we were quite calm.
>
> She was looking into my eyes with that way she had of looking that made you wonder whether she really saw out of her own eyes. They would look on and on after every one else's eyes in the world would have stopped looking. She looked as though there were nothing on earth she would not look at like that, and really she was afraid of so many things.
>
> "And there's not a damn thing we could do," I said.
>
> "I don't know," she said. "I don't want to go through that hell again."
>
> "We'd better keep away from each other."
>
> "But, darling, I have to see you. It isn't all that you know."
>
> "No, but it always gets to be."
>
> "That's my fault. Don't we pay for all the things we do, though?"

She had been looking into my eyes all the time. Her eyes had different depths, sometimes they seemed perfectly flat. Now you could see all the way into them.[142]

Without naming the conflict, Jake identifies that his wound to his groin, his inability to provide sexual satisfaction to Brett is the barrier in their ability to remain in a sustained, loving relationship. The implied issue is that Brett seeks out sexual gratification elsewhere in Mike Campbell, Robert Cohn, Pedro Romero, and others but remains emotionally unattached to all of them. Whereas Brett seems to have the most emotional attachment to Jake, she knows she is both unable to commit to a loving relationship, especially one that cannot be consummated. Hemingway shows us this in Brett's eyes; they "had different depths, sometimes they seemed perfectly flat. Now you could see all the way into them…(they) made you wonder whether she really saw out of her own eyes. They would look on and on after everyone else's eyes in the world would have stopped looking. She looked as though there were nothing on earth she would not look at like that, and really she was afraid of so many things." As opposed to having Brett express her desire to remain emotionally uncommitted in order to prevent herself from being emotionally crushed again, Hemingway shows us the "flatness" of her eyes, like the eyes of a shark without a developed limbic system, without the capacity to possess a range of emotions. And then paradoxically, Hemingway shows us that Brett has great emotional depth when she would stare intensely at a random object in a lost emotional reverie about her past loves. This contradictory emotional depth and emotional flatness make Brett maddeningly unable to return Jake's love, for she cannot reach the "desire to serve, to sacrifice for, to do things for." Brett knows the emotional consequences of doing so and has created an emotional barrier against getting hurt again.

It takes an entire novel worth of Brett's purely sexual relationships with others for Jake to conclude and, much to the reader's satisfaction, finally express to Brett that he cannot continue to harbor the illusion that they have a future as a couple in love. After sleeping with Pedro

Romero, a matador Jake deeply admires for both his skill in the bullring and his sincere and honest approach to love, Brett refuses Pedro's marriage proposal and concludes that "it makes one feel rather good deciding not to be a bitch" and then follows this with "it's sort of what we have instead of God."[143] Jake concludes that Brett is tragically unable "to sacrifice for the other, to serve the other," and unable to find love as a "religious feeling." The only religious feeling Brett has is the self-satisfaction of cutting off a relationship before it becomes too serious and before she hurts the other too much. This is a far cry from what Count Greffi meant by being "careful" about love as a religious feeling. So Jake, much to the satisfaction of the reader, rejects Brett's final assessment that "we could have had such a damned good time together" with the famous, acerbic rebuttal "Isn't it pretty to think so?" While we celebrate Jake's ability to extricate himself from the emotional pain he suffers from repeatedly hoping for a future relationship with Brett, my final thought at the end of the novel is about how the war ruined Brett's emotional capacity to love. This is the tragedy of *The Sun Also Rises*, and this asks the reader to empathize with all of the characters who fail in romantic relationships in Hemingway's texts. And with Hemingway who struggled in all of his marital relationships.

With a firm handle on multiple post-WWI relationships that are not defined by love, Hemingway writes brilliantly about what love is in the intense, but short-lived relationships of both Frederic Henry and Catherine Barkley in *A Farewell to Arms* and Robert Jordan and Maria in *For Whom the Bell Tolls*. As Lloyd Arnold—a hunting guide of Sun Valley Resort—provided a mentorship for how to love a good woman, Hemingway created in his novels older men who mentored his protagonists on how to love. It is helpful to recall that a discarded title for *A Farewell to Arms* was *The Sentimental Education of Frederic Henry*. Clearly, Frederic is educated by his experience at war to transcend beyond an idealistic, naive view of war and the empty platitudes of honor, courage, and glory often associated with an inexperienced view of war to a cynical, skeptical, irreverent view of war. But Frederic Henry also evolves from an uninformed view of love to an informed view of love through his passionate commitment to Catherine Barkley and his loss of this love when Catherine dies. Along the way to a more nuanced, appreciative view of love, Frederic receives some sage advice, as mentioned earlier in this chapter, from his mentors: the priest and Count Greffi.

After having his leg blown off eating cheese as he assisted the Italian army in a medical unit (akin to Hemingway's leg wound in the same war), Frederic is visited by the priest in the hospital, and they speak of faith, love, and service. When Frederic admits that he lacks faith and lacks love, the priest informs Frederic that he will have both love and faith in his life, but love of another will come before faith in God. In response to Frederic's query about how to tell if one is in love, the priest responds that you will know "when…you wish to do things for. You wish to sacrifice for. You wish to serve (another)."[144] Context is everything. While Frederic initially approached his relationship with Catherine as a game, as a step up from the physical encounters with the prostitutes of the Villa Rosa, a whorehouse where Frederic is stationed in the medical unit, Frederic's near-death experience and his candidness about his actual feelings for Catherine create an internal reflection on the need for love as an antidote to despair.

After Frederic escapes the codelessness of the Italian soldiers and military police during the retreat from Caporetto, Frederic and Catherine are back together in Milan. Frederic realizes that honor, courage, and valor cannot be achieved on the Italian front of WWI and recommits to being with Catherine, who is pregnant. It is implied through Frederic's actions that honor, courage, and valor stem from committing to the one you love, to sacrificing for the one you love, to serving the one you love. He wants to be with her, love her, and support her during the pregnancy. The priest's mentorship on how to tell when one is in love is present in Frederic's actions. Moreover, Frederic adds to his understanding of love by stating, when you are in love, you not only "wish to serve the other, wish to do things for the other," but also that you can be "alone but not lonely when together." That is, you can maintain your independence while being with the other. Hemingway writes of Frederic Henry's love of Catherine Barkley, "But we were never lonely and never afraid when we were together. I know that the night is not the same as the day: that all things are different, that the things of the night cannot be explained in the day, because they do not then exist, and the night can be a dreadful time for lonely people once their loneliness has started. But with Catherine there was almost no difference in the night except that it was an even better time."[145] This was certainly the feeling Ernest had for Marty Gellhorn in his first visits to Sun Valley. Hemingway loved deeply and with great intensity, and this passion for being in love emerges as one of the key code principles of the heroes in the novels and short stories.

Later on in *A Farewell to Arms*, Count Greffi also emerges as a mentor to Frederic Henry. Having escaped the war, Frederic has reunited with Catherine near the Swiss border, but they have to embark on their escape to Switzerland upon news that Frederic is in danger of being returned to the Italian medical unit. Before Frederic and Catherine leave, Frederic plays pool with Count Greffi—a ninety-four-year-old former acquaintance of Frederic. While playing pool, they have the following conversation:

> "You never seem old."
>
> "It is the body that is old. Sometimes I am afraid I will break off a finger as one breaks a stick of chalk. And the spirit is no older and not much wiser."
>
> "You are wise."
>
> "No, that is the great fallacy; the wisdom of old men. They do not grow wise, they grow careful."
>
> "Perhaps that is wisdom."
>
> "It is a very unattractive wisdom. What do you value most?"

"Someone I love."

"With me it is the same. That is not wisdom. Do you value life?"

"Yes."

"So do I. Because it is all I have.[146]

(my italics)

In this important exchange with his second mentor Count Greffi, Frederic learns that through life experiences one learns to be "careful" about the things that matter most: love and life. Frederic agrees with the count that being in love is the most valuable endeavor in life. Moreover, Frederic affirms that life is to be valued but with an important implied qualification: it must be a principled life. One can presume that a life worth living is one that follows the mutually enhancing code principles developed throughout the novels and short stories. Both the priest and Count Greffi emerge as mentors to Frederic for their faith in living lives worth living, and their sage advice states that a life worth living is one with a strong foundation in being in love.

Unlike Jake and Brett's failed relationship in *The Sun Also Rises*, and Francis and Margot's failed relationship in "The Short Happy Life of Francis Macomber," Frederic and Catherine can share a room in silence and feel alone but not lonely because they are in love. They have the deep connection, which Francis and Margot are lacking, that allows them to share special moments in silence. Frederic Henry's faith in love is tested but is not defeated. The concept of being emotionally, psychologically, or physically destroyed but not emotionally, psychologically, or physically defeated emerges famously in *The Old Man and the Sea*. While Santiago is unsuccessful in his quest to return with the marlin intact (sharks devour the marlin that is tied to the skiff), sell the marlin at a Cuban market, and break his eighty-four day dry spell, Santiago knows he has been emotionally, psychologically, and physically destroyed but not emotionally, psychologically, nor physically defeated.

As Catherine enters labor, she experiences some difficulties, and the baby and Catherine die. Frederic is emotionally destroyed because he loses the love of his life and his baby. However, when he leaves the hospital and walks "back to the hotel in the rain," his mind is cleared, and he realizes that the risk he took in loving Catherine was well worth it and that his quest for love isn't over. The code principle of valuing love that he learned from the priest propels Frederic to value his love for Catherine and develop faith that he will love again. In the weeds of an ugly divorce with Piper in the fall of 1939, Hemingway may have found solace in recalling both Frederic Henry's realization that one can love again and the mentorship of the deeply committed Sun Valley hunting guides' marriages: the Arnolds, the Purdys, and the Williamses also gave Hemingway encouragement to risk being in love again. His quick marriage to his third wife, Marty Gellhorn, in 1940 and his celebration of her courage and beauty in his writing of *For Whom the Bell Tolls* underscore Hemingway's belief that one can be emotionally destroyed in love but not defeated.

Hemingway's love for Marty Gellhorn was on full display during the early fall visits of 1939 and 1940 to Sun Valley Resort. Marty was most certainly the inspiration for Maria with her "golden tawny brown (skin) . . . high cheekbones, merry eyes and a straight mouth with full lips." In For Whom the Bell Tolls, Robert Jordan and Maria's relationship reveals how past atrocities can bring two individuals together to create a firmer bond, and how the fear of imminent death in war can intensify a bond. The mutual desire to heal the other to "get strong in the broken places" causes the love of Robert and Maria to be intense and admirable. Biographer Jeffery Meyer notes that Hemingway remarked to Fitzgerald, "War…speeds up the action and brings out all sorts of stuff that normally you have to wait a lifetime to get."[147] Hemingway fell deeply in love with Martha Gellhorn while they both covered the Spanish Civil War.

In contrast to the defensive, emotionless approach of Lady Brett Ashley in *The Sun Also Rises*, Maria finds a deep need to heal herself by committing wholeheartedly to love after being raped and tortured during the Spanish Civil War. In contrast to *The Sun Also Rises*'s Jake Barnes, who suffers from a physical wound, Robert Jordan in *For Whom the Bell Tolls* suffers from an emotional wound left by the suicide of his father. Both Robert and Maria are broken emotionally and need to heal themselves in the very place where they are broken: the need to love and be loved. This is the concept of "like finds like," as modernist contemporary William Faulkner put it in *Light in August*. Robert needs Maria as much as Maria needs Robert. Their relationship allowed Hemingway to show how love can become a "religious feeling" for those who "take risks in love," as an "antidote to despair."

Robert Jordan discovers early on that Maria has been raped by the enemy when she was a prisoner of war, and their bond solidifies further when he learns that both of her parents were murdered in front of her as well. As anyone would, Robert has great empathy for the atrocities Maria has suffered and for her emotional plight, but Robert is uniquely attuned to the loss of a parent since Robert lost his father to suicide. Cycling similar images as he did in *In Our Time*, Hemingway associates two moments involving mirrored reflections that link the emotional trauma of Robert and Maria. The first moment is when Maria sees her image reflected in the barbershop mirror while she is being tortured, and the second is when Robert recalls seeing his image reflected in the clear water of a mountain lake as he prepared to drop his father's fatal gun into it. Maria sees that her face has been altered by the grief. Hemingway writes:

> *My own face I could hardly recognize because my grief had changed it but I looked at it and knew that it was me. But my grief was so great that I had no fear nor any feeling but my grief.*
>
> *At that time I wore my hair in two braids and as I watched in the mirror one of them lifted one of the braids and pulled on it so it hurt*

> *me suddenly through my grief and then cut it off close to my head with a razor. And I saw myself with one braid and a slash where the other had been. Then he cut off the other braid but without pulling on it and the razor made a small cut on my ear and I saw blood come from it.*[148]

Maria saw her braids cut off, her blood run down her ear, and her face altered by grief but "knew that it was (her)," part of her but not all of her. In other words, Maria knew that her reaction to this horrible event would be a part of her. In two other code principles, "avoid self-pity" and "self-assess," it will be argued that Hemingway heroes "do not let the wrongs done to them," define them; they "get strong in the broken places" and know that we all live lives that struggle against psychological destruction. This torture, this humiliation, this disregard for her dignity are wrongs done to Maria, but this does not control her identity. She falls in love with Robert, opens up about the rape and the assassination of her parents, and "gets strong" in her ability to love again.

Similarly, Robert confides in Maria that his father's suicide bothered him and made him fear that he would have the same tendency in himself. Ironically, Ernest's own father committed suicide in 1928, and clearly, this manifested in Ernest's last moments in the Warm Springs house in Ketchum, Idaho, on July 2, 1961. In the description of how Robert disposes of his father's suicide gun, Hemingway draws a subtle parallel between the past griefs of Maria and Robert. Recalling his desire to rid himself physically and emotionally of the suicide gun, the omniscient narrator recalls that Robert:

> *had put the gun back in the drawer in the cabinet where it belonged, but the next day he took it out and he had ridden up to the top of the high country above Red Lodge, with Chub, where they had built the road to Cooke City now over the pass and across the Bear Tooth plateau, and up there where the wind was thin and there was snow all summer on the hills they had stopped by the lake which was supposed to be eight hundred feet deep and was a deep green*

color, and Chub held the two horses and he climbed out on a rock and leaned over and saw his face in the still water, and saw himself holding the gun, and then he dropped it, holding it by the muzzle, and saw it go down making bubbles until it was just as big as a watch charm in that clear water, and then it was out of sight.[149]

Beyond the common grief of Maria and Robert, they both see themselves in reflective images while preparing to overcome grief. As Maria remarks, "I could hardly recognize my face because my grief had changed it but I looked at it and knew that it was me." But not all of her. It is the same for Robert Jordan. He sees that his grandfather's gun that his grandfather had used heroically in the American Civil War was now tainted with the memory of its use by his father to take his own life. In the reflective image, Robert sees that the gun's associations with suicide and despair are a part of the image reflected by the mountain lake water, but this reflected image, like Maria's, is not definitive of Robert's being. Moreover, when the gun is "out of sight," solely Robert's face is reflected in the mountain lake. This is Robert's sense of self without being defined by his father's suicide. Both Robert and Maria get "strong in the broken places" by filling their need to be loved through their intensely passionate relationship in the mountains of Spain.

The need "to serve" the needs of the other, "to sacrifice for" the other, "to do things for" the other is beautifully captured by Robert Jordan's ability to provide cover while Pilar and Maria escape the enemy's advance at the end of the novel. Robert Jordan dies with his coded self intact and fully commits to "finding faith in love" because he holds off the enemy's advance long enough for Maria to survive, while knowing his broken leg will prevent him from joining her. So when Robert ruminates that "you never had (love) before and now you have it. What you have with Maria, whether it lasts just through today and a part of tomorrow, or whether it lasts for a long life is the most important thing that can happen to a human being," we know that their love burned brighter due to the intense need to heal each other.[150] We also know Hemingway's most coded characters, his best versions of himself, found faith in love and knew that, as the code principle states, "love is an antidote to despair."

And Hemingway knew something about intense, but short-lived love. His marriages were short-lived but intense. Hemingway was not always able to achieve the ideal commitment to love in his real life and was often in love with more than one woman while married, and this resulted in the ends of multiple marriages. While he often failed to achieve the ideal love of Frederic Henry and Catherine Barkley and Robert Jordan and Maria, it is helpful to recall that Hemingway wrote about male heroes who were successful in love. Hemingway wrote about what he hoped he could be, about his ideal self, but was not always able to achieve this ideal in his life. And he knew that if one "takes risks in love as an antidote to despair," it can lead to "a religious feeling."

5
Self-Assess

Avoid overvaluing false praise or meritless condemnation; value your awareness of the principles upon which you act.

Sun Valley Stories: Self-Assess

"When a man has the ability to write and a desire to write, no critic can damage his work if it is good, or save it if it is bad."[151]

While he was not known for taking negative criticism of his writing in stride, Ernest Hemingway's aspirational mantra asserts his desire to be the ultimate evaluator of his own work. Wyndham Lewis once commented, "Hemingway invariably invokes a dull-witted monosyllabic simpleton and dummy, a super-innocent, queerly-sensitive village idiot of a few words and fewer ideas"[152] Meritless condemnation? Of course. But Hemingway struggled with criticism that isolated his lack of education. He never went to college but chose the education of World War I and work as a journalist. Nonetheless, Hemingway possessed a sustained, jealous rejection of academia. But he knew his first successful short story collection *In Our Time* (1925) spoke to his prodigious intellectual talent. In a comic understatement, Hemingway once remarked that his innovative short story collection *In Our Time* had "a pretty good unity." This underscores his confidence that the visual images of firelight, folded legs, blankets, and auditory images of silences ("Nick said nothing…Krebs said nothing") unify the seemingly tangential short stories in the collection. He knew that, for the ideal reader, the short story collection has the taut, cyclical unity of an intricate tapestry. He knew his *In Our Time* worked, even if many readers failed to read it well.

Critics did not damage *his* self-assessment of his work. But when he expanded into the nonfiction texts of *Green Hills of Africa* and *Death in the Afternoon* and the novel *To Have and Have Not* in the 1930s, Hemingway was less sure the critics' proclamations that his well had dried up were inaccurate. While Hemingway did not take criticism well, he made the ability to self-assess a vital code principle in his fictional characters and an aspirational principle in his own life.

Hemingway was also keenly aware of the need to value tasks completed well for how they strengthen one's sense of self. Hemingway writes in a letter to Bernard Berenson, "I think we should never be too pessimistic about what we know we have done well because we should have some reward and the only reward is that which is within ourselves… publicity, admiration, adulation…are all worthless."[153] The only reward for writing well, hunting well, loving well is that feeling of intrinsic self-worth that resides "within ourselves."

As we have stated with many of the code principles, Hemingway's actions often belie the advice he so willing provides on how to live well. This is the fun of taking the measure of his life next to the ideal lives of his heroes in his fiction. Hemingway aficionado and contemporary writer, Cormac McCarthy helps us grasp the gap between aspirations and the actual; McCarthy writes, "The world is quite ruthless in selecting between the dream and reality, even where we will not. Between the wish and the thing the world lies waiting."[154] Between the ideal self of the fictional characters and the reality of living, Hemingway's biography unfolds.

Nevertheless, the desire to self-assess—to be self-aware, to be conscious of the principles upon which you act, to see through both false praise and unmerited condemnation—is a core code principle in the heroes of Hemingway's best novels and short stories. And this ability to self-assess also manifested in a few Sun Valley moments.

Famous Spanish photographer Robert Capa joined Hemingway in Spain while both covered the Spanish Civil War in the mid to late 1930s and then visited Hemingway in Sun Valley. Capa and Hemingway went on waterfowl hunts together in south central Idaho, and Capa took pictures of their hunting adventures. Robert Capa published a "full page spread" on Hemingway in *Life* magazine in 1940 with Hemingway holding up a cock pheasant. Under the picture, the caption read "Photographer Capa reports that dead-shot Hemingway, in ten days of hunting, never missed a bird."[155] (Is Hemingway showing a false portrayal of bravado in this letter?)

As Arnold notes in his *Hemingway: High on the Wild*, this angered Hemingway. They both knew that "countless gunners would laugh up their sleeves, knowing full well that the best wing shots do well in averaging 60%." Hemingway did not like false portrayals of bravado or expertise. In a letter to both Lloyd Arnold and Taylor Williams, Hemingway writes, "When he saw Capa again he'd have a boot poised for him-sidewise, so it would lift him!"[156] (Is Hemingway showing a false portrayal of bravado in this letter?)

Nonetheless, this fear of developing a false reputation as a "never miss" bird shooter came home to roost with the man who was responsible for Sun Valley Resort's existence. Hemingway ran into Averell Harriman in the Sun Valley Lodge, and Hemingway told Harriman, Union Pacific Chief and founder of Sun Valley Resort, about the hunting on Silver Creek and "how it was good duck weather, a little rainy… how he had made some good shots and missed a few."[157] Harriman in response said, "I am slightly disappointed in you…(you) didn't live up to his reputation as an unbeatable shot." Harriman stated this without a hint of irony. Hemingway wanted to fill him in on the fact that the best hunters hit 60 percent of the time, but Hemingway told Lloyd, "I kept my mouth shut, for once."[158] Hemingway resented the "false praise" of the caption in *Life* magazine and the "meritless condemnation" from Averill Harriman about his hunting skills. But he knew he was a good shot, so the overstated praise and unfounded criticism never affected Hemingway's self-assessment of his hunting skills.

Hemingway knew where he stood as a hunter and marksman, and the men who knew his hunting skills in Sun Valley: Bud Purdy, Taylor Williams, and Lloyd Arnold admired his skill. But what motivated Hemingway in hunting well as in writing well was the "self-awareness" and "self-confidence" that stem from doing a thing well and its ability to strengthen one's sense of self. All the while knowing that his shots and drafts of his writing missed nearly half of the time.

To grasp the code principle "self-assess," it is helpful to recall the tragic hunting death of Sun Valley publicist Gene Van Guilder in 1939 and Hemingway's self-assessment of his involvement in Van Guilder's death, even though Hemingway was not on the hunt. You will recall that Gene Van Guilder was hunting ducks on the Snake River with a young Sun Valley apprentice guide Dave Benner and head guide Lloyd Arnold. Gene shoots from the bow of the canoe, rocks the canoe with his recoil, and Dave Benner's gun swings and fires into the back of Van Guilder. Gene bleeds out on the banks of the Snake River within a half an hour. Hemingway is there to receive Lloyd Arnold when he returns distraught from this tragedy. Hemingway tells Lloyd Arnold that Gene's death was more than bad luck. Hemingway admonishes Lloyd, "How can we call it anything else but impulsive action? No, you and Gene were a fine team, and didn't go about telling each other what to do, and I admire your stand, but I won't buy it... *I'm involved too.*"[159] (my italics) The "I'm involved too" comment is instructive. Having hunted with Gene and Lloyd from a canoe, having allowed the hunts possibly to go on without addressing the unspoken rule about only shooting from a fixed, anchored boat, Hemingway seems to be self-assessing about his implicit involvement in Gene's death. Hemingway knew he could have addressed these rules in previous hunts. He did not. With Lloyd he is self-assessing about his involvement in and contribution to the carelessness and code breaking that led to Gene's death, and he is asking Lloyd to do the same. Lloyd's reaction to Hemingway's comments was "(Hemingway) was sympathetic and very severe about the rule-breaking"[160] Both men become self-aware that it is an obligation of all who hunt to ensure that the safety rules are followed. Hemingway valued fair, substantive self-criticism, and he wanted Lloyd to value his merited criticism as well. Lloyd did. Hemingway remained lifelong friends with Lloyd, in part, because they both "value their self-awareness of the principles upon which they act."

HEMINGWAY AND LLOYD ARNOLD, HUNTING GUIDE AND PHOTOGRAPHER FOR SUN VALLEY RESORT. *The Community Library, Ketchum, Idaho.*

NOVELS AND SHORT STORIES: SELF-ASSESS

We all receive both false praise and unmerited criticism. Being able to distinguish between substantive, merited praise and meaningless praise and criticism is a difficult task. Some of the great characters in Hemingway's fiction give us help.

In *A Moveable Feast*, Hemingway openly criticizes F. Scott Fitzgerald for overly and openly praising Hemingway's writing. Hemingway recalls, "I was very curious to see (Fitzgerald) and had been working hard all day…Scott did not stop talking and since I was embarrassed by what he said—it was about my writing and how great it was—I kept on looking at him closely…instead of listening. We went under the system, then, that praise to the face was an open disgrace"[161] Here, Hemingway overtly states that open praise in person is "a disgrace." This open praise embarrasses Hemingway, and he considers it to be meritless praise. In this moment with Fitzgerald, Hemingway seems desirous of staying focused on the process of his writing and regrets any attempt to make him conscious of the merits, even if they were substantive, of his writing. "You must be prepared to work without applause," Hemingway once stated.[162]

In *A Farewell to Arms*, Ettore is an egotistical, braggart about his heroic achievements in the famous WWI novel. In a familiar move, Hemingway develops a character who fails to possess a code principle in order to show the value of those who do. He defines by negation, by developing the opposite of self-assessing. Ettore values the praise of others (even false praise) over one's honest assessment of oneself. Ettore asks Frederic Henry about "getting the silver medal" for being wounded in battle. Frederic denies that he will receive it and implies he does not deserve it. Ettore retorts, "You're going to get it. Oh boy, the girls…will think you are fine then. They'll think you killed 200 Austrians or captured a whole trench by yourself."[163] As opposed to mocking the false, meritless praise that others will bestow upon Frederic for having a silver medal from the Italian army, Ettore seems ecstatic that Frederic will be the recipient of false commendations. Frederic is quietly disgusted.

Ettore keeps going, as he is regrettably known to do, and brags that "'I've got the bronze twice and three silver medals…I got three wound stripes.' The stripes were parallel silver lines on a black background sewed to the cloth of the sleeve…'When you've got three you've got something.'"[164] Unselfconscious of being overly satisfied with the conferred symbols of his supposed bravery, Ettore says he was wounded in the foot and states "every morning I take a few little pieces out and it stinks all the time."[165] Developing a conversation between Simmons and Ettore on how Ettore received the wound, Hemingway writes:

> "*A hand-grenade. One of those potato mashers. It just blew the whole side of my foot off.*
>
> *You know those potato mashers?*" *He turned to me.*

"Sure." (Frederic responded)

"I saw the son of a bitch throw it," Ettore said. "It knocked me down and I thought I was dead all right but those damn potato mashers haven't got anything in them. I shot the son of a bitch with my rifle. I always carry a rifle so they can't tell I'm an officer."

"How did he look?" asked Simmons.

"That was the only one he had," Ettore said. "I don't know why he threw it. I guess he always wanted to throw one. He never saw any real fighting probably. I shot the son of a bitch all right."

"How did he look when you shot him?" Simmons asked.

"Hell, how should I know," said Ettore. "I shot him in the belly. I was afraid I'd miss him if I shot him in the head."[166]

Ettore lacks self-awareness of his boasting and the disgust of his audience at both his boasting and false boasting. Frederic is uninterested in Ettore's supposed heroism and conveys this by his halfhearted response of "sure." Simmons presses harder and wants to know how the enemy looked after Ettore shot him. So obsessed with his supposed heroism, Ettore misses the social cue to show some humility and admit the horrors of war. Finally, Ettore answers Simmons's second inquiry by stating, "I shot him in the belly. I was afraid I'd miss him if I shot him in the head." Revealing his lack of skill and empathy in his cowardly, merciless killing, Ettore is unaware that the others are disgusted by the disconnect between Ettore's enthusiasm for his own bravado and the reality that Ettore shot the man in the belly and watched him bleed out. Catherine Barkley captures the moment well when she says to Frederic, "We have heroes too, but they are much quieter."[167] Ettore overvalues the symbols of his heroism: the medals and the stripes. He does not self-assess that often the atrocities of war are not worth describing and certainly not worth boasting of for the purpose of self-aggrandizement.

Frederic Henry knows where he stands when it comes to his involvement in the capricious violence of war that descended upon him while he was drinking wine and eating cheese. The explosion of a trench mortar shell forced Frederic's patella to the shin of his leg, yet he was able to put a tourniquet on Passini, whose leg was blown off. But Passini dies shortly thereafter. Later on in the novel after Frederic's wound heals, he returns to the front and is involved in the Italian retreat from Caporetto. During the retreat, Aymo is shot "low in the back of the neck and the bullet ranged upward and out under the right eye. He died while (Frederic) was stopping up the two holes."[168] Frederic sees through Ettore's meritless self-satisfaction with being wounded, because Frederic knows the randomness of violence at war and knows that his actions to help others, while heroic to some, were futile and what anyone else would have done in the moment. Frederic does not mention these moments and does not want medals for being wounded and supposedly acting bravely. He knows where he stands on bravery. In a conversation Frederic tells Catherine, "The coward dies a thousand deaths, the brave but one," but Catherine updates this familiar adage with "the brave dies perhaps two thousand deaths if he's intelligent." He simply doesn't mention them."[169] Because Frederic is trying too hard to impress Catherine with a quip on bravery, Catherine admonishes him with her take that all who think they are brave become victims of moments that reveal they are not. This echoes the familiar Hemingway concept that "a man can be destroyed but not defeated."[170] In other words, Catherine knows that a true self-assessment leads one to know that we are "destroyed" emotionally, physically, and psychologically by both self-inflicted wounds and wounds made by others. We just don't mention them nor let them "defeat" us. "To get strong in the broken places"—another familiar aphorism from *A Farewell to Arms*—encourages one to become emotionally, physically, and psychologically strong in the very place where one is injured. Catherine is living proof of this. Having lost her first love to the war, she finds love in Frederic and takes the risk of opening herself up emotionally, while knowing that Frederic too has a strong chance of losing his life at war. Encouraging honest self-assessment and substantive self-reflection on the setbacks in life that make one less sure one is brave, Catherine gets through to Frederic. And Frederic admits to Catherine, "I know where I stand. I've been out long enough to know. I'm like a ball player that bats .230 and knows he's no better."[171] This is the opposite reaction of Ettore. Frederic actually performed what many would consider noble actions both while injured and during a chaotic and frightening retreat, but he knows the silver medal for bravery at war from the Italian army means nothing in the face of his memory of being terrified and doing what anyone would do to help those around them and, not to be ignored, to no avail. Frederic helps us realize both the importance of rejecting meritless praise and valuing self-awareness of the principles upon which you act. Frederic does not brag nor look favorably upon anyone who wants to overpraise him for his actions.

This leads us to Frederic's encounter with Rinaldi in the hospital when Frederic is recovering from his leg wound from the trench mortar shell explosion. Rinaldi—a capable surgeon during the war—brings Frederic cognac and seems ecstatic about the prospect of Frederic receiving the silver medal for his "valorous conduct." Frederic rejects both the idea that he acted "valorously" and that the Italian army will reward him. Developing the differing views of medals between Rinaldi and Frederic, Hemingway writes:

> *". . . you are gravely wounded. They say if you can prove you did any heroic act you can get the silver. Otherwise it will be the bronze. Tell me exactly what happened. Did you do any heroic act?"*
>
> *"No," I said. "I was blown up while we were eating cheese."*
>
> *"Be serious. You must have done something heroic either before or after. Remember carefully."*
>
> *"I did not."*

> "Didn't you carry anybody on your back? Gordini says you carried several people on your back but the medical major at the first post declares it is impossible. He has to sign the proposition for the citation."
>
> "I didn't carry anybody. I couldn't move."
>
> "That doesn't matter," said Rinaldi.
>
> [...]
>
> "I think we can get you the silver. Didn't you refuse to be medically aided before the others?"
>
> "Not very firmly."
>
> "That doesn't matter. Look how you are wounded. Look at your valorous conduct in asking to go always to the first line."[172]

This is exactly the praise Ettore told Frederic he would get and that Frederic should relish. But this is exactly the kind of "false abstraction" about war that Frederic learns to loathe. Frederic is disgusted by the effusive praise and false account of heroism that Rinaldi wants to bestow upon Frederic.

Ernest Hemingway did receive the Silver Medal in WWI for assisting Italian soldiers when he was struck by a trench mortar and the citation read:

> *Gravely wounded by numerous pieces of shrapnel from an enemy shell, with an admirable spirit of brotherhood, before taking care of himself, (Hemingway) rendered generous assistance to the Italian soldiers more seriously wounded by the same explosion and did not allow himself to be carried elsewhere until after they had been evacuated.*[173]

Notice the language Hemingway would have hated: "admirable spirit of brotherhood," and "rendered generous assistance." False abstractions. Hemingway and Frederic can only recall the white light, the heat, the pain, and the terror when they were wounded. And Frederic has the additional horrifying memories of watching Passini die, then seeing the "doctors with their sleeves rolled up to the shoulders and red as butchers."[174] No heroism. No bravery. Just chaos and terror. Frederic prevents Rinaldi from any future false praise by stating, "You are…uninformed. Inexperienced, stupid from inexperience."[175] Form his experiential knowledge of the atrocities of war, Frederic self-assesses: he knows where he stands "on bravery" and knows the horrifying realities of war.

In the post-WWI novel *The Sun Also Rises*, Pedro Romero emerges as a coded hero by self-assessing as well. While Pedro becomes a "valued mentor" for Jake Barnes by helping Jake see what a man should do when he realizes love is not returned, Pedro also helps Frederic see how to "do things well for the self" and not for the praise it may evoke. Pedro is a young, handsome, confident, and accomplished matador. He honors the ritualistic life and death spectacle of the bullfight by honoring the bull in the risks he takes to his own life in the taking of the life of the bull. Jake helps Brett Ashley "see" that Pedro's actions are expert and honorable. He shows her how Pedro "never wast(es) the bull" and leaves the bull "not winded and discomposed but smoothly worn down."[176] Hemingway writes, "Romero had the old thing, the holding of his purity of line through the maximum of exposure, while he dominated the bull by making him realize he was unattainable, while he prepared him for the killing."[177] Of course, this is all well and good, but it is the fact that Pedro performs well in the bullring after he loses a fistfight to Robert Cohn over an argument about Brett Ashley that matters more. Instead of wallowing in "self-pity" over losing a fight to an intolerably immature American man-boy, Pedro wipes out his presumed self-criticism for losing the fight by performing well with the bull. More importantly, Pedro does this for himself and values his "self-awareness of the principles upon which he acts" in the bullring. Brett and Jake watch Romero regain his strength and confident sense of self by brilliantly wearing down a bull. Hemingway writes, "Pedro Romero had the greatness. He loved bull fighting, and I think he loved the bulls, and I think he loved Brett. Everything of which he could control the locality of he did in front of her all that afternoon. *Never once did he look up. He made it stronger that way, and did it for himself,* too, as well as for her. *Because he did not look up to ask if it pleased he did it all for himself inside, and it strengthened him,* and yet he did it for her, too. But he did not do it for her at any loss to himself. He gained by it all through the afternoon."[178] (my italics) After witnessing Romero complete the task of wearing down the bull well, Brett remarks, "He's wiped out that damned Cohn."[179] Pedro Romero restored his sense of self, his self-confidence, and his pride not by awaiting on the praise from others, nor even the approving gaze of Lady Brett Ashley, but by self-assessing. When people in the crowd pick up Pedro and carry him on their shoulders out of the ring, Pedro is embarrassed. It is the equivalent of Rinaldi overpraising Frederic Henry for being brave at war in *A Farewell to Arms*. Pedro and Frederic know where they stand. They are aware of what matters to them, and how doing things well for a strong, but honest sense of self "makes the difference." Frederic's commitment to his love of Catherine is akin to Pedro's fine performance in the bullring. And Jake Barnes of *The Sun Also Rises* takes Pedro's lead and finally self-assesses at the end of the novel and rejects the unrequited love of Brett Ashley. Pedro, Jake, and Frederic are better off though their ability to self-assess.

In *For Whom the Bell Tolls*, Robert Jordan is often able to self-assess in the extended interior monologues in this text. Unlike the terse "tip of the iceberg" writing in *In Our Time*, *The Sun Also Rises*, and *A Farewell to Arms*, Hemingway in *For Whom the Bell Tolls* allows multiple characters to have prolonged self-reflections about the code principles upon which they follow or fail to follow. Unlike Frederic who conveys his self-reflection in dialogue and Pedro who shows us by "not looking up" at the crowd that he is strengthened by his self-awareness, Robert Jordan *tells us* that he is in pursuit of the "chastity of mind" of "young doctors, priests and soldiers" and how this self-awareness of the principles upon which he acts can lead to the "inner dignity" he so admires in his valued mentors.

But context matters. After witnessing the "barbarous" slaughter of the Nationalists who took control of his hometown, Pablo—one of the most uncoded characters in Hemingway's works—is disgusted with the undisciplined, inebriated actions of his fellow Republican soldiers. He believes in the Republican cause, in the ideals of a democratically elected government, in separation of church and state, in the protection of civil liberties of his people. But when Pablo bears witness to the hacking of a priest to death with a sickle and the launching of men off the cliff while still alive, this leads Pablo to "eddy in his own weakness" and suffer from "a disinclination to action." "I would restore all of the (Nationalists) to life…We should have killed them all or none," Pablo says to American volunteer soldier Robert Jordan and his fellow Republican guerilla fighters.[180] We have empathy for Pablo and agree with his assessment of the undisciplined, inhumane nature of some of the Republican resistance, but Hemingway has the reader reject Pablo's self-pity, his wallowing in despair, and his unwillingness to fight for the cause.

So how does Robert Jordan—our coded hero—resist the undisciplined "disinclination to action" and "eddying in his own weakness" that paralyze Pablo? Jordan self-assesses about both the shortcomings of the battles and his awareness that there were moments when he "did the thing there was to do and knew he was right."[181] In a prolonged moment of self-reflection about why he carries on orders that seem impossible, Robert Jordan lets readers know that the allegiance to an ideal and deep connection to those connected to the same cause provide a religious experience for him. Robert Jordan thinks:

> *You felt, in spite of all bureaucracy and inefficiency and party strife, something that was like the feeling you expected to have and did not have when you made your first communion. It was a feeling of consecration to a duty toward all of the oppressed of the world which would be as difficult and embarrassing to speak about as religious experience and yet it was authentic as the feeling you had when you heard Bach, or stood in Chartres Cathedral or the*

> *Cathedral at Leon and saw the light coming through the great windows; or when you saw Mantegna and Greco and Brueghel in the Prado. It gave you a part in something that you could believe in wholly and completely and in which you felt an absolute brotherhood with the others who were engaged in it. It was something that you had never known before but that you had experienced now and you gave such importance to it and the reasons for it that your own death seemed of complete unimportance; only a thing to be avoided because it would interfere with the performance of your duty.*[182]

Robert Jordan took communion but, admittedly, felt no allegiance to the faith pronounced around him nor to the people who were working toward a collective reinforcing of this faith. Not so in the best moments of the Spanish Civil War for Robert Jordan. "The brotherhood with others," the pure focus on "the performance of duty," the "consecration" to a resistance to tyranny" created a spiritual experience for Robert. Not unlike the "religious feeling" achieved by finding faith in love, by serving the other, sacrificing for the other that Frederic Henry learns in *A Farewell to Arms*, Robert Jordan finds the transcendent experience in battle constitutes a self-awareness of what they are fighting for, the dedication of those around him to the cause, and the "selfless pride" that emerges when a soldier's duty is performed well.

Akin to Krebs's recollection in "Soldier's Home" of the times at war "when you felt cool and clean inside" from knowing you did the thing that needed to be done well, Robert Jordan describes the famous "grace under pressure" of the committed soldier. He recalls "the fear that dries your mouth and your throat, in the smashed plaster dust and the sudden panic of a wall falling, collapsing in the flash and roar of a shell burst" and how the soldier's necessary suppression of reality—the "negation of apprehension"—allows him to engage in "clearing the gun, dragging those away who had been serving it, lying face downward and covered with rubble, your head behind the shield working on a stoppage, getting the broken case out, straightening the belt again, you now lying straight behind the shield, the gun searching the roadside again; you did the thing there was to do and knew that you were right."[183] This is what kept Hemingway returning to war. In the 1948 introduction to *A Farewell to Arms*, Hemingway answers the question "why is (he) so preoccupied and obsessed with war...the constant, bullying, murderous, slovenly crime of war"? He answers this question by writing, "The closer to where they are fighting, the finer people you meet...(but) I believe that all the people who stand to profit by a war and who help provoke it should be shot on the first day it starts...and the author of this book would be very glad to take charge of this shooting."[184] Prefiguring this response, Hemingway in 1940 allows Robert Jordan to state, "The closer to the front, the finer the people." The more dire the circumstance, the more likely you will find out about people's character. To round off this self-assessment, Robert Jordan concludes that "(he) learned the dry-mouthed, fear-purged, purging ecstasy of battle" and that "fighting for all the poor in the world, against all tyranny, for all the things that you believed" taught him "how to endure and how to ignore suffering." Robert Jordan's self-assessment allowed him to recognize the value of his "inner dignity"—"a deep and sound and selfless pride."[185]

Of course many mutually enhancing code principles manifest here: complete tasks well, embrace the present, and value mentors committed to an ideal with equal fervor. The most coded hero of Hemingway's works, Robert Jordan self-assesses by being conscious of the principles upon which he acts. And it is this self-awareness that allows him to fight wholeheartedly for the Republicans of Spain, who had no reason to believe their side would be successful. And they were not. But he carries on with the cause he believes in for "it is only in the performing of (the orders) that they can prove to be impossible."[186] And it is only the principles exhibited in the performance that matter and not the end results.

6

Develop Experiential Knowledge

Be skeptical of any knowledge divorced from experience and seek out experiences that will allow you to become an expert.

Sun Valley Stories: Develop Experiential Knowledge

A result of following the code principle "valuing mentors" is the experiential knowledge one gains by learning from mentors who are expert at what they do. This is exactly what Ernest Hemingway did on his duck hunts at Silver Creek, elk and deer hunts in the Frank Church Wilderness, and pronghorn hunt in the Pahsimeroi Valley. He developed knowledge of where the hunting was good, how to set decoys to attract the ducks, how to stalk mallards in small tributaries, where the elk and deer were bedding down, and how to track pronghorn on ridge after ridge from hunting experts Taylor Williams, Lloyd Arnold, and Bud Purdy, among other local Sun Valley hunting guides and companions.

As we know from *The Sun Also Rises*, to be an "aficionado" is to have great passion for an endeavor, and in that novel's case, it was Jake Barnes's great passion and expert knowledge of bullfighting that made him a "buen hombre" in the eyes of the aficionados staying at the Hotel Montoya in Pamplona. As an aficionado, one can be an expert observer and critic of an event, but the code principle of "develop experiential knowledge" asks of us to be more *participant* than observer, to learn through the trials and tribulations of the ebb and flow of experience, and to be skeptical of any "false abstractions" removed from the reality of the experience. In short, developing experiential knowledge allows one to develop the famous Hemingway "bullshit detector." As Hemingway put it, "The essential gift for a good writer is a built-in, shockproof, bullshit detector."[187] Not only did this allow Hemingway to edit out what was not real as a writer, it allowed him to reject false abstractions from people who did not have the life experience to speak accurately about a subject. In *Death in the Afternoon*, Hemingway writes, "I found the greatest difficulty, aside from knowing truly what you really felt, rather than what you were supposed to feel and had been taught to feel, was to put down what really happened in action."[188] At his best, Hemingway gave us "what really happened in action." He let readers determine their emotional reaction; he let the image itself carry the idea and the emotion. Avoiding how we are socially constructed to feel, "how we are supposed to feel or had been taught to feel," about war violence or marital fighting or the loss of a loved one, Hemingway just presents these moments in the terse, elliptical, objective journalistic manner he learned at *The Kansas City Star*. The "bullshit" flies when one writes about what one does not know. Hemingway's experiential knowledge and thirst for life, for adventure, for moments that flush out one's character, and for conversations as they actually occurred allowed him to write about "what really happened" on a vast variety of subjects.

In his letters, Hemingway also theorized on the need to write about life as it was experienced. In a letter to his father, Hemingway is trying to assuage his parents' concern that their son is writing about immoral behavior and producing licentious stories. Hemingway's open portrayal of sex out of wedlock, violence, racism, and cruelty disturbed his parents to the point that his mother, Grace, threatened to avoid reading her son's work again. Hemingway pleads to his father:

> *I am trying in all of my stories to get the feeling of actual life across…to actually make it alive. So when you have read something by me you actually experience the thing. You can't do that without putting in the bad and the ugly as well as what is beautiful. Because if it is all beautiful you can't believe in it. Things aren't*

that way…three dimensions and if possible four. So when you see anything of mine that you do not like, remember that I am sincere in doing it and that I am working toward something. If I write a story that might be hateful to you and mother, the next one might be the one you like exceedingly.[189]

A student of mine once remarked, "Maybe the fourth dimension in Hemingway's mind is time." Hemingway is asking his father to stay with him in his stories, for he is "working toward something," and that over the time covered in the fictional stories, there will be "the bad and the ugly as well as what is beautiful." The expanded sense of time through the stories and chapters in *In Our Time* certainly allows the reader to see much of the "bad and the ugly" in and out of war but also allows the reader to witness Nick Adams grow from a nine year old "who felt quite sure he would never die" to a married man, father, and veteran of WWI who conducts himself in a very careful and coded manner on his return to the rivers of his youth in America after the war. We see that Hemingway is "up to something," that out of the flux of "the bad and the ugly as well as what is beautiful," we see Nick Adams distil a greater appreciation for the river, the trout, and, we hope, his wife and kid. With the expanded sense of time, we witness Nick become a man though all his has gained from his experiences. He hoped his parents would keep reading, for indeed, he was "working toward something."

As we know, Hemingway valued his friends, hunting guides, and significant others in Sun Valley as "the family" because they did not dispose of the flatteries that usually attended Hemingway admirers, they did not shower Hemingway with "bullshit" praise, but they did admire Hemingway's great facility with a shotgun and rifle and his desire to learn the local country by going out hunting. Hemingway liked being around people who are active and who are willing to learn from an experience that might reveal the brilliance and/or limitations of their skill.

Hemingway knew what fly to use and where to cast it to send a rainbow trout shooting up to smash the fly on the surface. He learned this from his father. Hemingway knew how to jig for marlin, where they would be according to the currents and birds working on the surface, how to set the hook so it will not release, and how not to attempt to bring the marlin in "too green." He learned this from the captain of his boat, the *Pilar*, and model for Santiago in *The Old Man and the Sea*, Gregorio Fuentes. Hemingway knew how to track pronghorn, where they will hold after being spooked, and where to shoot so that the pronghorn can be easily tracked over a short distance. He learned this from Sun Valley Resort's head hunting guide Taylor Williams.

Aware of the negative impact the exploding jackrabbit population was having upon the hay crop for farmers in the south central Idaho towns of Shoshone, Dietrich, and Gooding in the 1940s, Hemingway asked permission to hunt for rabbit on their fields to help alleviate the infestation. On one particular hunt, Hemingway asked the Frieze family to hunt the "hordes of jackrabbits," so "with Gary Cooper, son Jack Hemingway and the Frieze sons, Hemingway trapped the rabbits by advancing toward an irrigation ditch."[190] When the rabbits came back from the water "it looked like the earth was moving and…Mr. Frieze and his sons collected 1,700 jackrabbits, selling the hides for five cents apiece and saving the hay crop. The family was quite appreciative and always treated everyone to a chicken dinner."[191] Attune to the local jackrabbit infestation, aware that the rabbits will not swim across the irrigation ditch, and interested in the local people he celebrates as possessing a "peasant wisdom" in many of his texts, Hemingway used his experiential knowledge of how to hunt to help the local farmers of central Idaho.

In "The Shot"—the only piece Hemingway ever wrote about his time in Idaho—Hemingway depicts a pronghorn hunt in the Pahsimeroi valley. While he does celebrate his 275-yard rifle shot of a big buck pronghorn, he also celebrates the experiential knowledge of the hunting guides who knew this country and could put him onto the shot.

On the hunt with guides Lloyd Arnold and Taylor Williams, Hemingway celebrated how much these Sun Valley Resort hunting guides knew about where the good hunting was and how to hunt it. As Larry Morris recounts it in *Hemingway and Cooper in Idaho: An Enduring Friendship*, "Hunting in the Pahsimeroi with his sons (Patrick and

Gregory), Lloyd (Arnold), and Taylor (Williams), Hemingway got off the shot of his life when he halted suddenly from a dead run, aimed and fired in one motion and brought down a buck (pronghorn) from 275 yards away."[192] After hunting the Pahsimeroi Valley (a two hour drive from Sun Valley) with Lloyd Arnold, Hemingway tells him, "I'm hooked...I'm glad you got connection in this country...we old Shoshones will see it again." The cheeky Shoshone Indian reference is a telling one. Hemingway valued the "native" knowledge of the local hunting guides and the opportunity for him to push his talent as an expert marksman to a level he had never done before. "Value those who live by the other principles of the code" and "be skeptical of any knowledge divorced from experience" are the combined definitions of the code principles: "value mentors" and "develop experiential knowledge." In "The Shot," Hemingway gets to the pronghorn through the knowledge of mentors and pushes his expertise to the next level.

HEMINGWAY LOOKS TO SUN VALLEY HUNTING GUIDE TAYLOR WILLIAMS DURING A HUNT ON A FARM IN SOUTH CENTRAL IDAHO. *The Community Library, Ketchum, Idaho.*

In much of his time in central Idaho, Hemingway created an opportunity for others to develop experiential knowledge, to learn by doing, to develop a self-awareness of their strengths and weaknesses out in the field. For example, in a recent talk given by local Sun Valley real estate agent Jed Gray, he recalled that Hemingway would only allow ten-year-old Jed to have "one shotgun shell in the barrel when jump shooting ducks."[193] This, Hemingway insisted, would allow Jed to learn why he missed or why he made his shot. Hemingway wanted to instill both good hunting techniques in others and develop a reverence for the predator-prey relationship in the uninitiated. In the Wood River Valley, the code principles of valuing mentors, developing experiential knowledge, and valuing nature as an ethical arena were mutually enhancing as they often are in the texts.

Hemingway often insisted on taking the wives of hunting companions out on hunting adventures in central Idaho. Hoping the experience of hunting would encourage them to value the skill involved, the patience involved, and the accumulated experiential knowledge needed to be successful, he relished the chance for the wives to learn by doing.

Mary Hemingway, Ernest Hemingway, Tillie Arnold, and Lloyd Arnold snacking after a hunt. *The Community Library, Ketchum, Idaho.*

In a Wendy Warren interview in 2000 with Anita Gray, Jed Gray's Mom, she remembered a chukar hunt on Cove Ranch south of Bellevue. Hemingway was the leader of the hunt, and they heard chukar—a small partridge native to central Idaho—moving up the rocky hillside. As they approached the toe of the sage and rocky hill, "two ducks flew up from a puddle." Anita shot at the ducks and missed. The chukar quickly flew up the hill and ran for cover in the rocks high on the hill. "(Hemingway) was so mad," recalled Anita, "He scolded me, 'when you go for one kind of game, you do not go for another.'"[194] The unexpected experience of having mallards flush when chukar were the intended prey allowed for a teachable moment. A lesson only the experience would convey.

HEMINGWAY AND MARY ON A CHUKAR HUNT. *The Community Library, Ketchum, Idaho.*

Whether exhibiting his own experiential knowledge, appreciating it in the hunting guides, or sharing his knowledge with others, Hemingway knew the difference between those who are knowledgeable from experience and those who are not.

Novels and Short Stories: Develop Experiential Knowledge

In many mountain resort towns of the American West, there is a love-hate relationship with tourists and tourism. Without the influx of money tourists bring to these remote areas, many locals would not have jobs, the towns' infrastructures would be cash poor, and there would not be the cultural events that create vibrant, intellectual communities far from the intellectual centers of the country. But that notwithstanding, in Ernest Hemingway's bitter introduction to the 1949 edition of *A Farewell to Arms*, he lets the wealthy tourists of Sun Valley have it. He describes watching the wealthy resort goers tuck their "over-inflated bellies" under a stick as they drink and do the "Limbo" at Trail Creek Cabin. Not embracing the festive mood, Hemingway tells Ingrid Bergman, "This is going to be the worst year yet."[195] He then goes on to say that there will always be war, for wars are made by those who do not fight them. He proposes to shoot those who make war and offers that they can then shoot him too and leave his unburied body to rot on the ground, if they so choose. Yikes. But as a man who received shrapnel in his leg from a mortar shell explosion in WWI, who covered the Greco-Turkish War in 1922 as a reporter, who covered the Spanish Civil War as a reporter, and who returned to war as a correspondent for WWII in the 1940s, Hemingway was speaking from experience.

It is not surprising, then, that one of the major concepts that informs a reading of *A Farewell to Arms* is the idea that false abstractions about the importance, heroism, and valor of war are only made by those who are "stupid from inexperience." You will recall from the chapter on the code principle "self-assess" that this is the phase Frederic Henry uses to describe his closest friend and surgeon, Rinaldi, when Rinaldi claims that Frederic should get the Italian Silver Medal for bravery due to his "heroic actions" while injured at war. According to Frederic, Rinaldi is "uninformed...stupid from inexperience."[196]

Hemingway knows he was handing out chocolates to wounded Italian soldiers when a trench mortar shell exploded shrapnel into his leg; Frederic Henry knows he was drinking wine and eating cheese when a mortar shell bursts close enough to force his patella onto his shin. Despite Frederic's admonitions that he was not heroic, Rinaldi persists in his questioning. From his experiential knowledge of war, Frederic knows the randomness of a mortar strike, the chaos that ensues, and the terror that unfolds in the young men. This makes him increasingly irritable about Rinaldi's insistence that he receive a medal of honor for his actions. Rinaldi rejects Frederic's denial of heroism and states, "Look how you are wounded. Look at your valorous conduct in asking to go always to the first line."[197] This phrase "valorous conduct" pushed Frederic over the edge of civility. It is a false abstraction with no grounding in his experience of the war thus far. While Rinaldi is an expert surgeon and knows many things about saving lives that Frederic will never know, Rinaldi does not know about the randomness of being shelled and the often lack of heroism that accompanies the chaos of being shelled. Harsh and to the point, Frederic's criticism that Rinaldi is "stupid from inexperience" is really an admonishment that those who are not expert from experience should not try to categorize the meaning of an experience. This is why maps become so meaningful to Krebs in "Soldier's Home": only the names of battles and rivers and towns meant anything of value for those who have "experiential knowledge of war." The names of towns, rivers, battlefields, and regiments are factual and allow the *participant* in these battles for towns in regiments that crossed specific rivers to recall the actual experience without any "false abstractions" that celebrate the "sacrifice" of the men and the saving of the "sacred, hallowed" ground. While Ernest Hemingway did receive the Italian Silver Medal for bravery from the Italian army in WWI, he knew the knowledge from the experience behind the medal meant more than the false abstraction of bravery that the medal depicted.

In an often-overlooked short story / nonfiction essay titled "Natural History of the Dead" (1932), Hemingway furthers his definition of the code principle "develop and value experiential knowledge" by putting his ongoing internal battle over his faith in God to the test. Taught by his father to be a keen observer of nature, to know the names of the plants, the different species of fish he caught, and the genders of the fish he caught, and to sketch the plants, fish, and waterfowl they shot, Ernest Hemingway was raised to be a naturalist. So he applies the attention to detail of a naturalist to his actual observations of the dead on a battlefield, of an exploded ammunitions factory in which he picked up skull fragments of the female workers from barbed wire fences, and of a scene in which a doctor refuses to treat a soldier's head injury because he needs to attend to the wounded soldiers who might survive. "Natural History of the Dead" captures the sentiment of Frederic's criticism that false abstractions only come from those who are "stupid from inexperience."

Early on in "Natural History of the Dead," Hemingway introduces Bishop Stanley, a naturalist who concludes that the study of "any branch of Natural History" can lead one to "faith, love and hope." This, of course, is right out of the literary Romantic tradition that one's faith in God is enhanced by experiencing God firsthand through the splendor of nature, especially wild nature that has not been altered by man. Hemingway then goes on to share the story of exotic traveler Mungo Park, who nearly gave up on his life when lost and without water in the Sahara desert. But having witnessed the tiniest flower grow in the arid desert, Park is convinced that there must be a God and that if God allowed a tiny flower to flourish in the arid desert, then God's will must be able to guide him "who is made in God's image" to safekeeping. Not surprisingly, Mungo Park gets up and walks out of the desert and is more convinced than ever of the beneficence of divine providence.

In a wry, irreverent tone in "A Natural History of the Dead," Hemingway asks, "I wonder what the persevering traveler Mungo Park would have found on a battlefield to restore his confidence" in God's good will in the world. Hemingway goes on to describe in shocking detail the "accurate observation" of the dead after the Austrian offensive in June 1918: "The dead's skin goes yellow, green black...bloat to a bursting point...with paper everywhere, heat, flies."[198] He shares with us the shocking detail of the long strands of hair accompanying the skull fragments of the women who were blown to bits when the ammunition factory exploded. Hemingway was assigned to collect the body parts of the female workers after an ammunition factory exploded in Italy during WWI. His "tip of the iceberg" writing implies an answer to the rhetorical question "what would the persevering traveler Mungo Park have found on a battlefield to restore his confidence" in God's good will in the world? Nothing.

The experiential knowledge of the brutality of war prevented Hemingway from sustaining a consistent faith in God. But his struggles with faith also provide the context in which he endeavored to create a self-imposed code for his heroes and heroines in order to keep the godless, capricious world from destroying their faith in themselves. Raised a Congregationalist and having converted to Catholicism before his marriage to Pauline Pfeiffer and prior to the writing of "A Natural History of the Dead," Hemingway must have been enormously conflicted in writing this story in 1932. But Hemingway wanted to ground truth abstractions through experiential knowledge. And in this short story / nonfiction essay, Hemingway finds nothing at war to engender faith.

In *For Whom the Bell Tolls*, Robert Jordan finds Anselmo to be a coded mentor because Anselmo completes tasks well, endeavors to take responsibility for the killing of his fellow countrymen in the Spanish Civil War, and self-assesses about his actions. But in the very beginning of the novel, Robert Jordan states that he wants to trust Anselmo, but he has not yet learned to trust Anselmo's judgment. Hemingway writes, "Robert Jordan trusted the man, Anselmo, so far, in everything except judgment. He had not yet had an opportunity to test his judgment."[199] This discipline to take the time to develop experiential knowledge of others' judgment before entrusting significant tasks to them proves to be the critical discipline in the novel. Yes, Anselmo's judgment proves to be sound, reliable, and consistent, but Jordan only arrives at this through experiencing Anselmo's independent decision-making. In contrast, Pablo's judgment proves to be untrustworthy, inconsistent, and immoral, yet Jordan trusts Pablo even though Jordan had experienced Pablo's poor decision-making. When Pablo returns to the cave and indicates that he will aid in the blowing of the bridge and in the retreat after the bridge is blown, Jordan believes him while knowing Pablo has repeatedly shown that he is only interested in self-preservation. And Pablo betrays Jordan, steals the dynamite and detonator, and makes it very difficult to blow the bridge safely. As a result, Jordan loses his true mentor Anselmo in the blowing of the bridge, for they had to get too close to the bridge to detonate the explosives, and Anselmo is hit by a fatal piece of the bridge. Knowing whom to trust and whom not to trust stems from experiential knowledge. Failure to act on the experiential knowledge of whom to trust is the fatal flaw of Robert Jordan. And Gene Van Guilder, the Sun Valley publicist who was shot and killed accidentally by a young apprentice hunting guide.

But in *The Sun Also Rises* we witness Jake Barnes's ability to learn from past mistakes in his relationship with Lady Brett Ashley. By witnessing how his mentor Pedro Romero approaches love and by applying what he learns from Romero's coded approach to love to Brett at the end of the novel, Jake leaves Lady Brett Ashley. Unable to physically consummate his love for Brett due to his war wound, Jake is nonetheless hopelessly in love with Brett. However, she will not commit to him due to his physical limitations. This tortures Jake, and he hangs around Brett and her lovers and foolishly hopes that things will change. When Brett takes up with the young, studly matador Pedro Romero, Pedro is coded about love, asks her to marry him, and refuses to share her with the other men. Brett states she cannot marry Pedro and moves on, as does Pedro. But Jake is paying attention and is learning from Pedro's direct, honest marriage proposal and Pedro's ability to move on when the love is unrequited. So when Jake is asked by Brett to be a shoulder to cry on at the end of *The Sun Also Rises*, we are disgusted with him when he acquiesces to her request. But our opinion of Jake perks up when he rejects Brett's empty comment "we could have had such a damned good time together" with the famous, "isn't it pretty to think so?"[200] There is nothing in Jake's experience of Brett Ashley's actions and character that will allow him to conclude that she could love him. There is nothing in their experiences of war that allowed Hemingway and Frederic Henry to sustain a belief that all wounded soldiers are brave and that God's good will is in the world. "Isn't it pretty to think so."

7

EMBRACE THE PRESENT

You are what you do now, and not what you have done or will do.

SUN VALLEY STORIES: EMBRACE THE PRESENT

In a candid conversation with lifelong friend and hunting companion Lloyd Arnold in 1939, Hemingway expressed his enthusiasm and gratitude for the present state of Silver Creek as an intact ecosystem replete with robust populations of trout, duck, dove, deer, elk, moose, pheasant, and songbirds. Hemingway told Lloyd, "The truly good and wonderful things you can know but once in life…Those things nothing can ever take from you."[201] Upon his first trip to Silver Creek, Hemingway got to shoot doves "on the move to water after their morning feed…Ernest was flabbergasted that the hunting pressure on the nation's number one game bird was nonexistent" on Silver Creek.[202] Stopped for a view of the creek and the surrounding hill, Lloyd told Hemingway, there are "40 odd square miles of shotgun heaven spread out before us," and Hemingway responded, "If there is such a thing, and if not, I think this will do." Ernest followed with a comment to fiancée Marty Gellhorn: "Must be a thousand…big ducks, mallards, everyone one…Tuck it between your ears, Marty. Keep your fingers crossed for another fall.[203]

Of course, Ernest Hemingway not only appreciated the pristine state of Idaho's intact ecosystems but also appreciated being able to write well in the peaceful, calm, and cool mornings of late summer and fall. After one hunt and during dinner with the Arnolds, Lloyd's wife Tillie recalled Hemingway stating that his "work on (*For Whom the Bell Tolls*) continued as scheduled and it went better in the mountain cool than it had in months of heat in a hotel in Havana" . . . and that "he was on the rough of Chapter 13."[204] In Sun Valley, Hemingway focused on the immediate task of writing *For Whom the Bell Tolls* well. No matter how late the night was, no matter how much drinking was involved, and no matter if the words were not flowing, Hemingway would wake at dawn in room 206 of the Sun Valley Lodge and write. The discipline of staying present, of committing to the moment in case inspiration did come allowed Hemingway to produce some of his favorite moments in *For Whom the Bell Tolls*. He even worked Sun Valley, Idaho, into the novel and told Tillie and Lloyd Arnold he did so. Hemingway wanted to acknowledge the positive influence of Sun Valley upon his work on *For Whom the Bell Tolls*. "I wrote a 1,000 words that morning and each word was worth a dollar," Hemingway once told hunting guide Bud Purdy at lunch at the Alpine Restaurant in Ketchum[205] Hemingway did not wallow in despair about the critical rejection of his last three texts of the 1930s: *Death in the Afternoon*, *To Have and Have Not*, and *Green Hills of Africa*. He was able to write *For Whom the Bell Tolls* with a sustained commitment to developing the coded protagonist in Robert Jordan.

HEMINGWAY AT HIS TYPEWRITER IN SUN VALLEY. *The Community Library, Ketchum, Idaho*

Hemingway filled his days in the late summers and falls of 1939 and 1940 with flush material for his book on the Spanish Civil War and his afternoons flushing the big mallards of Silver Creek and enjoying the "shotgun heaven." After two failed marriages and the longest dry spell between best-selling novels (nearly a decade), Hemingway had found the Wood River Valley to be a place where he could "embrace the present" for he knew a man is "what he does now, and not what he has done or will do." Writing with abandon, hunting with great intensity, enjoying his new found love, Hemingway relished being present in Sun Valley in the falls of 1939-40. These were the moments that were the impetus for his remark "the truly good and wonderful things you can know but once in life…Those things nothing can ever take from you."

Novels and Short Stories: Embrace the Present

Arguably one of the most salient "embrace the present" moments occurs in the opening pages of the novella *The Old Man and the Sea*. After eighty-four days without a marlin, Santiago does not wallow in despair about his previous fruitless days fishing but decides to go out again with a sustained commitment to completing tasks well. Santiago places his baits at precise depths to ensure that he is placing the bait in the likely spots for feeding marlin. In a reflective interior monologue, Santiago recalls his past fishless days and his commitment to being precise with his placement of the bait in the water column and concludes, "I keep them with precision. Only I have no luck anymore. But who knows? Maybe today. Every day is a new day. It is better to be lucky. But I would rather be exact. Then when luck comes you are ready."[206] Purposefully attained luck: pluck. Willed fortune is the idea that you make your own luck by completing tasks well so that when fortune strikes, you will be ready. Santiago's rumination reveals his ability to retain hope for good fortune in the present. But no good fortune is fully appreciated without recognition of a strong will to accompany it. As Hamlet reminds us in preparation for his duel with Laertes, "the readiness is all…let be."

Santiago wants to be ready with his baits at precise depths, so that when the luck of a *feeding* marlin comes, his baits will be in the right place. Santiago rejects careless, casual fishing and redoubles his efforts to be "ready" for good fortune; he states, "I could just drift, he thought, and sleep and put a bight of line around my toe to wake me. But today is eighty-five days and I should fish the day well." And the narrator states, "Just then, watching his lines, he saw one of the projecting green sticks dip sharply."[207]

After Santiago is rewarded for his precise placement of bait and hooks the marlin with a hand line, he knows he needs the help of Manolin—a young deck hand— whom he instructed not to come with him that day. But in order to remain strong for the prolonged fight, Santiago fishes so he can eat to retain his strength. Again, remaining present in the moment with a focused will to eat to keep his energy, Santiago states, "Now is no time to think of what you do not have. Think of what you can do with that there is."[208] In Santiago's remarks, one can hear Hemingway coaching himself to stay present in his writing. While we all know that the marlin is eaten by sharks before he can bring it to the harbor and to market, the end result is not the focus of Santiago's attention, but it is the process and doing the best with what he has, "with what there is," in the present moment that matters to him and to us as readers.

In a powerful reflection on the need to embrace the present, Santiago recalls informing Manolin that he will commit himself as ever to the task at hand, to finding where marlin are feeding and to bringing a marlin to market, even though he is alone. After Santiago hooks into the marlin, the omniscient narrator reflects, "*Now* is when (he) must prove it. The thousand times that he had proved it meant nothing. *Now* he was proving it again. Each time was a new time and he never thought about the past when he was doing it."[209] "We are what we do now, not what we will do or have done," is the definition of the Hemingway code principle "embrace the present." Santiago has to prove his skill as a fisherman that day—his eighty-fifth day without a marlin—because it matters not that his previous days were fishless nor that his days before this drought were filled with record marlin. Coded heroes in Hemingway's novels and short stories never think of the past when committing to present action. Santiago proves to himself and to the fish that he is up to the task of landing a nine-foot marlin with a hand line. But he loses the marlin to the sharks, for he does not have Manolin to help fend off the sharks that attack the marlin. Santiago's act of "going out too far" alone violates the code principle to "value mentors and community." As a result, like Robert Jordan whose *fatal* flaw is his failure to reject Pablo and follow the principle of "value mentors and community," Santiago's *tragic* flaw is his inability to value the support of the community, the assistance of Manolin in bringing a marlin to market. The Hemingway code principles are mutually enhancing. They do not work in isolation. Of course, the aphorism that nothing of significance can be achieved well alone is a major lesson of Santiago's experience and the novella, yet the remarkable commitment to the present that Santiago sustains, even while he futilely attempts to deter sharks from eating the marlin, is an equally important lesson.

    This idea of holding on to faith in yourself in the face of adversity was also an early theme in Hemingway's tightly unified collection of short stories in *In Our Time*. After witnessing the codeless, random, merciless violence of WWI and sustaining a near-fatal spinal injury in the war, protagonist Nick Adams returns to the Upper Peninsula of Michigan, a place where he fished as a youth with his father and uncle. Hoping to recall some of the "old feeling" of his innocence, Nick backpacks, camps, and fly-fishes alone in the final story of the collection, "Big Two-Hearted River." Nick has told his post-WWI mate George that he will return to the United States, marry Helen, and attempt to build a life in the States. But he conveys this plan without enthusiasm for it and with great anxiety about being a veteran with post-traumatic stress disorder *and* a husband *and* a father. In response to George's query "It's hell, isn't it?" Nick responds unconvincingly "Not exactly." Hoping to gain some confidence in himself, Nick commits to being exact in *how* he selects his bait, where he chooses to fish, how he fishes, how he handles the trout when releasing them, and how he kills and cleans the trout he keeps for dinner. And this commitment to the present moment with careful attention to completing tasks well strengthens him. As critic Carl Wood poignantly puts it:

> *The main means by which a correct way of living can be found, however, lies in ritual, for it allows one to concentrate on giving meaning to life through attention to the slightest details in the performance of an action...In a world in which chaos and violence abound and the only certainty is death, man needs to adhere to a set of rules he erects himself. Through religious observance of them some semblance of meaning can be restored.*[210]

Complete tasks well. Value nature. Self-assess. Embrace the present. These mutually enhancing code principles allow the reader to conclude that "ritual" is vital to Nick's self-renewal. He is on a pathway to being "restored" at the end of *In Our Time* by following these edifying code principles, but most importantly, he is keeping the potential "hell" of his recollection of WWI trauma at bay by defining himself by what he does now and not what he did or did not do at war. The question begged by the tip-of-the-iceberg writing at the end of *In Our Time* is: will Nick develop "meaning to (his) life through attention to the slightest details in the performance of" his duties as a husband and father? An optimistic interpretation and one that I favor is that he does, for Hemingway gives readers enough in the surface of the iceberg in fishing, camping, and "valuing nature as an ethical arena" in "Big Two-Hearted River" to conclude that he will be as disciplined about his present relationship with Helen and their newborn as he is while fishing. Similarly, readers of *The Old Man and the Sea* have enough to go on from the text that Santiago will embrace the present of being a mentor to Manolin and being supported by the Cuban fishing village. We know that Santiago will fish with the help of others in the future. Both Santiago and Nick conclude that "you are what you do now and not what you have done or will do."

Often in his novels and short stories, Hemingway provides the reader with uncoded individuals who "are messy" because they do not adhere to the principles of the heroic code. And in contradistinction, Hemingway also provides characters in the same text who adhere to the "notion of a code, some notion of honor...which distinguishes him from people who merely follow their random impulses, and who are, by consequence, messy."[211] But it is most interesting when Hemingway develops a character who begins messily by "followi(ng)...impulses" and then develops honor in his adherence to the code. "The Short Happy Life of Francis Macomber" is one of these texts; Macomber does not embrace the present in his first hunting experience and then learns to speak through actions and embrace the present in his second hunt.

As you recall in "The Short Happy Life of Francis Macomber," Hemingway presents Francis to us from the point of view of the omniscient narrator, the coded hunting guide Wilson, his wife Margot, and the lion. This allows us to see the whole man or the empty shell of a man for most of the story. On a hunting safari with his wife, Francis quickly reveals that he is not up to the task of embracing the present in either his marriage or his hunting adventures. As for the relationship, the omniscient narrator informs us, "Margot was too beautiful for Macomber to divorce her and Macomber had too much money for her to leave him."[212] Margot is ashamed at his cowardly behavior on the lion hunt but even more at his inability to stand up for himself in their failed marriage. Margot controls him, and Francis does not resist. And the narrator continues to explore the paradox of Francis Macomber by stating, "(Francis) always had a great tolerance which seemed the nicest thing about him if it were not the most sinister."[213] "(Margot) was through with him," and Francis knows she is just sticking around for his money, but he tolerates it. In Hemingway's heroic code, this is "sinister" for it violates the code principle of "finding faith in love" as an antidote to despair. In Francis's case, his attenuated love is a *cause* of his despair. This is all to say that Francis does not recognize the reality of his failed marriage and does not "embrace the present," for he lives in a vestige of a memory of when they were once in love.

This refusal to recognize reality and embrace the present manifests in Francis's first hunting experience on this safari. Having spotted a lion at seventy-five meters, Wilson instructs Francis to shoot, but Francis attempts to shoot from the car. "You don't shoot them from cars," Wilson informs Francis.[214] Shifting from the perspective of Wilson to the perspective of the lion who is gutshot by Francis, Hemingway writes, "(the lion) heard the cracking crash and felt the slam of a .30-06 220-grain solid bullet that bit his flank and ripped in sudden hot scalding nausea through his stomach."[215] Hemingway forces the reader to feel what the lion feels when it is shot in the gut. And then Hemingway informs us "Macomber had not thought how the lion had felt as he got out of the car."[216] Not only does Francis shoot from the car, he shoots the lion in the stomach, does not think of the lion bleeding internally, and then, worse, does not want to do the humane act and go into the bush to finish off the lion. Of course, Francis is reluctantly shamed into going in after the wounded lion and then, of course, he runs in a cowardly panic. Francis Macomber "follows" his "random impulses," does not have a code of behavior, and is, by consequence, "messy."

But since this is "The Short Happy Life of Francis Macomber," Hemingway has to have Francis exhibit positive characteristics in the present, however brief this moment and the attending happiness may be. So Francis gets another chance to embrace the present and complete tasks well on a water buffalo hunt. Francis shoots and wounds a water buffalo in the head, this time not from the car. With "the bull coming, nose out, mouth tight closed, blood dripping, massive head…coming in a charge…Macomber fired…and fragments like slate burst from the huge boss of horns."[217] Francis Macomber exhibited courage in the present moment for "the buffalo's huge bulk (was) almost on him and his rifle almost level with the oncoming head."[218] As Hemingway puts it, this is the "sudden precipitation into action without opportunity for worrying beforehand" that is necessary in hunting an animal that can kill you or, at war, in hunting a man who can kill you. Hunting guide Wilson reflects on the "American-boy men" he has seen on many of these safaris and regrettably "how some stay little boys so long…sometimes all their lives."[219] But this short-lived moment of happiness wiped out Macomber's boyishness, naïveté, and cowardliness. But, in one interpretation of an ambiguous ending of this famous short story, Margot shoots Francis in the back of the head for fear that he will now leave her. Having recognized Francis's newfound courage, maturity, and ability to embrace the present, Margot cannot stand the fate of being left by her husband, so a hunting accident seems the best way to avoid a humiliating divorce. With a tragic ending bordering on the absurd, "The Short Happy Life of Francis Macomber" still provides a wonderful example of a character who fails to embrace the present his whole life but then evolves and learns to do so.

In his best-selling Spanish Civil War epic *For Whom the Bell Tolls* that Hemingway tellingly worked on in Sun Valley in 1939-40 when he badly needed "a good book" to keep the critics and self-doubt demons at bay, Hemingway provides us with Pablo, who fails to embrace the present, and Robert Jordan, who succeeds in embracing the present with "what (he) can do with what there is," to steal a line from *The Old Man and the Sea*. We first meet Pablo in the cave in the mountains and join Pilar and Robert Jordan's mistrust of and disgust for him. Pablo—once an inspired leader of the peasant fighters of the Spanish Republican cause—has become both disillusioned with and disenfranchised by the immoral behavior of soldiers in the resistance to the Nationalist and Fascist control of Spain. Recalling the horrific treatment of his fellow villagers who identified with the Nationalist cause, Pablo cannot shake the images of hacking the priest with sickles in his own town hall and the chucking of fellow townspeople over a cliff to their deaths. This leads Pablo to conclude, "I am tired of being hunted. Here we are all right. Now if you blow a bridge here, we will be hunted. If they know we are here and hunt for us with planes, they will find us. If they send Moors to hunt us out, they will find us and we must go. I am tired of all this."[220] Pablo wants to live out the Civil War hiding in the caves in the mountains, for he (correctly) surmises that the Republican cause is outmatched by Fascist military power and that further immoral treatment of fellow Spanish countrymen will only add to the misery after the Civil War. However, this inability to commit to the present moment without paralyzing thoughts about the future, to defend the democratic principles that one knows are right, to embrace the present by completing tasks as well as one can, even if the end result cannot be achieved, forces Pablo to be viewed as one of the most uncoded characters in Hemingway's texts.

Robert Jordan derisively cuts to the bone in his assessment of Pablo's unwillingness to help with the blowing of the bridge when he thinks, "Pablo I know is smart. But rendered useless by his fear and his disinclination to action…He wants to stay in the eddy of his own weakness.'"[221] This assessment accurately captures how Pablo is a victim of his past and how Pablo believes his past immoral actions and ineffective efforts will repeat themselves in the present. So Pablo's conclusion is to refuse to contribute to the Republican resistance and remain out of the current of action by wallowing in self-pity in an "eddy of his own weakness."

"Judge a man by the companions he sought—that will tell you what the real Ernest Hemingway was like," Sun Valley's Dr. John Moritz once said, according to Tillie Arnold in her book *The Idaho Hemingway*.[222] Interestingly, while Robert Jordan is an excellent judge of Pablo's character and Pablo's inability to "embrace the present," Robert Jordan does not disassociate himself enough from Pablo, and this ends with Pablo thwarting Jordan's ability to blow the bridge well.

Hemingway, however, admired the extended "family" of his Ketchum hunting companions so much, he is now surrounded by them in the Ketchum Cemetery. He was "severe" with Lloyd Arnold about the shooting from a moving canoe that led to Gene Van Guilder's tragic death, but he forgave Lloyd and trusted him because he embodied so many of the mutually enhancing principles of the heroic code. The Arnolds, the Williamses, the Purdys, the Atkinsons, the Spiegels, and the Grays, among others, were the "companions (Hemingway) sought" in Ketchum, and they, he felt, were some of finest people he had ever met. Robert Jordan felt the same way about the guerilla fighters in the mountains of Spain. Pilar, Maria, Anselmo, El Sordo, and Andres, among others, were the "companions (Jordan) sought," and they were some of finest people he had ever met. But Jordan's inability to reject Pablo for his uncodedness, specifically Pablo's inability to embrace the present, became Jordan's undoing.

However, Robert Jordan does emerge as one of the most coded heroes in all of Hemingway's novels and short stories. In an iconic moment of self-reflection on the need to remain present and committed to a principle by "completing tasks well" and "finding faith in love," Jordan ruminates:

> *You have it now and that is all your whole life is; now. There is nothing else than now. There is neither yesterday, certainly, nor is there any tomorrow. How old must you be before you know that? There is only now, and if now is only two days, then two days is your life and everything in it will be in proportion. This is how you live a life in two days.*[223]

While in this moment Jordan is thinking of both his love affair with Maria and his task of helping the Republican cause in Spain, he reveals to us the need to embrace the present by not thinking of what could have been done "yesterday" or what you could possibly do "tomorrow." Pondering how he has lived and loved more in the seventy hours since he first met Maria and the band of Spanish Republican guerilla fighters than he has in his whole life leading up to these three days, Jordan concludes, "There is no yesterday, nor tomorrow: only now."[224] He is committed to loving Maria now. No "disinclination to action" that results from focusing on the bleak prospect of their ability to be together in the future. Jordan concludes, "It is possible to live as full a life in seventy hours as in seven years."[225] This description dovetails with Hemingway's new romance with Mary Gellhorn in Sun Valley; this marriage lasted, ironically, seven years. Also, in his nostalgic recollection of his first marriage with Hadley in *A Moveable Feast*, he writes, "We should live in this time now and have every minute of it."[226] Robert and Maria in the mountains of Spain, Frederic and Catherine in the mountains of Switzerland, Hemingway and Marty in the mountains of Idaho, and Hemingway and Hadley in the streets of Paris all had foreshortened but intense love.

In *For Whom the Bell Tolls*, Robert Jordan also informs readers of an important Hemingway concept: the "negation of apprehension" before and during the completion of a task. The denial of the prospect of imminent death that plagues soldiers is necessary to any soldier's successful completion of tasks. Holding back his thoughts on the futility of blowing the bridge and his and his peers' almost-assured deaths in the retreat after blowing the bridge, Jordan thinks, "Carry out (the orders to blow the bridge and retreat) because it is only in the performing of (the orders) that they can prove to be impossible. How do you know they are impossible until you have tried them?"[227] The omniscient narrator also informs us that "(Jordan) would not think himself into any defeatism... he was serving in a war and he gave...as complete a performance as he could give while he was performing."[228] To embrace the present as a soldier is to disallow the paralyzing thoughts of past ineffective action from negatively affecting present action. To embrace the present as a soldier is to ignore that current action may result in one's death and the death of others. In one of the most revealing passages on the necessary eternal present of the soldier, Hemingway writes:

> *In the fear that dries your mouth and your throat, in the smashed plaster dust and the sudden panic of a wall falling, collapsing in the flash and roar of a shellburst, clearing the gun, dragging those away who had been serving it...getting the broken case out, straightening the belt again: you did the thing there was to do and you knew that you were right. You learned the dry-mouthed, fear-purged, purging ecstasy of battle...you learned that fall how to endure and how to ignore suffering in the long time of cold and wetness, of mud and of digging and fortifying.*[229]

Here Jordan reflects on his collective actions as a soldier and the things he did in the present moment: clearing the gun, getting injured soldiers to safety, and resetting the ammunition belt. He informs us that he had to "ignore suffering" in order to "endure." He had to deny the reality of his misery, his fear, and his thoughts of imminent death to embrace the present and complete the necessary tasks well. This is the "sudden precipitation into action without opportunity for worrying beforehand" that hunting guide Wilson claims is necessary to embrace the present in hunting an animal that can kill you.[230] This is the "negation of apprehension" of the soldier, the matador, the big game hunter, the boxer, the writer, and the athlete that affords a cleansed mental space that allows for an unconscious commitment to an action. This is what allows for grace under pressure, for greatness in the face of external and internal adversity.

As Robert Jordan is in the process of setting the grenades on the bridge (recall that Pablo stole dynamite and the remote detonation device), Robert Jordan is in the present moment and interestingly notices the eternal present of nature. Hemingway writes, "Now as he worked, placing, bracing, wedging, lashing tight with wire, thinking only of demolition, working fast and skillfully as a surgeon works...Finishing wiring the grenades down, he no longer heard the firing from up the road. Suddenly he was working only with the noise of the stream."[231] Robert Jordan achieves the "negation of apprehension" by denying the sound of the machine gun fire and his imminent demise. What is left is the sound of the stream, the eternal present of nature. Jordan then sees a trout rise to an insect on the river below the bridge and notices the trout commit to an action necessary to its survival. Hemingway continues, "As (Jordan) looked (at the river) a trout rose for some insect and made a circle on the surface...as he twisted the wire tight with the pliers that held the two grenades in place, he saw, though the metal of the bridge, the sunlight of the green slope of the mountain. It was brown three days ago, he thought."[232] This juxtaposition of Jordan committing to the detonation of the bridge and the trout feeding and mountain greening with renewed life conveys that nature and Jordan are in the eternal present in order to survive and thrive.

After the successful blowing of the bridge to keep the Fascist troops at bay, Robert retreats and in doing so breaks his leg when his horse is shot and falls on him. When Maria approached Jordan after having his leg crushed by the injured horse, Maria asks him "What hast thou?"

The stilted "hast" and "thou" are anomalies in Hemingway's accurate, terse, realistic dialogue for which he is rightly famous. But Hemingway is reminding the reader that all of the conversations in *For Whom the Bell Tolls* are occurring in Spanish. Robert Jordan is a volunteer American soldier (the United States committed one hundred thousand volunteer soldiers for the Republican cause in Spain), and he is, conveniently, a professor of Spanish at the University of Montana. When the lover of Jordan, Maria is asking Robert, respectfully, "Qué tiene usted?", she is asking in the present tense "What do you (currently) have?" Of course, Maria is asking Jordan what ails him that he cannot move, but, it can be argued, she is also asking him what he still has left as a coded individual.

Avoiding despair at his injury that will likely lead to his death, Jordan thinks, "I hate to leave (the world) very much and I hope I have done some good in it. I have tried to with what talent I had. *Have, you mean. All right, have*…The world is a fine place and worth the fighting for and I hate very much to leave it"[233] Jordan updates his past tense "had" with the present tense "have." He amends his summation of his current situation from wallowing in self-pity and regret to embracing the present by reflecting on "what (he) can do with what there is" left. What's left to do is to hold off Lt. Berrendo—a Fascist soldier who massacred El Sordo's group and had their heads cut off. What's left to do is shoot at Lt. Berrendo and his troops as his lover Maria and the undaunted gypsy Pilar escape. "And if you wait and hold them up even a little while or just get the officer that will make all the difference. One thing done well can make—," Robert Jordan thinks to himself.[234] The unfinished "one thing done well can make" invited the reader to finish the statement with "all the difference." The reader knows that Robert still has his coded self intact, and his "negation of apprehension" of his broken leg, of his imminent death, and of his imminent loss of Maria remains strong. Jordan *has* the ability to embrace the present and complete the task of holding off the enemy well. Hemingway informs us that Robert Jordan's "submachine gun lay across lay across his saddle in the crook of his left arm…and (he) lay behind the tree holding onto himself very carefully and delicately to keep his hand steady."[235] This is "embracing the present." We witness Jordan "holding onto himself"; that is, he is answering Maria's query "what do you have?" by showing that he still "holds on." He still *has* the capacity to commit to a cause greater than himself and in a manner that is consistent with the code principles. Embrace the present. Complete tasks well. Speak through actions. Self-assess. All of these mutually enhancing code principles coalesce in this moment. And while the text does not explicitly state that Jordan kills Lt. Berrendo in order to allow Maria to get to safety, we know that he does.

So what is the final lesson of Robert Jordan? What can we learn from his ability to embrace the present? Reflecting on his short life in his final moments of his life, Robert Jordan ruminates, "I have fought for what I believed in for a year now. You've had just as good a life as grandfather's though not as long. You've had just as good a life as any one because of these last days. You do not want to complain when you have been lucky. I wish that there was some way to pass on what I've learned."[236] While his life was tragically cut short, Robert Jordan has experienced the fullness of love, the "feeling of consecration" to a cause he so wholeheartedly believes in, and the religious feeling of brotherhood in fighting for and with others who are coded. Fortunately for us as readers, Hemingway captured and "passed on what (Robert Jordan) learned." The value of embracing the present.

8
SPEAK THROUGH ACTIONS

Your character is exhibited in what you do.

SUN VALLEY STORIES: SPEAK THROUGH ACTIONS

When Ernest Hemingway first arrived in Sun Valley in the fall of 1939, things were also a bit of a mess in his life. His visit with second wife, Pauline, and the boys on a ranch in Montana did not go well, for Pauline left before the vacation was over. Hemingway knew this marriage was over. So he invited Martha Gellhorn to join him and stay at Sun Valley Resort. In addition, Hemingway was overly sensitive about the poor critical reception of his two nonfiction books *Death in the Afternoon* (1932) and *Green Hills of Africa* (1935) and his novel *To Have and to Have Not* (1937). As you know, Hemingway needed a good book. He needed a book that would restore his reputation as a major literary figure. He needed to prove to critics, especially the critic within, that he had not gone the way of F. Scott Fitzgerald, who only produced impactful novels early in his career.

Well, Hemingway produced a good book in *For Whom the Bell Tolls*. He put the final touches on *For Whom the Bell Tolls* in the fall of 1940 and published in October 21, 1940. The book was a "Book of the Month Club" selection and sold 491,000 copies in six months. In the middle of a practice shoot at Sun Valley Gun Club, he sold the novel's movie rights to Paramount Pictures. Hemingway exhibited his grit and determination by producing one of the greatest war novels of the twentieth century. And the protagonist of *For Whom the Bell Tolls*—Robert Jordan— spoke to Hemingway's fundamental belief that one must commit to principles even if and especially if positive outcomes are unlikely. In the end of the novel, Robert Jordan holds off the Nationalist soldiers to show his love for Maria and his love for the Spanish Republicans who were fighting for democracy, separation of church and state, and equal access to land ownership. Robert Jordan's action of holding off the Nationalist soldiers speaks to his ideals.

While writing and editing *For Whom the Bell Tolls*, Hemingway had many hunting adventures in central Idaho. You will recall that Hemingway went hunting on Silver Creek with John and Anna Boettiger (Anna was President Franklin D. Roosevelt's daughter) and the Sun Valley Resort's black Lab, "Bullet." John did not put his safety on his shotgun when he placed it in the canoe, and when he picked up the gun, he accidentally shot the hind leg of Bullet—"one of the fine Arden Labradors given to Sun Valley (Resort) by Averell Harriman."[237] Hemingway was furious and disgusted by the event and how easily it could have been avoided. Dorice Taylor recalls, "As always, Hemingway was furious enraged when a gun was handled carelessly, and the two men had to be taken back to (Sun Valley) lodge in separate cars."[238] John was profusely apologetic and regretful to all who would listen. Disgusted from being witness to such codeless behavior, Hemingway

> *retired to…suite (206) but Marty (Gellhorn) was having a drink on the terrace…when two shots rang out. "Good God," said Marty, "Papa has shot John Boettiger." Actually two wild geese, one badly hurt with a leg trailing, flew past the French doors (of room 206). Hemingway had grabbed a gun and shot the cripple from inside the room.*[239]

Here, Hemingway "exhibited his character," not to others but to himself through the "action" of humanely taking the life of a wounded goose. He was frustrated by the carelessness of John Boettiger's poor hunting skills and unmoved by John's remorse, so when he saw a goose, possibly wounded by another careless hunter, he put it out of its misery. Your "character is exhibited in what you do, not what you say you will do" nor say you regret doing.

Hemingway also spoke through actions during his time in Sun Valley by demonstrating his love for Martha Gellhorn by marrying her as they exited Sun Valley en route to Cuba. In a telegram from Cheyenne, Wyoming, after marrying Marty Gellhorn on November 21, 1940, Hemingway wrote to the Wood River Valley couple he most admired, Lloyd and Tillie Arnold, "We hope we can live up to our wedding pictures and also to be as good a pair as you two."[240] More than just "speaking" of his desire to love Marty as well as Lloyd loved Tillie, Hemingway showed his love in committing to her in marriage.

But this marriage flamed out in seven short years. They were too alike, in my view. Too egotistical. Too independent. Too committed to their work. On assignment as a war correspondent in 1944, Ernest Hemingway met Mary Welsh in London during WWII. They fell in love and were married in 1946 in Cuba. In 1945, Hemingway's first son, Jack, was released from a German prison camp, as the war came to a close.

PATRICK, JACK, HEMINGWAY, AND GREGORY. *Ernest Hemingway Collection. John F. Kennedy Presidential Library and Museum, Boston.*

On August 20 of 1946, Hemingway and Mary packed to go to Sun Valley from Casper, Wyoming, to join the boys, Jack, Patrick, and Gregory, who were hunting with Taylor Williams in Sun Valley. However, Mary had a "tubular pregnancy that had burst. Her heavy internal hemorrhaging caused the anesthesiologist to believe Mary would die. Hemingway took over the plasma infusion…Mary revived, and the surgeon…operated and her life was saved. One fallopian tube was removed and the other damaged…It was unlikely that she would bear children."[241] Hemingway used his training as an ambulance driver and first responder medic in WWI to aid Mary: the taking "over of the plasma infusion" is the grace-under-pressure ethic he created in his most coded characters. Hemingway conveyed his love in his act of preparing her for the surgery properly. Knowing what to do because he had given plasma infusions many times during WWI, Hemingway applied his experiential knowledge to assist in saving the life of his wife. Hemingway was able to apply what he knew by experience calmly and was an able participant in his wife's recovery. Hemingway never spoke about this harrowing experience, but he conveyed his love for Mary in his actions, and his "grace under pressure" was evidenced in knowing what to do and doing it in the immediacy of the moment. Hemingway believed "you could not judge a man until you had seen him in action."[242]

Since Hemingway's *A Farewell to Arms* depicts the fatal pregnancy of Catherine Barkley and death of the child, the fictional account proves bizarrely prescient. But Mary did not succumb to the difficult miscarriage.

Before Ernest and Mary purchased the Warm Springs house in Ketchum, Idaho, they stayed in the McDonald cabins just south of Ketchum.

JUST SOUTH OF KETCHUM ARE MCDONALD'S CABINS, AN OCCASIONAL PLACE OF RESIDENCE FOR HEMINGWAY IN THE VALLEY. *The Community Library, Ketchum, Idaho.*

In Dorice Taylor's account *Sun Valley Stories*, she recalls watching Ernest Hemingway in August of 1946 walk by the McDonald cabins in a short robe and then in shorts and a T-shirt and then in just shorts.[243] He was pacing nervously, and only later did Dorice Taylor learn that Hemingway was pacing nervously over Mary's recovery from the miscarriage. Akin to Frederic Henry's nervous pacing about the potential loss of Catherine Barkley and child in *A Farewell to Arms*, Hemingway was anxious over Mary's recovery from the surgery and was pacing frantically. Deeply in love with Mary in Ketchum in 1946, Hemingway was fearful of experiencing what *his* Frederic Henry and Catherine Barkley experienced. Thankfully, fiction did not prefigure fact.

NOVELS AND STORIES: SPEAK THROUGH ACTIONS

As was established in the "Develop Experiential Knowledge" chapter, we know that Hemingway emphasizes the disconnect between the "false abstractions" of the inexperienced and virtues exhibited by the actions of experts. In *A Farewell to Arms*, Rinaldi speaks of bravery and "valorous conduct" to injured Frederic, who knows he was not brave when he was under fire. The battle police in the same novel speak of "treachery" and desertion and "losing the fruits of victory" to Frederic, who has just participated in the chaos of the retreat at Caporetto.[244] And Gino tells Frederic that the fighting of "the summer could not have been done *in vain*."[245] (my italics) These three moments in *A Farewell to Arms* reveal the tension between those "uninformed" by experience who speak about bravery, honor, and victory and those informed by experience who know the reality of the actions behind these false abstractions.

In a self-reflective moment in *A Farewell to Arms*, Frederic Henry derisively rejects speeches and false abstractions as divorced from the reality of actions. Frederic ruminates:

> *I was always embarrassed by the words sacred, glorious, and sacrifice and the expression in vain. We had heard them, sometimes standing in the rain almost out of earshot, so that only the shouted words came through, and had read them, on proclamations that were slapped up by billposters...now for a long time, and I had seen nothing sacred, and the things that were glorious had no glory and the sacrifices were like the stockyards at Chicago if nothing was done with the meat except to bury it. There were many words that you could not stand to hear and finally only the names of places had dignity. Certain numbers were the same way and certain dates and these with the names of the places were all you could say and have them mean anything. Abstract words such as glory, honor, courage, or hallow were obscene beside the concrete names of villages, the numbers of roads, the names of rivers, the numbers of regiments and the dates.*[246]

Hemingway loathed the hollowness of speeches from those who are "stupid from inexperience." Moreover, he valued those who could convey what they believed solely through their actions. "Abstract words such as glory, honor, courage, or hallow were obscene beside the concrete names of villages, the numbers of roads, the names of rivers, the numbers of regiments and the dates," thinks Frederic. In "Soldier's Home," Krebs echoes this thought by pining for more good war maps and histories to be published post-WWI. The actions in the battles, in the towns, next to the rivers are deeply ingrained in the memories of soldiers; all that is needed to evoke the memory of these actions are "concrete names" of villages, roads, regiments, and rivers. This is not to say that there were not courageous moments at war and honorable actions that were both effective and ineffective in saving the lives of others at war. But even to have these moments spoken of as courageous and honorable moments is to devalue them. Worse yet, to have horrific moments of moral failure (like the retreat from Caporetto in which Frederic kills one Italian officer and wounds another, and Passini dies from friendly fire) spoken of as honorable, courageous, and hallowed is disgraceful. Character is exhibited in actions and not in the recounting of actions.

In many short stories, Hemingway shows us how characters convey their love or lack of love through their actions and inactions. And not in their speeches about love. In "Hills Like White Elephants," the American repeatedly says he loves his recently pregnant girlfriend, Jig, and will do anything for her, but his inaction belies his speech, his "false abstraction" about love. The American refuses to marry Jig, settle down, and raise their child. He encourages her to have an abortion. This selfish unwillingness to show his love lets both Jig and the reader conclude that he is not in love despite his speeches to the contrary. In the end of the story, Jig says to the American, "There is nothing wrong *with me*. I feel fine." (my italics)[247] She conveys her disgust with his unwillingness to act on love and get married. And we know Jig is moving on from him at the end of the story.

In another failed post-WWI relationship story, "Cat in the Rain," published in *In Our Time* (1925), the husband "speaks through his actions" and reveals how he is not in love. He shows that he is not in love with his wife by refusing to stop reading when she speaks to him, by refusing to acknowledge her desire to settle down, and most tellingly, by refusing to get the cat out of the rain for his wife. Character is exhibited both in actions and inactions. The woman in the story empathizes with the cat caught in the rain, in its inability to extricate itself from its oppressive surroundings beyond its control. At the end of the story, the concierge of the hotel ("the padrone") has his maid retrieve the cat from the rain and bring it to the wife after the wife has shared her desire to save the cat. Hemingway writes, "In the doorway stood the maid. She held a big tortoise shell cat pressed tight against her and swung down against her body. 'Excuse me,' she said, 'the padrone asked me to bring this for the signora.'"[248] The padrone shows he cares for the wife by his action of having the maid retrieve the cat; the husband shows he is not in love by "reading again" and ignoring his wife's desires. Both "Hills Like White Elephants" and "Cat in the Rain" are stories in which a husband or lover's actions belie their professed love. This stands in sharp contrast to Hemingway's conveyance of his love for Mary when he did "the one thing…easily and naturally,"—the plasma infusion—to aid her ability to survive this traumatic tubular pregnancy.

    A chapter in *In Our Time* in which a soldier prays to God to be saved from the heat of battle provides our first glimpse at the well-known Hemingway pattern of actions exposing false speech. In this moment, a soldier who is being shelled by mortars prays to God he will live. This is "foxhole faith." Praying for divine intervention in order to live is a disingenuous faith that occurs only when death is imminent. This supposed faith in Jesus Christ as his savior is contradicted by this soldier's later actions. In a one paragraph vignette ironically labeled as a "Chapter VII," Hemingway writes:

> *While the bombardment was knocking the trench to pieces at Fossalta, he lay very flat and sweated and prayed oh Jesus Christ get me out of here. Dear Jesus please get me out. Christ please please please Christ. If you'll only keep me from getting killed I'll do anything you say. I believe in you and will tell everyone in the world that you are the only one that matters. Please please dear Jesus. The shelling moved farther up the line. We went to work on the trench and in the morning the sun came up and the day was hot*

and muggy and cheerful and quiet. The next night back at Mestre he did not tell the girl he went upstairs with at the Villa Rosa about Jesus. And he never told anybody.[249]

In "Chapter VII" (this excerpt is the entire chapter), we know the soldier's prayer is hollow and that his feigned belief in divine providence is only momentarily and selfishly rendered, because his actions contradict his speech. He never tells "anybody" about how he was saved from imminent death by Christ. Sleeping with a prostitute at the Villa Rosa "the next night" underscores that his speech about faith in divine providence is a "false abstraction." This soldier know he survives because the mortar shells fortunately missed and not because of the benevolent hand of divine providence answering the soldier's prayer. And this soldier does not have faith in Jesus Christ as his savior as his actions of sleeping with a prostitute in the whorehouse and never mentioning Christ's teachings to anyone reveal. For Hemingway, this soldier wallowed in self-pity, and in his depth of despair falsely called out for divine intervention. What he needed to do was complete tasks well, speak through actions, embrace the present, and effect positive change by fighting back or retreating to a safer place to fight. In short, Hemingway believed that one's character and one's beliefs can only be accurately assessed by one's actions and not in false speeches about one's beliefs.

Of course, "Chapter VII," quoted above in its entirety, is not a chapter. Hemingway started out as a poet and was heavily influenced by the modernist focus on the image itself as "an emotional and intellectual complexity in an instant of time."[250] Some modernist poems were two or three lines long and solely comprised of images. For example, Ezra Pound, Hemingway's friend and editor, writes in 1917:

In a Station of the Metro

The apparition of these faces in the crowd;

Petals on a wet, black bough.

This is the whole poem. The title is key to its meaning. The image of the ghost-like faces of those waiting for work in the early morning in a subway / metro station is startling. They are dead to life, uninspired about the daily grind, and look like dead, lifeless, decayed "petals on a wet, black bough." In 1918, Ernest Hemingway followed his mentor Ezra Pound's lead and wrote:

POETRY

> So now,
> Losing the three last night,
> Taking them back today,
> Dripping and dark the woods…[251]

Hemingway titled his four line and sixteen-word poem "Poetry" while knowing that most contemporary readers would not consider this to be a poem. But it is a powerful poem that conveys the despair of taking back the three fatally wounded who drip blood in the woods dripping from the recent rain. So when Hemingway labels the above vignette from *In Our Time* "Chapter VII," we know he is following Ezra Pound's dictum "make (literature) new." Hemingway anticipates the reader's complaint that this is not a chapter but believes in Pound's advice that one image is "an emotional and intellectual complex in an instant of time." In Chapter VII, we get one auditory image of a prayer for personal safety and one visual image of the soldier with a prostitute. And they work together to convey the soldier's false faith.

In *For Whom the Bell Tolls*, Hemingway develops that Robert Jordan's fatal flaw resides in Robert's struggles with "whom to trust and not to trust." While Jordan rightly trusts and values the mentorship of Anselmo, Jordan foolishly trusts Pablo in the end. Robert Jordan's willingness to trust Pablo's sincerity in assisting the blowing of the bridge violates the code principle "value mentors and community" for this principle states, "develop and maintain faith in others who embody and exhibit the other principles of the code." Jordan has been provided with ample evidence that Pablo does not support the blowing of the bridge and does not support resisting the enemy forces at all. Pablo tells Robert this to his face. In addition, Pilar recounts the horrible massacre in Pablo's hometown in which Pablo oversaw the Republican soldiers who threw Pablo's Nationalist-aligned neighbors over the cliff and hacked a local priest to death with sickles. The undisciplined and undignified actions of his band of Republican fighters and the fact that his hometown was retaken by the Nationalists three days later led Pablo to state that he wished all the deceased Nationalists "were restored to life." "We should have killed all or none," Pablo says to Robert and others.[252] In addition, Pablo says to his former band of Republican guerilla fighters, "You are a group of illusioned people...led by a woman with her brain between her thighs and a foreigner who comes to destroy you."[253] This "eddying in his own weakness," this "disinclination to action" are criticized by Robert and the other Republican guerrilla fighters as well. They acknowledge the atrocities committed in the attempt to return Pablo's town to the Republicans, but they also know that they have to "get strong in the broken places" and fight again because they know their fight for democratic ideals is just.

So when Robert and the other Republican fighters discuss the notion that Pablo cannot be trusted and must be removed from their group, Robert Jordan openly states that he knows he must kill Pablo or suffer the consequences of having a dissenter in the group. When Fernando says, "(Pablo) is a danger to the Republic...he should be eliminated in order that the operations projected should be insured of the maximum possibility of success," Robert Jordan responds, "Estoy listo...it is a service I can do."[254] It is important to recall that Pablo has stepped outside to check on his horses when Robert says this in the cave. At that moment, "the blanket fastened across the opening of the cave was lifted and Pablo put his head in."[255] Did Pablo overhear Robert Jordan's affirmation that he will eliminate Pablo? It seems so. The reader then hears Pablo's change of heart and willingness to rejoin the Republican band of fighters, help blow the bridge, and fight again for the Republicans with the skepticism that Robert Jordan fails to muster. Pablo tells all in the cave, "I have changed my opinion...I am with thee."[256] Up until this moment, Pablo is drunk on wine and wallows in self-pity; Robert Jordan knows this. So Pablo's claim to rejoin the Republican cause and desire to aid Robert Jordan and the others is untrue and only motivated by self-interest and self-preservation. Had Robert Jordan trusted his ability to evaluate individuals by their actions, he would have heard it as a false statement of solidarity.

However, Robert allows Pablo to rejoin the fight, and Robert later regrets this lapse of judgment of character. Pablo steals Robert's remote detonator, caps, fuses, two horses, and some of the dynamite. Pablo exhibits his weak character, his codelessness, his inability to "complete tasks well," "avoid self-pity," and "embrace the present." The result? Anselmo is killed in the blowing of the bridge from too close of a distance, and Robert Jordan is wounded in their hasty, chaotic attempt at escaping the Nationalist surge after the blowing of the bridge. Robert Jordan should have interpreted Pablo's character by assessing Pablo's actions: his excessive drinking and previous unwillingness to act to aid their efforts. "Your character is exhibited by what you do," not what say you will do. Like Santiago who fails to follow the code principle of "valuing mentors and community" in his solo attempt to bring in a giant marlin to market, Robert Jordan fails to judge others by their actions and not their "false abstractions."

Robert Jordan reacts to the stolen detonator, dynamite, caps and fuses by stating, "The dirty, vile, treacherous, sod...ugly bastard. The dirty cabron (coward)."[257] But Robert's anger is misplaced. He should be angry at *his* uncodedness, at *his* inability to judge Pablo by Pablo's actions/inactions.

However, Robert does have moments in *For Whom the Bell Tolls* in which he is able to recognize the fallacy of his own "false abstractions." In thinking about the "impossible" orders from Russian General Golz to blow the bridge and successfully take Segovia, Robert thinks "you have no responsibility...except in action...you should carry (the orders) out because it is only in the performing of them that they can prove to be impossible."[258] While this is an admirable interior monologue about committing to action to show your allegiance to the Republican cause and to prove the success or failure of the orders by acting on them, Robert should also recognize that it is his "responsibility" to know whom to trust and not trust by judging people by their actions. Anselmo has always followed Robert's orders and while Anselmo regrets the killing of his fellow Spaniards during the Spanish Civil War, he has shown that he will follow orders, even an order to kill. Pablo's inaction should have confirmed to Robert Jordan that Pablo believes in the "impossibility of the orders" and will be unwilling to prove the success or failure of the orders by carrying them out. Later on in this same interior monologue, Robert wonders:

> *Was there ever a people whose leaders were as truly the enemies of the people as this one? Enemies of the people. That was a phrase he might omit. He had gotten to be as bigoted and hidebound about his politics as a hard-shelled Baptist and phrases like enemies of the people came into his mind without his much criticizing them in any way. Any sort of clichés both revolutionary and patriotic. His mind employed them without criticism…Bigotry is an odd thing. To be bigoted you have to be absolutely sure that you are right and nothing makes that surety and righteousness like continence. Continence is the foe of heresy…When you were drunk or when you committed either fornication or adultery you recognized your own personal fallibility.*[259]

At the writing of *For Whom the Bell Tolls* in 1939 and 1940, Hemingway knew plenty about "personal fallibility" through his affairs with Pauline Pfeiffer while married to his first wife, Hadley, and through his affairs with Jane Mason and Martha Gellhorn while married to his second wife, Pauline. Adultery was familiar to Hemingway leading up to his writing of *For Whom the Bell Tolls*. But this is Hemingway's point in the passage above. Those who are unaware of their personal shortcomings, those who do not "self-assess" and adhere to valid, substantive self-criticism and criticism from others, are uncoded. And in this passage, Robert Jordan fears that "righteousness" and "bigotry" stem from those (including himself) who are not self-aware of their incontinence, "personal fallibilities," and shortcomings. To call all of the Nationalists and Germans and Northern Italians "enemies of the people" is a "false abstraction" that could only be sincerely stated by one who believes one is always right, always acting correctly, and incapable of spurious reasoning. Robert Jordan reads the letters of the Nationalist soldier he kills and learns that the boy from Navarra was engaged to be married, deeply religious, and the son of a blacksmith. Jordan knows that while the "leaders" of the Nationalists and the Fascists may be condemnable, the soldiers, like the boy from Navarra, are not. Some Nationalist soldiers are caught up in the machine of war and do not have political motivations and are most certainly not "enemies of the people"—enemies of all the politically disenfranchised of the world. Robert knows he "does not always kill who he wants to kill in war" and knows he is aware of his "personal fallibilities." This allows Robert to judge *his character* by *his actions* and ditch false abstractions like "I am killing all the enemies of the people." Your character is not exhibited in your speeches and catchphrases but in what you do. And Robert knows, through the sage advice of his mentor Anselmo, that he will have to commit to actions that serve as a penance for the killing after the war. Robert Jordan and the reader learn that actions convey values, ideals, and virtues.

9
TAKE RESPONSIBILITY FOR WRONGS

Do not blame others for wrongs caused by yourself; cleanse the self by both avoiding repeating mistakes and "get(ting) strong in the broken places."

SUN VALLEY STORIES: TAKE RESPONSIBILITY FOR WRONGS

Hemingway spent some of his last moments in Ketchum writing *A Moveable Feast* to honor both his enormously productive period of writing in Paris from 1921–1926 and his love for Hadley Richardson, his first wife. In the 1920s, Hemingway produced his famous short story collection *In Our Time (1925)*, *The Sun Also Rises (1926)*, and *A Farewell to Arms (1929)*. While *A Farewell to Arms* was finished in Key West, much of this writing was produced in Paris when "we did not think of ourselves as poor. We did not accept it. We thought we were superior people and other people that we looked down on and rightly mistrusted were the rich. It did not seem strange to me to wear sweatshirts for underwear to keep warm. It only seemed odd to the rich. We ate well and cheaply and slept well and warm together and loved each other."[260] Writing *A Moveable Feast* was an attempt to recall those days when he felt he possessed enormous potential as a writer with endless fodder for his stories, when he was deeply in love with his first wife, Hadley, and when the hunger to write stemmed from the need to make money and the need to prove himself as a writer.

Mary Hemingway writes that "Ernest started writing (*A Moveable Feast*) in Cuba in the autumn of 1957, worked on it in Ketchum, Idaho in the winter of 1958-9, took it with him to Spain…brought it back to

Cuba, and then to Ketchum late that fall. He finished the book in the spring of 1960 in Cuba, after having put it aside to write…*The Dangerous Summer*…He made revisions of (*A Moveable Feast*) in the fall in 1960 in Ketchum."[261] Many critics argue that Hemingway left the autobiographical snapshot *A Moveable Feast* unfinished, along with *Islands in the Stream*, *The Garden of Eden*, and another book on his travels in Africa *True at first Light*. Nonetheless, Hemingway's desire to return to when he and Hadley "loved each other" and the stories were flowing shows us more than Hemingway's nostalgia for a better time in his life; it shows us his desire to take responsibility for relinquishing a love and a life.

In the fall of 1959 and toward the end of his life, Hemingway tells Ketchum native Clayton "Stu" Stewart that "you never own anything until you have given it away."[262] In typical trademark ambiguity with multiple antecedents for the pronoun "it," Hemingway could be referring to his first marriage, to his deteriorating relationship with Mary, to the Finca Vigia in Cuba that was appropriated by Castro during the revolution, or to his memory that was fading and his consequent inability to write well. All of these losses exacerbated Hemingway's mental state in the years from 1959 to 1961, the year of his suicide in his Ketchum home. A man always in love, Hemingway believed he had outlived his ability to complete tasks well, value community, and value being in love.

But in this comment, "you never own anything until you have given it away," Hemingway is "taking responsibility for wrongs." The operative phrase is "given it away." He did not willfully give away his control over his mind and his enthusiasm for life. But he did willingly give away his love for and marriage to Hadley, and this, in essence, is what *A Moveable Feast* is about. In the Hemingway heroic code "to take responsibility for wrongs" is to avoid blaming others for wrongs caused by yourself and to cleanse the self by both avoiding repeating mistakes and "get(ting) strong in the broken places." Well, one could argue that Hemingway was writing an unflattering portrayal of his foolish attempt to sustain a married relationship with Hadley and have an affair with Pauline Pfeiffer. But *A Moveable Feast* is more about not knowing how deeply he was in love with Hadley until he "gave her away" in his pursuit of the more fashionable and more cosmopolitan Pauline.

The writing of *A Moveable Feast* conjured up both an irrecoverable time when writing came fluidly and when Hemingway and Hadley "slept well and warm together and loved each other."[263] Local Ketchum historian Taylor Pasley archived all of the material in the Hemingway Ketchum house, and in his perusal of the books in the house for potential marginalia, he discovered a postcard from Hadley to Mary on July 21—Ernest's birthday—stating, "I remember this day well." This postcard arrived after Ernest's death, and Mary held onto a token of this first marriage, of Ernest's first love in marriage, and knew from her reading *of A Moveable Feast* what "he had given away." His last near-finished work took responsibility for this wrong, for as Hemingway remarked with contrition, how does one know that the first love will be the finest?

In a reflective moment about falling in love with Pauline while married and deeply in love with Hadley, Hemingway writes, "All things truly start from an innocence. You lie and you hate it and it destroys you and every day is more dangerous."[264] Hemingway finds some cathartic release here in taking responsibility for ruining his first marriage. In an even more poignant moment of avoiding the tendency "to blame others for wrongs caused by yourself," Hemingway writes:

> *When I saw my wife (Hadley) again standing by the tracks..., I wished I had died before I loved anyone but her. She was smiling, the sun on her lovely face tanned by the snow and sun, beautifully built, her hair red gold in the sun, grown out all winter awkwardly and beautifully...I loved her and I loved no one else and we had a lovely magic time while we were alone. I worked well...this is how Paris was in the early days when we were very poor and very happy.*[265]

Whatever one thinks about the influence of recalling his great period of writing well and loving well in the 1920s in Paris had upon Hemingway in his final years, Hemingway certainly took responsibility for his wrongs, for losing Hadley "destroy(ed)" him, and as he writes, he wished he "had died" in love with her.

In 1960, the year before his tragic suicide in Ketchum, as Hemingway attempted the final edits on *A Moveable Feast*, he knew his "natural talent" had been "marred," and he "became conscious of his damaged wings and of their construction and he learned to think and could not fly any more because the love of flight was gone and he could only remember when it had been effortless."[266] While this quote was written by Hemingway in reference to F. Scott Fitzgerald's waning talent, it applies well to Hemingway in his last few years of his life. His unfinished texts are a testament to his consciousness of his waning capacity to write. Was Hemingway self-aware that his depression, alcoholism, paranoia, and memory loss from multiple concussions and electroshock treatments exacerbated his declining writing powers? Did he blame himself for allowing himself to get to this state of mind? No one will ever know. Hemingway may have hoped to rekindle some of the hunger, confidence, and love he felt in the early 1920s by writing *A Moveable Feast*, but it seemed only to widen the gulf between his previous literary powers and his current state. He was unable to "get strong in the broken places." He may have felt responsible, in part, for his declining powers and could not "get strong" where he felt most broken: his capacity to write and to love well.

In contrast, a moment at the end of Hemingway's life in Sun Valley reveals Hemingway's ability to change course and recognize his wrongs

HEMINGWAY AND HIS FIRST WIFE, HADLEY, AND FIRST SON, JACK, OR "BUMBY."
Ernest Hemingway Collection. John F. Kennedy Presidential Library and Museum, Boston.

and work to ameliorate them. On January 1, 1959, news came to the Hemingways that Fidel Castro had taken over Havana. According to Mary Hemingway, Ernest wrote to a paper "I believe in the historical necessity of the Cuban revolution and I believe in its long range aims."[267] The New York Times followed up on the report and phoned Hemingway in the Ketchum house on January 1. Hemingway told the reporter he was "delighted" with the news from Cuba. Mary asked him to retract his word "delighted…You don't want that on record."

Hemingway responded, "One bloody word." And Mary retorted, "You're a man of words. You know their power." [268]

Hemingway revised "delighted" to "hopeful." Recognizing the negative way readers of *The New York Times* would perceive the notion that Hemingway was "delighted" with the Cuban Revolution, Mary encouraged Hemingway to take responsibility for the overly charged word and amend it. That he did shows his respect for the power of one word, his respect for Mary, and his ability to take responsibility for selecting the wrong word.

HEMINGWAY AND MARY IN THE KETCHUM WARM SPRINGS HOUSE. *The Community Library, Ketchum, Idaho.*

In addition, the moments hunting in central Idaho are also instructive in assessing the code principle "take responsibility for wrongs." The hunts that ended badly because of poor behavior of others bothered Hemingway. And we often witness Hemingway either admonishing the poor behavior or so deeply bothered by it that he needs time to himself. Three hunting stories come to mind.

First, you recall that on a hunt for chukar near Silver Creek, Ketchum resident and novice hunter Anita Gray shot at ducks that flushed from a large puddle and caused all the chukar to scare up the hillside to safe cover in the rocks. Hemingway upbraided her for not knowing the unspoken hunting code: when one goes for one species, one does not shoot at another species. Hemingway wanted Anita to be able to avoid this mistake in the future and take responsibility for it, if it were to happen again.

Second, you recall the hunt in Silver Creek during which John Boettiger failed to put his safety on his gun and shot the leg off the Sun Valley Resort Lab, "Bullet," when he accidentally pulled the trigger when reaching for his gun. Hemingway left this hunt immediately in a separate car from Boettiger. Hemingway was disgusted with Boettiger's carelessness with the gun, heartsick over the innocent lab, and impatient with Boettiger's contrition. Certainly, Boettiger took responsibility for Bullet's leg, but it was the general lack of responsibility with firearms that infuriated Hemingway.

Third, the most instructive Idaho moment involving the code principle "take responsibility for wrongs" occurred during the tragic hunt on the Snake River when Sun Valley publicist Gene Van Guilder was killed by a shotgun blast to the back. You will recall that Dave Benner and Gene Van Guilder both shot from a moving canoe that was steered by Sun Valley hunting guide Lloyd Arnold, and the rocking of the canoe from Gene's shot from the bow caused Dave Benner's shotgun to swing inadvertently toward the back of Gene. But it is Hemingway's reaction to the tragic death that underscores his desire to take personal responsibility for the wrong and for others to do so as well. Hemingway tells Lloyd Arnold that Lloyd should own the carelessness that led to Gene

Van Guilder's death. He tells Arnold that Gene's death was more than bad luck; he states, "How can we call it anything else but impulsive action? No, you and Gene were a fine team, and didn't go about telling each other what to do, and I admire your stand, but I won't buy it...I'm involved too."[269]

Having hunted with Gene and Lloyd from a canoe, having allowed the hunts to go on without addressing the unspoken rule about only shooting from a fixed, anchored boat or having only one person shoot, Hemingway is "taking responsibility" for his implicit involvement in Gene's death. Hemingway could have addressed these rules in previous hunts. He did not. With Lloyd he is taking responsibility for his involvement in and contribution to the carelessness and code breaking that led to Gene's death, and he is asking Lloyd to do the same. Lloyd's reaction to Hemingway's comments was "(Hemingway) was sympathetic and very severe about the rule-breaking"[270] While Hemingway wrote a beautiful eulogy for Gene Van Guilder, I am confident that he never allowed hunting from an unfixed craft (even though he was not directly involved) and "cleansed the self by avoiding repeating mistakes." Lloyd Arnold and Taylor Williams enjoyed hunting with Hemingway all the way up to his last days in Ketchum.

NOVELS AND SHORT STORIES: TAKE RESPONSIBILITY FOR WRONGS

Lady Brett Ashley is the most famous Hemingway character who fails to take responsibility for actions. Hemingway's *The Sun Also Rises* depicts Brett as a woman who refuses to take responsibility for the ruined lives she leaves in her wake as she moves through men with unprecedented celerity. But, again, context matters. Having lost her first two loves to the war (one is killed and one suffers from PTSD), Brett evokes empathy for her current emotionless state. Nonetheless, Brett views male-female relationships primarily as vehicles for sexual gratification and a means to ward off loneliness and boredom. Brett consciously breaks the hearts of Robert Cohn, Jake Barnes, Count Mippipopolous, and fiancé Mike

Campbell. But in breaking up with Pedro Romero—the immensely skilled young Spanish matador—, Brett reveals her inability to "take responsibility for wrongs." Depicting a conversation in which Brett reveals her love for Pedro to Jake, Hemingway writes:

> "I've got to do something. I've got to do something I really don't want to do. I've lost my self-respect."
>
> "You don't have to do that."
>
> "Oh, darling, don't be difficult. What do you think it's meant to have that damned Jew about, and Mike the way he's acted?"
>
> "Sure."
>
> "I can't just stay tight all the time."
>
> "No."
>
> "Oh, darling, please stay by me. Please stay by me and see me through this."
>
> "Sure."
>
> "I don't say it's right. It is right though for me. God knows, I've never felt such a bitch."[271]

It is worth noting that Brett is telling Jake about her new crush on Pedro while knowing full well that Jake is in love with her. She confesses that she "has lost" her "self-respect" and recognizes that she "cannot stay tight all the time" and feels remorseful when the numbing effect of alcohol wears off. Confessing that she is a "bitch" to Jake is as close to "taking responsibility" for her reckless behavior with men as Lady Brett gets. And it falls profoundly short of "not blaming others for wrongs caused by oneself" and dramatically short of "cleansing the self by avoiding repeating mistakes." Brett begs Jake to "stay by" her to distract her from her self-loathing, and Jake, much to the reader's regret, obliges.

After breaking it off with Pedro when Pedro honorably informs Brett that he wants to marry her, Brett again returns to the feeling of "not being a bitch." Exposing Brett's unselfconsciously ironic pride in refusing Pedro's marriage proposal, Hemingway writes::

> *"You know, he'd only been with two women before. He never cared about anything but bull-fighting."*
>
> *"He's got plenty of time."*
>
> *"I don't know. He thinks it was me. Not the show in general."*
>
> *"Well, it was you."*
>
> *"Yes. It was me. You know I feel rather damned good, Jake."*
>
> *"You should."*
>
> *"You know it makes one feel rather good deciding not to be a bitch."*
>
> *"Yes."*
>
> *"It's sort of what we have instead of God."*[272]

Jake's highly ironic and terse responses allow the reader to conclude that Jake is mocking Brett's inability to hear what she is saying; to comprehend her inability to take responsibility for breaking the heart of a young, sincere matador; and, by the way, for breaking Jake's heart as well. Brett claims she "feels rather damned good," for it "makes one feel rather good deciding not to be a bitch." Brett proudly goes on to say to Jake, "I will not be one of those bitches that ruins children." Of course, the reader sees through the false pride of Brett in refusing marriage and raising children only to leave the marriage and the children. This is a far cry from "taking responsibility for wrongs," for it leaves out the wake of men she has emotionally destroyed. Moreover, Brett is falsely proud of her ability to break off a relationship before it gets too serious because she knows she is incapable of love. To go further and claim that this is a religious, confessional purging of sin with "what we have instead of God" would be laughable, if it weren't so sad. Jake learns here that Brett is uncoded, ruined from her first two losses of love, and profoundly unable to "cleanse the self by both avoiding repeating mistakes and "gett(ing) strong in the broken places."

But Santiago in *The Old Man and the Sea* is a character who acknowledges he broke the code principle of "valuing mentors and community" and takes responsibility for the wrong of going "out too far" without support. Santiago fishes alone and hooks a giant marlin with great skill, but he knew he alone would be unable to honor the marlin's life, get it to shore, and get it to market without sharks destroying it. Santiago repeatedly confesses that he wished he had the boy, Manolin, to help him ward off the sharks and bring the marlin to market intact. To underscore Santiago's recognition that no one achieves anything alone, he often refers to baseball and the other eight players that allowed Joe DiMaggio to achieve greatness, of the pride of lions on the beaches of Africa, and of the "school of porpoises" that hunt together in unison. Hemingway writes:

> *He did not dream of the lions but instead of a vast school of porpoises that stretched for eight or ten miles and it was in the time of their mating and they would leap high into the air and return into the same hole they had made in the water when they leaped. Then he dreamed that he was in the village on his bed and there was a norther and he was very cold and his right arm was asleep because his head had rested on it instead of a pillow. After that he began to dream of the long yellow beach and he saw the first of the lions come down onto it in the early dark and then the other lions came and he*

rested his chin on the wood of the bows where the ship lay anchored with the evening offshore breeze and he waited to see if there would be more lions and he was happy.[273]

(my italics)

Santiago conflates the communal work of porpoises and lions, while longing for the support of the "village," a community that honors him with food he cannot afford and moral support by wishing him well as he embarks on his eighty-fifth day without a marlin. Santiago ruminates aloud "I wish I had the boy. I'm being towed by a fish and I'm the towing bitt."[274] One of the great themes of the novella is Santiago's realization that nothing of significance can be achieved alone. Santiago thinks, "After it is light, he thought, I will work back to the forty-fathom bait and cut it away too and link up the reserve coils. I will have lost two hundred fathoms of good Catalan *cordel* and the hooks and leaders. That can be replaced. But who replaces this fish if I hook some fish and it cuts him off?...Aloud he said, 'I wish I had the boy.' But you haven't got the boy, he thought. You have only yourself and you had better work back to the last line now, in the dark or not in the dark, and cut it away and hook up the two reserve coils."[275] When Santiago returns with only the head of the marlin intact after the sharks devour the body of the marlin, he knows he disrespected both the marlin and the code principle "value mentors and community." In keeping with the "tip of the iceberg" writing style, Hemingway lets the reader conclude that Santiago will only go for marlin in the future with Manolin or others and will "cleanse the self by both avoiding repeating mistakes and 'get(ting strong in the broken places.'"

Beyond Santiago's implied resolve to fish with others and ability to take responsibility for his mistakes, Anselmo in *For Whom the Bell Tolls* is a character who overtly states the need to cleanse the self through contrition. Immediately emerging as a man Robert Jordan can both trust and revere as a mentor, Anselmo informs Robert that "it is a sin to kill man. Even the Fascists who we must kill…No. I am against the killing of all men."[276] Anselmo goes on to tell Robert, "if I live later, I will try to live in such a way, doing no harm to any one, that it will be forgiven." Without a religious confession "since we do not have God anymore," Anselmo informs Robert that "a man must be responsible to himself." Anselmo informs Robert that the enemy—the Catholic supported Nationalists—have claimed God and want to maintain mandatory religious teachings in Spanish schools and that "if there were a God, never would He have permitted what (he) has seen."[277] In keeping with the necessity for Hemingway's code to replace the chaos of a world without divine providence, Anselmo is instructing Robert to confess his killings at war *to himself* and to seek out repentance and reconciliation for the killings. Later in the novel, Anselmo argues that "there must be some form of civic penance organized that all may be cleansed from the killing or else we will never have a true and human basis for living."[278] Anselmo underscores this with the comment "we must do something very strong to atone for (the killings at war)."[279] It is instructive to recall that Anselmo knows he is killing his fellow Spaniards, and, in particular, the Spanish "poor" who have been caught up in the machine of war and who "have no politics." Anselmo watches the "enemy" soldiers of the sawmill near the bridge sentry post and concludes "they are the same men as we are. I believe I could walk up to the mill and knock on the door and I would be welcome except that they have orders."[280] Anselmo "takes responsibility for the wrongs" of killing his fellow countrymen and knows in order to "cleanse" himself and get "strong in the broken places," he will need to rebuild trust with his fellow Spaniards by physically working to demonstrate his good will toward all Spaniards and the future of Spain.

This advice from his mentor is not lost on Robert Jordan, for when Robert reads the letters of the "enemy" soldier he kills, he realizes that he too must not "forget anything" and "not believe in the killing," for "if you believe in it the whole thing is wrong."[281] In reading the slain soldier's letter, Robert realizes that the boy was very religious and was engaged to be married. Robert wonders how many "enemies" he has "killed have been real fascists." "Not many," he thinks. Taking responsibility for killing this boy whom "he had probably seen run through the streets... at the Feria in Pamplona," Robert concludes that "you never kill anyone you want to kill in a war."[282] This boy has a family at home in Tafalla who loves him and has a fiancée who is "completely hysterical with concern for his safety."[283] Echoing Anselmo's suggestion that they all must cleanse themselves by serving a penance for the wrongful but necessary killing, Robert states, "I believe in the people and their right to govern themselves ... but... I mustn't believe in the killing. You must do it as a necessity but you must not believe in it...You have no right to forget anything. You have no right to shut your eyes to any of it nor any right to forget any of it nor to soften it nor to change it."[284] Robert learns to "not blame others for wrongs caused by himself" and to "get strong in the broken places." The killing of people he would otherwise greatly admire and befriend is necessary to help the Republicans fight "to govern themselves," but Robert knows that only through a penance, a life lived according to a self-imposed code that includes causing no unnecessary harm to others in the future, can he be "responsible to himself" and "cleanse" his self in the future.

10

AVOID SELF-PITY

Do not let the wrongs done to you and by you define you; "get strong in the broken places" psychologically, emotionally, and physically.

NOVEL AND SHORT STORIES: AVOID SELF-PITY

As a code principle, this is the one principle, even more than "find faith in love," that is most problematic when applying the heroic code to Ernest Hemingway's life. We understandably expect the man who created the heroic code principles in his characters to follow these principles in his own life. But this is precisely the tension in life. As Cormac McCarthy notes, "The world is quite ruthless in selecting between the dream and reality, even where we will not. Between the wish and the thing the world lies waiting."[285] We all have aspirations for ourselves that we fail to meet on a daily basis, if we are honest. We all have an idea of what we hope to be: in our families, in our friendships, in our professional lives, and this often is belied by the reality of ourselves in the world. "Between the wish and the thing," we live out our lives.

We know Hemingway created ideal loving relationships in his texts and, in his own life, at times, failed to achieve his own definition of love. But we struggle with the code principle "avoid self-pity" and its demands on us to "not let the wrongs done to you and by you define you and to 'get strong in the broken places' psychologically, emotionally, and physically," while knowing Hemingway took his own life on July 2, 1961, in the cold room of his home in Ketchum, Idaho. We struggle with Hemingway's overt criticism of suicide in *For Whom the Bell Tolls* as a selfish act that could only be committed by someone who is "awfully preoccupied with (one)self," when we know he placed a double barreled shotgun in his mouth and pulled the trigger with his big toe.[286]

But isn't this part of our fascination with the end of Hemingway's life in Ketchum? We want to know why he took his life. We want to know how a Nobel Prize winning author with love, money, and fame could take his own life. We want to know how he could allow himself to do it when a principle of his code, "avoid self-pity," denounces behavior that may lead up to it. We want answers, but I will warn readers that *definitive* answers do not exist. I hope to offer a context that will illuminate the tragic end of Hemingway's life but not definitive explanations, nor excuses, nor justifications. In addition, this chapter will explore whether Hemingway struggled to avoid self-pity precisely because he was unable to meet the aspirational goals of the other code principles.

The order of this chapter is reversed: moments of self-pity and avoiding self-pity in the texts will be developed first, and then how Hemingway struggled to avoid self-pity will follow second. Moments abound in Hemingway's texts in which characters are not able to avoid self-pity and who "let the wrongs done to them and by them define them." Recall that Hemingway was as interested in code breakers as he was with code followers. But there are also key characters who emerge as heroic because they are able "get strong in the broken places" psychologically, emotionally, and physically.

In order to define the code principle of avoiding self-pity, it is helpful to learn from the experiences of Hemingway's characters who fail to achieve it, who let the wrongs done to them and by them define them. In one of his most famous short stories "Soldier's Home" published in *In Our Time*, Hemingway develops the eponymous veteran Krebs who clearly suffers from post-traumatic stress disorder. Krebs's coping mechanism is avoiding painful conversations and relationships, and he devolves to an emotional numbness as an antidote to his despair. Krebs will not engage with the women he admires from his front porch for fear of the emotional consequences of having to open up to them about what he witnessed at war. In Krebs's mind "it was not worth it."[287] Moreover, Krebs tells his mother that he does not love her, does not love anyone, and does not love nor believe in God. After this emotionally charged conversation during which his mother sobs, Krebs, we are informed, "felt sick and then vaguely nauseated...but not of it touched him."[288] He believes he will leave for Kansas City and live out a life without meaningful relationships. He believes he will oscillate between an emotionally numb state and, it is implied, wallowing in self-pity. The horrors of war have left Krebs in a state of detachment from life and emotions, and the reader feels immense empathy for him. But nonetheless, Krebs is letting the wrongs done to him and by him define his existence. And both the reader and Hemingway take "Soldier's Home" as a cautionary tale.

Also in *In Our Time*, Hemingway writes "A Very Short Story" that is ripped right out of the pages of his life. Of course, the self-consciously ironic title is true to its name: the story is a page and a half long, but many do not know that the relationship described in the story is based on Hemingway's WWI relationship with British nurse Agnes Von Kurowsky. Hemingway fell in love with Agnes while he was convalescing in a hospital in Milan. Hemingway hoped to marry Agnes, but upon returning to the States, she broke it off with him in an "Ernie, dear boy" letter and informed Hemingway that she planned to marry on Italian officer. All of this happens to the unnamed soldier in "A Very Short Story." However, the story ends by stating that the nurse "never got an answer to the letter to Chicago about it. A short time after he contracted gonorrhea from a sales girl in a loop department store while riding in a taxicab in Lincoln Park."[289] This familiar, yet unnamed veteran wallows in self-pity, gives up on the idea of loving relationships with women, views women solely as objects of sexual gratification, and ends up with gonorrhea to add to his broken heart. He "lets the wrongs done to him define him" and does not get stronger emotionally or psychologically in the very places where he was hurt. He does not avoid self-pity. You recall that Hemingway commented on the shocking end of his relationship with Agnes by writing in a letter, "I loved her once and then she gypped me. And I don't blame her. But I set out to cauterize out her memory and I burnt it out with a course of booze and other women and now it's gone."[290] Of course, this is not a great coping mechanism in response to a broken heart: excessive drinking and sex do not lead to a healthy state of mind that can keep self-pity at bay.

Beyond the shortcomings of characters in the short stories, in *For Whom the Bell Tolls*, the untrustworthy Pablo emerges as the most uncoded character Hemingway created. Specifically, Pablo wallows in his own self-pity regarding both the war and the bleak future for the Spanish Republican resistance to military dictatorship. As we know Pablo was once a great leader in the resistance, but the barbaric killing of his own townspeople, including the priest made Pablo question his moral high ground. When Robert Jordan meets Pablo in the mountains, Pablo reports, "I am drunk on wine and I would be happy except for those people, those people I have killed all of them fill me with sorrow…I would restore them all to life"[291] Pablo recognizes that in the civil war, they are killing their own countrymen and men and women who, for reasons possibly outside of their control, have not sided with the Republican resistance. So Pablo "eddies in his own weakness," drinks too much, distrusts Robert Jordan's plan to blow the bridge, and sabotages the effort to blow the bridge. His statement that he would restore all of the men he has killed to life underscores his defeatist attitude. As Hemingway reminds us in *The Old Man and the Sea*, "a man can be destroyed but not defeated."[292] Well Pablo is defeated for he lets the wrongs done *by* him define him and does not get stronger emotionally or psychologically. He gives up on the war, proposes to hide out in the mountains until it is over, and, most certainly, does not avoid self-pity. Krebs and the foxhole faith soldier from *In Our Time* and Pablo from *For Whom the Bell Tolls* encourage us to avoid the "living death" of giving oneself over to self-pity.

Hemingway's characters become heroes in his novels and short stories, not by successfully slaying the dragon or defeating the Fascists or bringing a marlin to shore, but by showing readers that the "the ultimate response to suffering, loss and grief is…proud stoicism." Moreover, Hemingway heroes achieve an inner victory of self-acknowledged perseverance after setbacks: they may lose the game but they finish up well. Jeffery Meyers adds that Hemingway's heroes, beyond possessing the mutually enhancing principles of the code, are able "to develop physical and moral strength" in the very places where they have been broken down physically and morally.[293]

"Peasant wisdom," as Hemingway called it, is a stoic response to suffering. He allows Andres—a peasant guerilla fighter for the Spanish Republican cause—to define "peasant wisdom" as the wise understanding of what can be realistically achieved by those who live under great oppression and with little social mobility. Andres states, "I think we were born into a time of great difficulty. I think any other time was probably easier. One suffers little because all of us have been formed to resist suffering."[294] Andres knows that his difficult life before the war as a farmer and his difficult time now as a soldier outmatched by the enemy in numbers and equipment have made him stronger than those who were not formed in the crucible of adversity. The wisdom of the peasant is the knowledge of controlling what one can control, effecting positive change when and where positive change can be achieved, and adhering to an ideal principle in one's actions (for Andres it is to sustain a democratic republican form of government). Peasants know they were born "to resist suffering."

Also in *For Whom the Bell Tolls*, both Robert Jordan and Maria emerge as characters who avoid self-pity and do not let, in particular, the wrongs that have been *done to them* define them. You will recall that Maria was a prisoner of war after the Nationalists murdered both her parents in front of her. Three Nationalist guards tie Maria to a barber chair, keep her from screaming by tying her pigtails across her mouth, and later rape her. Hemingway allows Maria to tell the story to Robert Jordan: "I saw my face in the mirror of the barbershop…My own face I could hardly recognize because my grief had changed it but I looked at it and knew that it was me. But my grief was so great that I had no fear nor any feeling but my grief."[295] Maria knows it is her image in the mirror, that it is she who is being tortured, despite her face being radically transformed by "grief." But Maria later tells Robert Jordan of advice Pilar gave her shortly after she was rescued. Pilar told Maria, "Nothing is done to oneself that one does not accept…love…would take it all away"[296] Of course, Maria is following a code principle by valuing the advice of a mentor in

Pilar, but it the substance of the advice that encourages Maria to avoid self-pity. Fearful that she will never trust a man again, let alone be able to both emotionally and physically love a man, Pilar tells her that the wrong of the rape done to her will not define her if she does not "accept" it. Moreover, Pilar informs Maria that she must "love" in order "to take it all away"; in other words, Pilar is demanding that Maria "get strong in the broken places." Of course, this is the advice from Frederic Henry in *A Farewell to Arms*: "The world breaks everyone and afterwards many are strong in the broken places."[297] To avoid all male relationships, to view all men as untrustworthy, to shut oneself off from emotional vulnerability would be to wallow in self-pity. But Maria takes Pilar's advice and opens herself up emotionally to Robert Jordan and starts the process of self-healing by doing so.

In a remarkable juxtaposition, Hemingway develops how Robert Jordan was also a victim of tragic circumstances outside of his control. Jordan's father committed suicide, as Hemingway's father committed suicide—with an American Civil War revolver. Both Hemingway's father, Dr. Clarence Hemingway, and Robert Jordan's father inherited the Civil War revolver from their fathers. Eleven years after his own father's suicide, Hemingway decides to write about it in *For Whom the Bell Tolls*. In an introspective moment before blowing the bridge, Jordan wishes to summon the courage and advice of his grandfather who, like Hemingway's grandfather, fought in the Civil War. Jordan thinks:

> *Hell, if I didn't get advice I'd just like to talk to (my grandfather). It's a shame there is such a jump in time between ones like us...he realized that if there was any such thing as ever meeting, both he and his grandfather would be acutely embarrassed by the presence of his father. Anyone has a right to do it, he thought. But it is not a good thing to do...I do not approve of it. Lache was the word... you have to be awfully preoccupied with yourself to do a thing like that.*[298]

Writing this, possibly, in 1939 in the cold fall mornings in Ketchum, Idaho, Hemingway could not have imagined that he would take his own life in Ketchum twenty-two years later. Through the ruminations of Robert Jordan, Hemingway informs us that suicide is universally wrong and that to commit suicide one would have to be completely unaware of the devastating wake that would be left afterwards. To wallow in self-pity is to allow the wrongs done to you and by you define you. To resolve to take your own life due to your self-loathing for the wrongs done to you and by you is the epitome of letting self-pity define you. Robert Jordan continues on in the same moment to lament that "so much fear...made a *cobarde* out of (my father)...I'll never forget how sick it made me the first time I knew he was a *cobarde*. He was just a coward and that was the worst luck any man could have."[299] Cowardice is to let fear define you, prevent you from acting to improve a situation. "Lache" is the Spanish word that means a failure to do something in the proper time; here, both Jordan's father and Hemingway's father failed to act to overcome their self-pity in the proper time, before it was too late. In the conclusion to his reflections, the omniscient narrator informs us that Robert Jordan "forgave his father...but was ashamed of him."[300]

As Maria hopes not to be defined by the torture and the rape, Jordan hopes he will not be defined by his father's suicide. He tells Maria that he took his grandfather's gun—the revolver his father committed suicide with—and rode a horse to a high mountain lake outside of Red Lodge, Montana, and dropped the revolver in the lake. But in a striking juxtaposition to the moment in which Maria sees herself in the mirror being raped, Jordan sees his face reflected in the cold, clean water of the high mountain lake. Hemingway writes, "He climbed out on a rock and leaned over and saw his face in the still water, and saw himself holding the gun, and then dropped it, holding it by the muzzle, and saw it go down making bubbles until it was...out of sight."[301] As Maria sees that it is indeed her in the mirror image being tortured by the enemy, Jordan also sees that the revolver that ended his father's life is indeed a part of his identity. But neither Robert Jordan nor Maria let the torture nor the suicide—wrongs done to them and outside of their control—define them. Maria drops her eyes from the mirrored image and resolves to love again and to be healed by love, and Robert Jordan drops the gun into the mirrored lake and resolves to never let cowardice, fear, and self-pity prevent him from loving the world, himself, and others.

At the end of the novel, Robert Jordan suffers in pain from his crushed leg and awaits the fast approach of the enemy who will surely spray him with bullets. Jordan reflects, "I do not want to do that business my father did…there is something you can do yet…one thing done well can make—" with the implied "all the difference."[302] Robert Jordan does not wallow in self-pity, does not decide to take his own life, "holds onto himself," and as Lt. Berrendo approaches him, Jordan has him in the crosshairs of his machine gun, as "his heart beat against the pine needle floor of the forest."[303]

SUN VALLEY STORIES: AVOID SELF PITY

Developing characters who fail to avoid self-pity and, thereby, lose the reader's respect was as central to Hemingway's works as developing characters who avoid self-pity and gain the reader's admiration. When we apply this aspirational goal of avoiding self-pity to the final chapters of Hemingway's life in Ketchum, Idaho, we see that there were numerous interwoven, contributing factors that led to his inability to "get strong in the broken" emotional, psychological, and physical places. Not the least of which was his inability, at the end of his life, to adhere to the other self-imposed code principles.

There are many documented contributing factors that led Hemingway to end his life. Many scholars have noted the deleterious effects of Hemingway's:

- post-traumatic stress disorder
- bipolar depression
- electroshock therapy and the loss of memory
- alcoholism

- four successive concussions later in life
- hypochondria
- paranoia
- despair over the US invasion of Cuba and potential loss of his Cuban home, the Finca Vigia, and his manuscripts
- a toxic cocktail of palliative medications
- physical ailments

It is important to note the overwhelming influence of the collective whole of these factors and their exacerbating effects on each other.

But it is even more important to add and underscore Hemingway's inability to live by the code principles to this list. Hemingway's inability to adhere to the other principles of the heroic code provides the thread through which we can navigate our way through this dark, last chapter of Ernest Hemingway's life.

At the end of his life, Hemingway could not follow the following code principles:
- Complete Tasks Well
- Find Faith in Love
- Speak through Actions
- Embrace the Present
- Self-Assess

In June of 1961, Hemingway told friend A. E. Hotchner, "What does a man care about? Staying healthy. Working good. Eating and drinking with friends. Enjoying himself in bed. I haven't any of those."[304] While Hemingway could still hunt well and did so up until his last days in Ketchum, it was his inability to remember well, to write well, to love well, and to "embrace the present" that bothered him.

HEMINGWAY SHOOTING CLAY PIGEONS NEAR HIS WARM SPRINGS HOUSE. *The Community Library, Ketchum, Idaho.*

HEMINGWAY WITH A HALF SMILE. *The Community Library, Ketchum, Idaho.*

In the spring of 1961, Hemingway once turned to his fourth wife, Mary Welsh Hemingway, and said, "I hope things do not look as bad to you as they do to me."[305] Ironically, the demanding code principles of the most famous and celebrated Hemingway characters provided a context for the self-deprecation that led Ernest Hemingway to succumb to paralyzing self-pity. In my view, he did not want to stick around and witness the prolonged deleterious effects of self-pity on his character and on the well-being of others.

However, it is interesting to remember that Hemingway's best times were in the Sun Valley area as well. You will recall that he achieved the familial love with the band of hunting companions in the Wood River Valley, a band he called "the family." He did not share the same affection for his Oak Park immediate family. And it is the group of Idahoan locals that surrounds Hemingway today at his grave in the Ketchum Cemetery.

HEMINGWAY'S GRAVE IN THE KETCHUM CEMETERY, *Wikicommon*.

In a candid conversation about shotgunning techniques with Sun Valley hunting guide and photographer Lloyd Arnold, Hemingway said that Lloyd was lucky to have such good shotgunning instruction from his father. Hemingway lamented his father's poor shotgunning instruction, but more importantly, he lamented his father's suicide. Bill Peschel recalls the untimely death of Ernest Hemingway's father; he writes:

> *In 1928, Dr. Clarence Hemingway spent the morning at his office, then entered his home in Oak Park, Illinois, for lunch. He burned personal papers in the basement furnace. Then he walked up the stairs to his second-floor bedroom and in the semi-darkness cast by the drawn shades, sat on the marital bed. In the next room, his 13-year-old son, Leicester, was laying in bed with a cold when he heard the gunshot. He knocked at the bedroom door and called,*

"Daddy!" Inside, in the semi-darkness, his father lay on the bed, breathing hoarsely. When Leicester put his hand behind his father's head, he felt the warm blood on his palm. Seriously ill with diabetes and heart disease, suffering losses from bad investments in Florida real estate and depressed, he had shot himself behind his right ear with his father's .32 Smith and Wesson revolver.[306]

The Hemingway family poses for a portrait in Oak Park, Illinois. Left to right: Clarence Edwards Hemingway, Carol Hemingway, Grace Hall Hemingway, Ernest Hemingway, Leicester Hemingway, Ursula Hemingway, Madelaine "Sunny" Hemingway, and Marcelline Hemingway. *Ernest Hemingway Collection. John F. Kennedy Presidential Library and Museum, Boston.*

Hemingway was writing *A Farewell to Arms* in Key West when his father took his own life. Hemingway was en route to New York City to assist Jack in getting settled at boarding school—the Storm King School—when Hemingway received the telegram on December 6, 1928: "Try to locate Ernest Hemingway in New York. Advise him of the death of his father today. Ask him to communicate with home immediately."[307] There is no easy way to deliver this news, but the telegram's necessarily terse, emotionless tone has to be one of the worst ways to deliver this news. Hemingway left Jack and went to Oak Park to attend to the funeral and family affairs. Hemingway told Pauline Pfeiffer's mother, Mary, that he had written his dad and told him "'not to worry about money because he could always borrow from Scribner's (publishing)…The reassuring letter reached the house 20 minutes after Ed had shot himself." As Peschel notes above, Hemingway's father was suffering physically and had recently experienced major financial losses in real estate investments. Hemingway was haunted by the realization that his letter to his father arrived too late to assuage him. "I will probably go the same way," was Hemingway's reaction to his father's suicide.[308]

But in a conversation at the Sun Valley Lodge, Hemingway told Lloyd Arnold that he most resented his father being dominated "by…mother; she had to rule everything, have it all her own way, and she was a bitch!" Hemingway went on to say that he envied Lloyd being surrounded by an older brother. Hemingway said, "And you were lucky in competition with your older brother, and it would have been awfully good for me too, if I'd had one to kick the hell out of me now and then and keep me in line…mine was a surrounding of sisters and a brother just a kid when I was grown up and on my own."[309] There is no self-pity here, just an awareness that the legacy his father left was less-than-stellar shotgunning instruction, the need to assert oneself in a marital relationship, and paralyzing self-pity that led to suicide. There is also an awareness that his family connections left a lot to be desired. In Ketchum, however, Hemingway felt a kinship with the men and women who shared his passion for hunting adventures and who shared his healthy sense of humor and penchant for sarcasm. He felt a part of a family here, and the fact that he never wrote about Sun Valley and the people here attests to his love for the place and the people and his desire to protect both it and them.

Beyond being haunted by the memory of his father's suicide and its negative effect on his mental state, Hemingway suffered physical ailments as well. In January of 1954, Hemingway and Mary were on an African hunting safari when they decided to take a sightseeing plane ride to Murchison Falls—the source of the Nile River—and the plane avoided some birds, clipped a telegraph wire, and crashed. Hemingway suffered a dislocated shoulder and a concussion. Bizarrely, a replacement plane came to pick them up but burst into flames on takeoff, and "Hemingway had to butt his way out of a burning plane with his head and shoulder." Hemingway recalled that "apart from the full scale concussion...injuries included a temporary loss of vision in left eye, loss of hearing in left ear, crushed vertebra, sprained right arm, sprained left leg, first degree burns on face and arms, and head."[310] We now know that multiple concussions in close proximity can lead to loss of cognitive function. With two violent plane crashes and blow to the head within a week, it is almost certain that Hemingway suffered two concussions. Reports that "both blood and cephalian liquid" flowed from Hemingway's skull underscore the severity of the second concussion.[311]

The late 1950s for Ernest and Mary Hemingway were filled with unfinished writing projects and vain attempts at returning to Cuba, Spain, and Italy to rekindle an enthusiasm for life that was once so palpable and that was now barely traceable. The years of 1960 and 1961 were difficult ones for Ernest and Mary and for the close friends in the family of Ketchum locals to witness. As Nick Adams hoped to recover his innocent perspective of life before WWI in *In Our Time* by returning to the rivers and woods of his youth after the war, Hemingway hoped to return to his home on the Big Wood River and rekindle a spark of the enthusiasm for life, love, and writing that he had in summers and falls in the 1940s in the Wood River Valley. But unlike Nick, who in "Big Two-Hearted River" finds solace in his ability to navigate the woods of the Upper Peninsula of Michigan without a map, find where the fishing is good, and fish well, Hemingway finds that he cannot write well nor love well nor love being with his family of friends. As lifelong friend Lloyd Arnold tragically put it, "You feel like crawling under anything at hand when trying to make (Hemingway) talk, get nowhere, no matter what you say—thinking: My God, is this Papa, like a deaf man who sees the fun going on before him, and joins in with a grin like on a mask?" This was written on April 22, 1960, and Lloyd sadly concluded to his wife Tillie, "Truth is, Papa was gone. No fight left."[312]

HEMINGWAY AND LLOYD ARNOLD. *The Community Library, Ketchum, Idaho.*

In the middle of July 1960, Hemingway stated that he "felt dead in the head and feared a complete physical and nervous breakdown."[313] Many know about the electroshock treatments Hemingway received at the Mayo Clinic in order to calm his nerves, but few know about how "the medications that Hemingway took also ruined his mental and physical health. These included Reserpine, Wychol, Ritalin, Serpasil, Equanil, and Seconal—the side effects and interactive effects of which were naturally not fully understood at the time. Accidents, illness, hypochondria, depression, alcoholism, and finally paranoia settled around Hemingway like a fog that would not lift."[314]

In addition to the toxic cocktail of medications, Hemingway's irrational paranoia and hypochondria escalated in Ketchum during the winter of 1961—the year of his death. "On March 6th 1961, Hemingway complained of phone calls being monitored by the FBI,…worried about Social Security Taxes for the (Ketchum) maid, and demanded to see Mary's checkbook."[315] Mary informed Hemingway that he was not being watched, but no one could convince him that he wasn't being tracked by the federal government. Mary also recalled his irrational paranoia over a fallen cottonwood tree across the Big Wood River that flows in front of his fourteen-acre riverfront property in Ketchum. She recalls a conversation with her husband over the tree. Hemingway remarked, "Anybody could get over here from there." Mary responded, "They could just come up the road…but we are surrounded by friends and good will."[316] Indeed, the Ketchum friends were "the family"—the people with whom for many years he felt most comfortable being himself. Hemingway's paranoia that people were out to ruin him was beyond his control.

In addition, Hemingway's solace was always being able to work well, to write well, to stand at the typewriter and will the inspiration to come. But this was lost too. Mary recalls that Hemingway's "pen hovered with nervous uncertainty in his attempt to write a note to the Kennedy family. It took a week for Hemingway to write four sentences."[317] In Boris Vejdovsky's *Hemingway: A Life in Pictures*, he reports that Hemingway was working on what came to be titled *A Moveable Feast* in both Cuba and Ketchum, but Hemingway lamented, "I can't finish (*A Moveable Feast*). Not this fall or next spring or ten years from now. I can't."[318] And he didn't. But it was published posthumously as a finished text.

With haunting prescience, Hemingway's narrator in the short story "The Snows of Kilimanjaro," reflects, "Each day of not writing, of comfort, of being what he despised, dulled his ability and softened his will to work."[319] The protagonist of this story, Harry, had stopped being disciplined about writing and then lost the will and ability to write. But unlike Harry, Hemingway had his ability to write taken away. With unfinished drafts of nonfiction and fiction: *Islands in the Stream*, *The Garden of Eden*, *A Moveable Feast*, and "the African book," to be posthumously titled *True at First Light*, and with his pen hovering over a simple celebratory letter to the Kennedy family, Hemingway was most troubled by his inability to write— a task that always renewed and strengthened his faith in himself. In the winter of 1961, Hemingway remarked, "Writing is the only thing that makes me feel I am not wasting my time sticking around."[320]

Both of Hemingway's doctors in Sun Valley, Dr. John Moritz and Dr. George Saviers, concur that Hemingway expressed existential despair in being unable to complete tasks well, in being unable to write well, in the end. In a 1990 interview, Dr. George Saviers recalled that Hemingway confessed to him that he was "trying to piece together the Paris book, but it was tough." Saviers recalls that Hemingway's "depressive moods were getting more serious" and frequent and concluded that the Mayo Clinic was trying to address a psychiatric problem "40 years too late."[321] In an inscription in a gifted copy of *A Farewell to Arms*, Saviers recalled that Hemingway wrote, "This is as good as I can get it." *A Farewell to Arms* was written when Hemingway was twenty-nine years old, so the sixty-year-old Hemingway was longing for the confident writing powers of his youth.

Dr. John Moritz remarked, "My impressions are so different than the biographical sketches...Hemingway was a gentle, sensitive, very caring man." But in the early 1960s, Moritz does recall Hemingway telling him "he was disappointed that he could not produce...his expression was 'the juices don't flow.'"[322] Without a doubt, the frustration with being unable to get the creative juices to flow, with being unable to finish writing projects, with being unable to write as he once did, dominated his despair.

HEMINGWAY DURING HIS FINAL YEARS IN KETCHUM, IDAHO. *The Community Library, Ketchum, Idaho.*

On top of the toxic cocktail of medications, escalating paranoia, and inability to write well, Hemingway received ten electroshock treatments by the winter of 1961. Electroshock therapy to the brain, while proven to ameliorate severe bipolar depression, has the most devastating side effect for a writer: the loss of long-term memory. Hemingway remarked to friend A. E. Hotchner, "If I can't exist on my own terms, then existence is impossible…that is how I lived, and that is how I must live—or not live."[323] Hemingway could still hunt well, but it was his inability to remember well, imagine well, and write well that ruined his will to live. And the electroshock treatments unintentionally ensured that he would not remember well, imagine well, and write well again.

Add to all of this the realization that Hemingway knew his beloved home in Cuba—the Finca Vigia—had been appropriated, as was all private land in Cuba, by the Cuban Revolutionary Armed forces in January of 1961. Moreover, by April 17, 1961, Hemingway learned of the botched US airstrike on Fidel Castro's airfields. More than ever, Hemingway was convinced that he would not return to his home in Cuba—a place that produced some of his best writing. And he was concerned that he would not be able to retrieve his manuscripts from Cuba as well.

On his way into Atkinsons' food market in Ketchum on April 20, 1961, three days after John F. Kennedy's Bay of Pigs announcement, Hemingway looked rushed and harried. He bumped into Tillie Arnold, longtime friend and wife of Sun Valley photographer Lloyd Arnold, and candidly told her, "There is no other way out for me…I am not going back to Rochester where they can lock me up."[324] Of course, Hemingway is referring to the Mayo Clinic in Rochester, Minnesota, where he endured electroshock therapy. This chance encounter preceded Hemingway's first suicide attempt by one day.

First Suicide Attempt: April 21, 1961

Four days after learning of the US invasion of Cuba and the potential loss of his beloved Cuban home, Hemingway took his shotgun to the "front vestibule of the house and (loaded) two shells." Mary calmed him down and got him to sit on the couch in the living room of the Warm Springs home. He was still holding his shotgun as he sat on the couch. She reminded Hemingway of all the people who loved him and needed his guidance. Mary told Hemingway, "I was thinking we might go to Mexico...Gregorio might get the *Pilar* over there...I read somewhere there's marvelous fishing off the Yucatan Peninsula...Honey, you wouldn't do anything to harm me as well as you...many people love you and need your strength, wisdom and counsel."[325] Mary hoped to give Hemingway something to look forward to—a fishing adventure on his beloved fishing boat *Pilar*—and remind Hemingway of his beloved friends who both admired and needed him. It worked. "Dr. George Saviers and Dr. Moritz arrived and took Hemingway to the Sun Valley hospital where they sedated him."[326] However, Mary candidly wrote of this moment, "Years later I wondered if we were not more cruel than kind in preventing his suicide."[327]

Second Suicide Attempt: April 24, 1961

All around him agreed that Hemingway must return to the Mayo Clinic for more psychiatric examinations and, yes, more electroshock therapy. Hemingway was nominally in agreement. As Hemingway loaded the car in his driveway of the Ketchum home, he let Don Anderson and nurse Joanie Higgins know that he forgot something inside. Don Anderson, a longtime Ketchum hunting companion, knew something could be amiss, and shortly thereafter both he and Joanie followed Hemingway into the home. Mary was upstairs in the bedroom. Hemingway took off to the gun rack in the living room, and "Don beckoned Joan to follow him; at the corner of the gun rack in the living room, from behind him, Don pinned Papa's arms as Papa closed the breech on the double barreled shotgun and managed to get a thumb on the opening lever. Joan pulled out the shells and the brief storm subsided...Papa went quietly to the hospital again...except with a single question 'Where are they taking me this time?'"[328] The helplessness and lack of autonomy are evident in Hemingway's question. He certainly does not want to return to the electroshock therapy of the Mayo Clinic and have his short- and long-term memory further ruined. He wants to complete tasks well, speak through actions, and embrace the present, but he cannot. His mind will not let him. As Lloyd Arnold reflected, "Papa's dilemma was many sided but I do know that paramount was a deep humiliation...he did not want to kill himself...he did care what would be thought about it, as he cared all his life what (people thought of him)...he was certain he wasn't his own man any more, and he was not about to face the living death."[329] The "living death" of constantly being reminded of his inability to do the very things that defined him was a horrifying prospect.

Third Suicide Attempt: April 25, 1961

The next day Hemingway and Don Anderson successfully boarded the plane in Hailey for the flight to the Mayo Clinic in Rochester, Minnesota. Hemingway reluctantly agreed, again, to return to the Mayo Clinic. In a candid reflection on the negative effects of electroshock therapy, Hemingway told A. E. Hotchner, "What these shock doctors don't know about writers is...what is the sense in ruining my head in erasing my memory, which is my capital, and putting me out of business."[330] En route to more electroshock therapy, Hemingway exits the plane when it touches down for refueling. As Anderson and Hemingway exit the plane, Hemingway "saw another plane taxiing down the ramp, and (Hemingway) walked straight toward the whirling propellers. Hemingway and Don were 50 ft away when the pilot cut the propellers and Hemingway lost interest."[331]

Fourth and Final Suicide Attempt: July 2, 1961

After months of therapy at the Mayo Clinic, Hemingway was able to persuade the doctors to allow him to return to his home in Sun Valley where he would be much more comfortable. He returned, but his mental state deteriorated. On July 1, 1961, he went to dinner with Mary at the

Christiania Restaurant on Sun Valley road in Ketchum. Two men at the bar were dressed in formal suits, and Hemingway was convinced they were FBI agents spying on him. They were real estate agents from Twin Falls. After dinner, Mary and Hemingway returned to their Ketchum home and prepared for bed. They slept in different bedrooms because Hemingway liked to get up early and work, and he did not want to disturb Mary. As they prepared for bed, Hemingway sang the Italian folk song, "Tutti mi chiamono bionda. Ma bionda io non sono," and then together they sang "Porto capelli neri."

"Good night, my kitten," were Hemingway's last words.

As Mary recalls it in her autobiography *How It Was*, "The next morning the sounds of a couple of drawers banging shut awakened me...I saw a crumpled heap of bathrobe and blood, the shotgun lying in the disintegrated flesh, in the front vestibule of the sitting room."[332]

Mary called Chuck Atkinson of Atkinsons' Markets in the Wood River Valley to come over, and he helped clean up, took the gun, and promised Mary that no one would ever see the gun again. Mary spent the night above Atkinsons' market. Chuck Atkinson broke the gun into pieces and buried it in an undisclosed location in the Wood River Valley. Chuck remained true to his word to Mary: no one would ever see the gun again.

While there was controversy over Mary reporting that Ernest was fatally wounded while cleaning his gun (she amended the report to the press that it was indeed a suicide), a larger controversy brewed over how Hemingway still had access to his guns. With three known suicide attempts, common sense dictates that Hemingway should have been kept away from his guns. In a candid explanation in her autobiography, Mary Hemingway writes, "Before leaving Ketchum (for the Mayo Clinic), I locked all the guns in a storeroom in the basement, leaving the keys among those on the kitchen window sill. I thought of hiding the keys and decided no one had the right to deny a man his access to his possessions, and I also assumed that Ernest would not remember the storeroom."[333] This honest account sparked great criticism from both within the Hemingway family and from friends and admirers. Mary's admission that she felt it was not her place to "deny a man access to his possessions" needs to be heard in the context of both the expectation of male and female roles in marital relationships in the late 1950s and early 1960s and Mary's other candid and reflective comment, "Years later I wondered if we were not more cruel than kind in preventing his suicide." Nonetheless, on July 2, 1961, the world lost a literary icon who shaped and still shapes contemporary prose styles, who gave us aspirational code principles and illustrative moments to learn about them, and who lived a life of adventure beyond one's wildest imagination.

The loss of Ernest Hemingway was strongly felt throughout the nation, but "the family" of friends in Ketchum felt the loss acutely, as if they had lost a beloved brother. On July 6, 1961, the pallbearers of Hemingway's coffin were Sun Valley doctor George Saviers, Sun Valley Resort hunting guides Lloyd Arnold and Bud Purdy, food market owner Chuck Atkinson, local friend and hunting companion Don Anderson, and Forrest McMullen, George Brown, and Toby Bruce. Sun Valley Resort hunting guide Bud Purdy confessed, "The ending of his life was kind of traumatic to me. He was such a great guy…I guess if he couldn't write, it got so life wasn't worth living for him."[334]

Even in death, Hemingway still teaches us about his aspirations and his shortcomings. Raised a Congregationalist in Oak Park, Illinois, Hemingway was a server during church ceremonies. As we know, the atrocities he witnessed in WWI, the Greco-Turkish War, the Spanish Civil War, and WWII called his religious faith into question, but his second wife, Pauline Pfeiffer, demanded that Hemingway join the Catholic Church before their marriage. He obliged. One thinks of the many references to the struggle for religious faith and visits to cathedrals by the characters in the novels. In *A Farewell to Arms*, Frederic Henry and Catherine Barkley debate a traditional marriage in a church, but Catherine balks and informs Frederic that "(love) is her religion."[335] Frederic is unsure this will suffice in the eyes of God. Also, Frederic regrettably witnesses the Italian soldiers mock the priest with rude gestures and false accusations about the priest breaking his celibacy vow at the whorehouse. Frederic admires the priest and the priest's hometown of Abruzzi where "it is not a dirty joke…to love God…and serve Him."[336] In *The Sun Also Rises*, Jake Barnes visits a cathedral and prays selfishly for money and good bullfights but dips his hand in the holy water and crosses himself as he leaves. Jake wants to have the "religious feeling," but the prayer and the formality of the church fall short. Hemingway respected those with deep, unwavering religious faith and desired this feeling of respect for God and the world. However, strict religious faith was a struggle for him, but he did find faith in the aspirational code principles of his heroic characters.

In his death by suicide, there was a question over whether he could have funeral services in the Sun Valley Catholic Church "Our Lady of the Snows." Of course, it is considered a mortal sin in the Catholic Church to take one's own life, so a decision had to be made about the funeral service. It was decided that a service would be held and presided over by the priest of "Our Lady of the Snows," but the service was to be held at the Ketchum cemetery and not in the Catholic Church. Even in being laid to rest, we experience the tension between Hemingway's aspirations for a religious faith and the reality of his struggles with it.

HEMINGWAY FUNERAL IN KETCHUM CEMETERY. *The Community Library, Ketchum, Idaho.*

Reflection

So what should we make of this tragic end to a remarkably inspiring life? What should we make of my argument that the principles of the Hemingway heroic code contributed to his failing desire to live when he could not achieve them? Jeffery Meyers aptly argues, "His code—formulated in youth, based on toughness and stoicism—was not suited to old age and failed him at the end."[337] In my view, Hemingway's tragic end underscores the gulf between our ideals and the realities of our lives. It underscores that *we* are our most devastating critics. It underscores the need to return to and follow his code principle "self-assess": to not overvalue meritless praise nor meritless condemnation, especially when the condemnation stems, as it often does, from us. Hemingway's tragic end does not, as some might argue, reveal the dangers of having such high self-imposed aspirational goals for ourselves. Rather, his tragic end underscores the need to have them with one additional principle: accept that life is lived between the "wish and the thing," between the dream and the reality.

Appendix

ERNEST HEMINGWAY SITES IN THE SUN VALLEY AREA:

1. Room 206 of the Sun Valley Lodge:

Built in 1936 by Union Pacific Chairman Averell Harriman, the Lodge allowed Sun Valley to become the first destination ski resort in the United States. In 1939, Ernest Hemingway was invited to stay in room 206 with the balcony overlooking the ice skating rink. He had free room and board in exchange for use of his image on Sun Valley advertisements for summer and fall recreation in the area. From the balcony of the "Glamour House," as Hemingway called it, he shot two geese after noticing one was wounded.

To view the balcony of Room 206, stand at the ice rink and face the lodge. It is the second story balcony on your left.

Location: 1 Sun Valley Rd, Sun Valley, ID

2. Hemingway Trail Creek Memorial

On Sun Valley / Trail Creek Road just up from the Sun Valley Lodge, the Hemingway Trail Creek Memorial consists of his bust overlooking Trail Creek and the surrounding sagebrush hills. His bust faces nearly the entire length of the trout stream. It was dedicated on July 21, 1966 on what would have been Hemingway's 67th birthday. The inscription on the plaque stems from the eulogy Hemingway wrote for Gene Van Guilder who was killed in a tragic hunting accident in the first months of Hemingway's first visit to Sun Valley in 1939. But it could easily apply to Hemingway himself:

> Best of all he loved the fall
> The leaves yellow on the cottonwoods
> Leaves floating on the trout streams
> And above the hills
> The high windless blue sky
> Now he will be apart of them forever.
> **Location:** just north of Sun Valley Golf Club (200 Trail Creek Rd)

3. Ernest Hemingway's grave at the Ketchum Cemetery

A visit to Sun Valley is not complete without spending time at Ernest Hemingway's grave in the Ketchum Cemetery. Buried next to his fourth wife Mary, Hemingway is also near two of his three sons Jack and Gregory. Beyond the family members, Hemingway's flat gravestone is flanked by many members of "the family" of hunters: Gene Van Guilder, Lloyd Arnold, Taylor Williams, Dr. George Saviers, and Chuck Atkinson, among others. Hemingway found "kindred spirits" in the Sun Valley hunting guides and friends. Now he is surrounded by them forever.

Location: 1026 North Main Street, Ketchum, ID

4. Ernest Hemingway Silver Creek Monument

> **THE HEMINGWAY LEGACY**
>
> ONE GENERATION PASSES AWAY, AND ANOTHER GENERATION COMES; BUT THE EARTH ABIDES FOREVER. THE SUN ALSO RISES, AND THE SUN GOES DOWN, AND HASTENS TO ITS PLACE WHERE IT AROSE.

The Hemingway Silver Creek Monument with the epigraph to *The Sun Also Rises* engraved on it is located on a trail by Silver Creek's Kilpatrick bridge. Before you walk up the trail to the memorial, walk out to the bridge and see the trout holding under the bridge. Think of Nick Adams and his admiration for the trout holding below the bridge in "Big Two Hearted River." Ernest Hemingway had many memorable days hunting ducks on Silver Creek. His first son Jack Hemingway was instrumental in The Nature Conservancy's acquisition of this area of Silver Creek. It is now a catch and release fly fishing only area with designated spots for waterfowl hunting as well. Recall that Ernest Hemingway turned to his third wife Martha Gellhorn and said, "Must be a thousand…big ducks, mallards, everyone one…Tuck it between your ears, Marty."

Location: 165 Kilpatrick Bridge Rd, Bellevue, ID

5. Michel's Christiania Restaurant

Frequented by Ernest and his fourth wife Mary, the Christiania Restaurant was one of Hemingway's favorite places for a drink and a meal after hunting. He could also gamble here as well as at the Casino Club and the Alpine (now Whiskey Jacques) on Main Street. Hemingway ate his last meal at the Christiania on July 1, 1961.

Location: 303 Walnut Ave, Ketchum, ID

6. Hemingway Boulders Wilderness Area

From his bedroom in the Warm Spring House, Hemingway looked out at the often snow-capped Boulder Mountains. While the house is not open to the public, it can be viewed from the Northwood Subdivision just north of Ketchum. Look for the home across the Big Wood River that resembles the Sun Valley Lodge.

When Hemingway looked out at the headwaters of the Salmon River and the Sawtooth Mountains, he remarked, "You'd have to come from a test tube and think like a machine to not engrave all of this in your head so that you never lose it." Well, Hemingway would be pleased to know that the Sawtooths became a wilderness area in 1972 and the Boulder Mountains became the Hemingway Boulders Wilderness Area in 2015. Now both areas that he loved will never be altered by man.

Location: 5 Northfork Canyon Rd, Ketchum, ID

Please respect private property while exploring the sites listed here.

Endnotes

1. Lloyd Arnold, *Hemingway: High on the Wild* (Caldwell, ID: Caxton Printers, 1968), 19.
2. Greg Foley, "Ernest Hemingway's Autumns in Idaho" *Sun Valley Guide*, accessed July 12, 2018, http://www.svguide.com/svg_hem.htm.
3. Ernest Hemingway, *Death in the Afternoon* (New York: Scribner's, 1932), 98.
4. Mary Dearborn, *Ernest Hemingway* (New York: Knopf, 2017), prologue.
5. Dearborn, *Ernest Hemingway*, prologue.
6. David Brooks, *The Road to Character* (New York: Random House, 2015), 494.
7. Brooks, *The Road to Character*, 520–1.
8. Ernest Hemingway, *The Complete Short Stories*, (New York: Scribner's, 1987), 111.
9. Robert Penn Warren, "Hemingway," *The Kenyon Review* 9, no. 1 (Winter 1947), 2.
10. Warren, "Hemingway," 11.
11. Warren, "Hemingway," 11.
12. Ernest Hemingway, *A Farewell to Arms* (New York: Scribner's, 1929), 122.
13. Warren, "Hemingway," 3.
14. Hemingway, *The Complete Short Stories*, 335.
15. Hemingway, *The Complete Short Stories*, 291.
16. Warren, "Hemingway," 6.
17. Warren, "Hemingway," 7.
18. Hemingway, *A Farewell to Arms*, 57.
19. Ernest Hemingway, *For Whom the Bell Tolls* (New York: Scribner's, 1929), 471.
20. Tillie Arnold, *Hemingway in Idaho* (Boston: Beacon Books, 1999), 47.
21. Arnold, *Hemingway in Idaho*, 20.
22. Jeffrey Meyers, *Hemingway* (Boston: Da Capo Press, 1999), 67.
23. Dorice Taylor, *Sun Valley Stories* (Sun Valley: Ex Libris Publishers, 1980), 137.

24 Taylor, *Sun Valley Stories*, 138.
25 Taylor, *Sun Valley Stories*, *138.*
26 Taylor, *Sun Valley Stories*, *136.*
27 Taylor, *Sun Valley Stories*, *136.*
28 Taylor, *Sun Valley Stories*, *139.*
29 Taylor, *Sun Valley Stories*, *139.*
30 Taylor, *Sun Valley Stories*, *139.*
31 Lloyd Arnold, *Hemingway: High on the Wild* (Caldwell, ID: Caxton Printers, 1968), 10.
32 L. Arnold, *Hemingway*, 26.
33 L. Arnold, *Hemingway*, 28.
34 Marilyn Bauer, "Papa's Legacy: An Interview with Jack Hemingway," *Sun Valley Guide*, accessed July 12, 2018, http://www.svguide.hemingway.htm .
35 Hemingway, *The Complete Short Stories*, 175.
36 Hemingway, *The Complete Short Stories*, 111.
37 Hemingway, *The Complete Short Stories*, 14.
38 Ernest Hemingway, *The Old Man and the Sea* (New York: Scribner's, 1952), 8.
39 Meyers, *Hemingway*, 486.
40 Ernest Hemingway, *The Sun Also Rises* (New York: Scribner's, 1926), 171.
41 Hemingway, *The Complete Short Stories* , 142.
42 Meyers, *Hemingway*, 118.
43 Hemingway, *The Sun Also Rises* , 223.
44 T. Arnold, *Hemingway in Idaho*, 18.
45 T. Arnold, *Hemingway in Idaho*, 18.
46 Warren, "Hemingway," 23.
47 Hemingway, *For Whom the Bell Tolls* , 33.
48 Hemingway, *For Whom the Bell Tolls*, 355.
49 Hemingway, *For Whom the Bell Tolls*, 436–8.
50 Hemingway, *For Whom the Bell Tolls*, 236.
51 Hemingway, *For Whom the Bell Tolls*, 470.
52 Meyers, *Hemingway*, 10.
53 Meyers, *Hemingway*, 12.
54 L. Arnold, *Hemingway*, foreword.
55 L. Arnold, *Hemingway*, foreword.

56 T. Arnold, *Hemingway in Idaho*, 43.
57 T. Arnold, *Hemingway in Idaho*, 43.
58 Ernest Hemingway, *A Farewell to Arms* (New York: Scribner's, 1929), ix.
59 Hemingway, *A Farewell to Arms*, xii.
60 T. Arnold, *Hemingway in Idaho*, 135.
61 "Remembering Hemingway." *YouTube*, uploaded, 26 Sept. 2015, accessed June 20, 2019, https://www.youtube.com/watch?v=d2fzox5JLGc.
62 "Remembering Hemingway."
63 "Remembering Hemingway."
64 Hemingway, *The Sun Also Rises* , 136.
65 Hemingway, *For Whom the Bell Tolls*, 404.
66 Hemingway, *For Whom the Bell Tolls*, 405.
67 Hemingway, *For Whom the Bell Tolls*, 410.
68 Meyers, *Hemingway*, 22.
69 Hemingway, *For Whom the Bell Tolls*, 235.
70 Hemingway, *For Whom the Bell Tolls*, 192.
71 Hemingway, *For Whom the Bell Tolls*, 196.
72 Ernest Hemingway, *Green Hills of Africa* (New York: Scribner's, 1935), 6.
73 L. Arnold, *Hemingway*, 19.
74 "Remembering Hemingway."
75 Beegel qtd. in Robert F. Fleming, ed., *Hemingway and the Natural World* (Moscow, ID: University of Idaho Press, 1999), 242.
76 "Remembering Hemingway."
77 "Remembering Hemingway."
78 David Butterfield, *Ernest Hemingway in Idaho: Hemingway the Autumn* (Ketchum, ID: Centennial Entertainment, 1999), DVD.
79 Hemingway, *The Complete Short Stories*, 15.
80 Hemingway, *The Complete Short Stories*, 13.
81 Fleming, *Hemingway and the Natural World*, 91.
82 Beegel qtd. in Fleming, *Hemingway and the Natural World*, 243.
83 Ernest Hemingway, *The Complete Short Stories*, 22.
84 Beegel qtd. in Fleming, *Hemingway and the Natural World*, 243.
85 Gifford Pinchot, "*The Fight for Conservation*," accessed August 8, 2018, http://wwnorton.com/college/history/america-essential-learning/docs/GPinchot-

86 John Muir, "Hetch Hetchy," *Sierra Club Bulletin*, accessed August 8, 2018, http://vault.sierraclub.org/ca/hetchhetchy/hetch_hetchy_muir_scb_1908.html .
87 Beegel qtd. in Fleming, *Hemingway and the Natural World*, 243.
88 Beegel qtd. In Fleming, *Hemingway and the Natural World*, 238.
89 Beegel qtd. in Fleming, *Hemingway and the Natural World*, 238.
90 Hemingway, *The Complete Short Stories*, 165.
91 Ezra Pound, "On the Principles of an Imagiste," accessed August 10, 2018, https://www.poetryfoundation.org/poetrymagazine/articles/detail/58900 .
92 Hemingway, *Death in the Afternoon*, 322.
93 "The Star Copy Style," *The Kansas City Star*, accessed August 10, 2018, http://www.kansascity.com/entertainment/books/article10632713.ece/BINARY/The%20Star%20Copy%20Style.pdf.
94 "The Star Copy Style," *The Kansas City Star*.
95 Hemingway, *The Complete Short Stories*, 208.
96 Hemingway, *The Complete Short Stories*, 175-6.
97 Hemingway, *The Complete Short Stories*, 176.
98 Hemingway, *The Complete Short Stories*, 163.
99 Hemingway, *The Complete Short Stories*, 165.
100 Hemingway, *The Complete Short Stories*, 159.
101 Hemingway, Ernest. *A Moveable Feast: The Restored Edition*, New York: Simon and Schuster, 147.
102 Hemingway, *The Complete Short Stories*, 144.
103 Hemingway, *The Complete Short Stories*, 145.
104 Hemingway, *A Farewell to Arms*, 8.
105 Hemingway, *A Farewell to Arms*, 13.
106 Hemingway, *A Farewell to Arms*, 249.
107 Hemingway, *A Farewell to Arms*, 259-60.
108 Hemingway, *A Farewell to Arms*, 232.
109 Hemingway, *The Sun Also Rises*, 106.
110 Hemingway, *Green Hills of Africa*, 29.
111 Hemingway, *The Sun Also Rises*, 124,130.
112 Hemingway, *The Sun Also Rises*, 121.
113 Hemingway, *The Sun Also Rises*, 238, 242.

114 Hemingway, *For Whom the Bell Tolls*, 431.
115 Hemingway, *Green Hills of Africa*, 129.
116 Bauer, "Papa's Legacy."
117 "Wilderness Connect," accessed August 10, 2018, http://www.wilderness.net/nwps/legisact.
118 T. Arnold, *Hemingway in Idaho*, 76.
119 *Ernest Hemingway: Wrestling with Life* (Arts and Entertainment Television Networks, 1998), DVD.
120 Hemingway, *For Whom the Bell Tolls*, 164.
121 L. Arnold, *Hemingway*, 56.
122 Meyers, *Hemingway*, 418.
123 Meyers, *Hemingway*, 41.
124 Hemingway, *The Complete Short Stories*, 75–76.
125 Hemingway, *The Complete Short Stories*, 80.
126 Hemingway, *The Complete Short Stories*, 81.
127 Ernest Hemingway, *The Complete Short Stories*, 90.
128 Boris Vejdovsky, *Hemingway: A Life in Pictures*, (Buffalo: Firefly Publishers 2011), 41.
129 Hemingway, *The Complete Short Stories*, 107.
130 Hemingway, *The Complete Short Stories*, 108.
131 "Agnes Von Kurowsky to Ernest Hemingway," *Hemingway*, accessed July 13, 2018, http://www.rjgeib.com/thoughts/hemingway/agnes-von-kurowsky.html.
132 Hemingway, *The Complete Short Stories*, 116.
133 Hemingway, *The Complete Short Stories*, 116.
134 Hemingway, *The Complete Short Stories*, 112–113.
135 Hemingway, *The Complete Short Stories*, 131.
136 Hemingway, *The Complete Short Stories*, 145.
137 Hemingway, *The Complete Short Stories*, 146.
138 Hemingway, *The Complete Short Stories*, 90.
139 Hemingway, *The Complete Short Stories*, 147.
140 Hemingway, *The Complete Short Stories*, 212.
141 Hemingway, *A Farewell to Arms*, 62.
142 Hemingway, *The Sun Also Rises*, 34.
143 Hemingway, *The Sun Also Rises*, 249.
144 Hemingway, *A Farewell to Arms*, 62.

145 Hemingway, *A Farewell to Arms*, 216.
146 Hemingway, *A Farewell to Arms*, 226.
147 Meyers, *Hemingway*, 22.
148 Hemingway, *For Whom the Bell Tolls* , 337.
149 Hemingway, *For Whom the Bell Tolls*, 351.
150 Hemingway, *For Whom the Bell Tolls*, 305.
151 A. E. Hotchner, *The Good Life According to Ernest Hemingway*, 1.
152 Meyers. *Hemingway*, 87.
153 Ernest Hemingway, *Selected Letters: 1917-1961* (New York: Scribner's, 2003), 837.
154 Cormac McCarthy, *All the Pretty Horses* (New York: Vintage, 2003), 238.
155 L. Arnold, *Hemingway*, 55.
156 L. Arnold, *Hemingway*, 55.
157 L. Arnold, *Hemingway*, 72.
158 L. Arnold, *Hemingway*, 72.
159 L. Arnold, *Hemingway*, 28.
160 L. Arnold, *Hemingway*, 28.
161 Ernest Hemingway, *A Moveable Feast* (New York: Scribner's, 1964), 149–150.
162 Ernest Hemingway, *By-Line Ernest Hemingway: Selected Articles and Dispatches of Four Decades (*New York: Scribner's 1998), 185.
163 Hemingway, *A Farewell to Arms*, 105.
164 Hemingway, *A Farewell to Arms*, 106.
165 Hemingway, *A Farewell to Arms*, 106.
166 Hemingway, *A Farewell to Arms*, 106.
167 Hemingway, *A Farewell to Arms*, 108.
168 Hemingway, *A Farewell to Arms*, 185.
169 Hemingway, *A Farewell to Arms*, 121-122.
170 Hemingway, *The Old Man and the Sea*, 103.
171 Hemingway, *A Farewell to Arms*, 122.
172 Hemingway, *A Farewell to Arms*, 55.
173 Meyers, *Hemingway*, 33.
174 Hemingway, *A Farewell to Arms*, 49.
175 Hemingway, *A Farewell to Arms*, 57.
176 Hemingway, *The Sun Also Rises*, 171.
177 Hemingway, *The Sun Also Rises*, 171.

178 Hemingway, *The Sun Also Rises*, 220.
179 Hemingway, *The Sun Also Rises*, 223.
180 Hemingway, *For Whom the Bell Tolls*, 209.
181 Hemingway, *For Whom the Bell Tolls*, 236.
182 Hemingway, *For Whom the Bell Tolls*, 235.
183 Hemingway, *For Whom the Bell Tolls*, 236.
184 Hemingway, *A Farewell to Arms*, ix.
185 Hemingway, *For Whom the Bell Tolls*, 236.
186 Hemingway, *For Whom the Bell Tolls*, 162.
187 Elizabeth Dewberry, "Hemingway's Journalism and the Realist Dilemma," *Cambridge Companion to Hemingway*, ed. Scott Donaldson (Cambridge: Cambridge University Press, 1996), 35.
188 Hemingway, *Death in the Afternoon*, 837.
189 Hemingway, *Selected Letters*, 153.
190 Morris, *Hemingway and Cooper in Idaho: An Enduring Friendship* (Charleston, SC: The History Press, 2017), 51.
191 Morris, *Hemingway and Cooper in Idaho*, 51.
192 Morris, *Hemingway and Cooper in Idaho*, 50.
193 "Jed Gray's Talk at The Community Library's 2016 Ernest Hemingway Festival," *YouTube*, accessed June 28, 2019, https://www.youtube.com/watch?v=JMD4jLKnQn8.
194 "Remembering Hemingway."
195 Hemingway, *A Farewell to Arms*, ix.
196 Hemingway, *A Farewell to Arms*, 57.
197 Hemingway, *A Farewell to Arms*, 55.
198 Hemingway, *The Complete Short Stories*, 337.
199 Hemingway, *For Whom the Bell Tolls*, 4.
200 Hemingway, *The Sun Also Rises*, 257.
201 L. Arnold, *Hemingway*, 135, 160.
202 L. Arnold, *Hemingway*, 9.
203 L. Arnold, *Hemingway*, 9.
204 Tillie Arnold, *Hemingway in Idaho* (Boston: Beacon Books, 1999), 47.
205 Butterfield, *Ernest Hemingway in Idaho*.
206 Hemingway, *The Old Man and the Sea*, 31.

207 Hemingway, *The Old Man and the Sea*, 65.
208 Hemingway, *The Old Man and the Sea*, 81.
209 Hemingway, *The Old Man and the Sea*, 106.
210 Carl Wood, "A Pretty Good Unity," accessed August 18, 2018, http://connection.ebscohost.com/c/literary-criticism/9609035268/hemingways-our-time-pretty-good-unity.
211 Warren, "Hemingway," 11.
212 Hemingway, *The Complete Short Stories*, 18.
213 Hemingway, *The Complete Short Stories*, 18.
214 Hemingway, *The Complete Short Stories*, 13.
215 Hemingway, *The Complete Short Stories*, 13.
216 Hemingway, *The Complete Short Stories*, 13.
217 Hemingway, *The Complete Short Stories*, 27.
218 Hemingway, *The Complete Short Stories*, 27.
219 Hemingway, *The Complete Short Stories*, 25.
220 Hemingway, *For Whom the Bell Tolls*, 15.
221 Hemingway, *For Whom the Bell Tolls*, 94–95.
222 T. Arnold, *Hemingway in Idaho*, 135.
223 Hemingway, *For Whom the Bell Tolls*, 169.
224 Hemingway, *For Whom the Bell Tolls*, 169.
225 Hemingway, *For Whom the Bell Tolls*, 166.
226 Hemingway, *A Moveable Feast*, 55.
227 Hemingway, *For Whom the Bell Tolls*, 162.
228 Hemingway, *For Whom the Bell Tolls*, 136.
229 Hemingway, *For Whom the Bell Tolls*, 236.
230 Hemingway, *The Complete Short Stories*, 25.
231 Hemingway, *For Whom the Bell Tolls*, 437–438.
232 Hemingway, *For Whom the Bell Tolls*, 438.
233 Hemingway, *For Whom the Bell Tolls*, 467.
234 Hemingway, *For Whom the Bell Tolls*, 470.
235 Hemingway, *For Whom the Bell Tolls*, 471.
236 Hemingway, *For Whom the Bell Tolls*, 467.
237 Taylor, *Sun Valley Stories*, 137.
238 Taylor, *Sun Valley Stories*, 137–138.

239 Taylor, *Sun Valley Stories*, 138.
240 L. Arnold, *Hemingway: High on the Wild*, (Caldwell, ID: Caxton Printers, 1968), 56.
241 Morris, *Hemingway and Cooper in Idaho*, 73.
242 Meyers, *Hemingway*, 35.
243 Taylor, *Sun Valley Stories*, 135.
244 Hemingway, *A Farewell to Arms*, 193.
245 Hemingway, *A Farewell to Arms*, 161.
246 Hemingway, *A Farewell to Arms*, 161.
247 Hemingway, *The Complete Short Stories*, 213.
248 Hemingway, *The Complete Short Stories*, 131.
249 Hemingway, *The Complete Short Stories*, 109.
250 Pound, "On the Principles of an Imagiste."
251 Ernest Hemingway, *88 Poems* (NY: Harcourt Brace, 1979), 41.
252 Hemingway, *For Whom the Bell Tolls*, 209.
253 Hemingway, *For Whom the Bell Tolls*, 215.
254 Hemingway, *For Whom the Bell Tolls*, 218.
255 Hemingway, *For Whom the Bell Tolls*, 219–220.
256 Hemingway, *For Whom the Bell Tolls*, 222–223.
257 Hemingway, *For Whom the Bell Tolls*, 369.
258 Hemingway, *For Whom the Bell Tolls*, 162.
259 Hemingway, *For Whom the Bell Tolls*, 163–4.
260 Hemingway, *A Moveable Feast*, 51.
261 Mary Welsh Hemingway, *How It Was* (New York: Knopf Publishing, 1976), 431.
262 T. Arnold, *Hemingway in Idaho*, 198.
263 Hemingway, *A Moveable Feast*, 51.
264 Hemingway, *A Moveable Feast*, 210.
265 Hemingway, *A Moveable Feast*, 210–211.
266 Hemingway, *A Moveable Feast*, 147.
267 M. W. Hemingway, *How It Was*, 458.
268 M. W. Hemingway, *How It Was*, 458.
269 L. Arnold, *Hemingway*, 28.
270 L. Arnold, *Hemingway*, 28.
271 Hemingway, *The Sun Also Rises*, 187–188.
272 Hemingway, *The Sun Also Rises*, 249.

273 Hemingway, *The Old Man and the Sea*, 80.
274 Hemingway, *The Old Man and the Sea*, 44.
275 Hemingway, *The Old Man and the Sea*, 50.
276 Hemingway, *For Whom the Bell Tolls*, 41.
277 Hemingway, *For Whom the Bell Tolls*, 41.
278 Hemingway, *For Whom the Bell Tolls*, 196.
279 Hemingway, *For Whom the Bell Tolls*, 197.
280 Hemingway, *For Whom the Bell Tolls*, 192–3.
281 Hemingway, *For Whom the Bell Tolls*, 304.
282 Hemingway, *For Whom the Bell Tolls*, 302.
283 Hemingway, *For Whom the Bell Tolls*, 303.
284 Hemingway, *For Whom the Bell Tolls*, 304.
285 McCarthy, *All the Pretty Horses*, 232.
286 Hemingway, *For Whom the Bell Tolls*, 338.
287 Ernest Hemingway, *In Our Time* (New York: Scribner's, 1925), 113.
288 Hemingway, *In Our Time*, 116.
289 Hemingway, *In Our Time*, 108.
290 "Agnes Von Kurowsky to Ernest Hemingway."
291 Hemingway, *For Whom the Bell Tolls*, 209.
292 Hemingway, *The Old Man and the Sea*, 103.
293 Meyers, *Hemingway*, 116.
294 Hemingway, *For Whom the Bell Tolls*, 367.
295 Hemingway, *For Whom the Bell Tolls*, 351.
296 Hemingway, *For Whom the Bell Tolls*, 73.
297 Hemingway, *A Farewell to Arms*, 216.
298 Hemingway, *For Whom the Bell Tolls*, 338.
299 Hemingway, *For Whom the Bell Tolls*, 338–339.
300 Hemingway, *For Whom the Bell Tolls*, 340.
301 Hemingway, *For Whom the Bell Tolls*, 337.
302 Hemingway, *For Whom the Bell Tolls*, 469–470.
303 Hemingway, *For Whom the Bell Tolls*, 471.
304 Morris, *Hemingway and Cooper in Idaho*, 113.
305 Butterfield, *Ernest Hemingway in Idaho*.
306 Bill Peschel, "Like Father Like Son," *Bill Peschel*, accessed July 15, 2018,

http://planetpeschel.com/2012/12/like-father-like-son-ernest-hemingways-father-kills-himself-1.

307 Vejdovsky, *Hemingway*, 126.
308 Meyers, *Hemingway*, 210.
309 L. Arnold, *Hemingway*, 31.
310 Morris, *Hemingway and Cooper in Idaho*, 91, 94.
311 Vejdovsky, *Hemingway*, 116.
312 L. Arnold, *Hemingway*, 160.
313 Morris, *Hemingway and Cooper in Idaho*, 97.
314 Morris, *Hemingway and Cooper in Idaho* , 98.
315 Morris, *Hemingway and Cooper in Idaho* , 110.
316 M. W. Hemingway, *How It Was* , 492.
317 M. W. Hemingway, *How It Was*, 496.
318 Vejdovsky, *Hemingway: A Life in Pictures*, 186.
319 Hemingway, *The Complete Short Stories*, 50.
320 Vejdovsky, *Hemingway*, 186.
321 "Remembering Hemingway."
322 "Remembering Hemingway."
323 Meyers, *Hemingway*, 550, 552.
324 Morris, *Hemingway and Cooper in Idaho*, 111.
325 M. W. Hemingway, *How It Was* , 498.
326 Morris, *Hemingway and Cooper in Idaho*, 119.
327 M. W. Hemingway, *How It Was* , 498.
328 L. Arnold, *Hemingway*, 154.
329 L. Arnold, *Hemingway*, 160.
330 Vejdovsky, *Hemingway*, 186.
331 Morris, *Hemingway and Cooper in Idaho*, 120.
332 M. W. Hemingway, *How It Was* , 502.
333 M. W. Hemingway, *How It Was*, 502.
334 "Hemingway," *Sun Valley Guide*, accessed August 1, 2015, http://www.svguide.com/svg_hem.htm .
335 Hemingway, *A Farewell to Arms*, 100.
336 Hemingway, *A Farewell to Arms*, 62.
337 Meyers, *Hemingway*, 558.

Bibliography

"Agnes Von Kurowsky to Ernest Hemingway." Accessed July 13, 2018. http://www.rjgeib.com/thoughts/hemingway/agnes-von-kurowsky.html.

Arnold, Lloyd. Hemingway: *High on the Wild*. Caldwell, ID: Caxton Printers, 1968.

Arnold, Tillie. *Hemingway in Idaho*. Boston: Beacon Books, 1999.

Bauer, Marilyn. "Papa's Legacy: An interview with Jack Hemingway." Sun Valley

Guide. Accessed July 12, 2018. http://www.svguide.hemingway.htm.

Butterfield, David. *Ernest Hemingway in Idaho: Hemingway in the Autumn*. Ketchum, ID: Centennial Entertainment, 1999. DVD.

Ernest Hemingway: *Wrestling with Life*. Arts and Entertainment Television

Networks, 1998. DVD.

Fleming, Robert F., ed. *Hemingway and the Natural World*. Moscow, ID: University of Idaho Press, 1999.

Foley, Greg. "Ernest Hemingway's Autumns in Idaho," Sun Valley Guide. Accessed July 12, 2018. http://www.svguide.com/svg_hem.htm.

Hemingway, Ernest. *A Farewell to Arms: The Hemingway Library Edition*. New York:

Scribner's, 2012.

———. *A Moveable Feast*. New York: Scribner's, 1964.

———. *For Whom the Bell Tolls*. New York: Scribner's, 1940.

———. *Green Hills of Africa*. New York: Scribner's, 1935.

———. *The Complete Short Stories*. New York: Simon and Schuster / Scribner's, 1987.

———. *The Sun Also Rises*. New York: Scribner's, 1926.

———. *The Old Man and the Sea*. New York: Scribner's, 1952.

———. *Selected Letters: 1917-1961.* New York: Scribner's, 2003.

Hemingway, Mary Welsh. *How It Was.* New York: Knopf Publishing, 1976.

Hotchner, A. E. *The Good Life According to Ernest Hemingway.* New York: Ecco Publishing, 2008.

———. *Hemingway in Love: The Untold Story.* New York: Macmillan, 2015.

"Jed Gray's Talk at The Community Library's 2016 Ernest Hemingway Festival."

Accessed September 4, 2018. https://www.youtube.com/watch?v=JMD4jLKnQn8.

Mooallem, Jon. "The Strange Story of the Teddy Bear and What It Reveals." TED

Talk. Accessed July 18, 2018. https://www.youtube.com/watch?time_continue=201&v=EE

Morris, Larry. *Hemingway and Cooper in Idaho: An Enduring Friendship.* Charleston: The History Press, 2017.

Lunde, Darrin. *The Naturalist.* New York: Crown Publishers, 2016.

McCarthy, Cormac. *All the Pretty Horses.* New York: Vintage, 2003.

Meyers, Jeffrey. *Hemingway.* Boston: Da Capo Press, 1999.

Muir, John. "Hetch Hetchy." Sierra Club Bulletin. Accessed August 8, 2018. http://vault.sierraclub.org/ca/hetchhetchy/hetch_hetchy_muir_scb_1908.html.

Peschel, Bill. "Like Father Like Son." Bill Peschel. Accessed July 18, 2018.

http://planetpeschel.com/2012/12/like-father-like-son-ernest-hemingways-father-kills-himself-1.

Pinchot, Gifford. "The Fight for Conservation." Accessed August 8, 2018.

https://wwnorton.com/college/history/america-essential-learning/docs/GPinchot-Conservation-1910.pdf.

Pound, Ezra. "On the Principles of an Imagiste." Accessed August 10, 2018.

https://www.poetryfoundation.org/poetrymagazine/articles/detail/58900.

"Remembering Hemingway." YouTube. Accessed September 26, 2018. https://www.youtube.com/watch?v=d2fzox5JLGc.

Spanier, Sandra, ed. *The Letters of Ernest Hemingway: Volume 2, 1923-1925.*

Cambridge: Cambridge University Press, 2013.

Strunk, William and White, E. B. *The Elements of Style.* New York, Harcourt, Brace &

Howe[, 1918.

Taylor, Dorice. *Sun Valley Stories.* Sun Valley: Ex Libris Publishers, 1980.

"The Star Copy Style." *The Kansas City Star.* Accessed August 10, 2018. http://www.kansascity.com/entertainment/books/article10632713.ece/BINARY/The%20Star%20Copy%20Style.pdf.

Vejdovsky, Boris. *Hemingway: A Life in Pictures.* Buffalo: Firefly Publishers, 2011.

Warren, Robert Penn. "Hemingway." The Kenyon Review 9, no. 1 (Winter 1947).

White, William, ed. *By-Line Ernest Hemingway: Selected Articles and Dispatches of*

Four Decades. New York: Scribner's, 1998.

"The Wilderness Act." Wilderness Connect. Accessed August 10, 2018. http://www.wilderness.net/nwps/legisact.

Winn, Harbour. "Hemingway's *In Our Time*: 'Pretty Good Unity.'" Accessed August 18,

2018. https://sites.google.com/a/communityschool.org/us-hemingway-huss/blended-learning-course/in-our-time-unit/criticism-pretty-good-unity.

Index

A

Adams, Nick 1, 10, 11, 18, 40, 50, 56, 60, 62, 63, 64, 65, 66, 68, 76, 86, 89, 97, 100, 101, 106, 108, 137, 152, 203
Africa xii, 25, 42, 43, 50, 51, 78, 80, 178, 186
alcoholism (Hemingway's) 180, 197, 204
Anderson, Don 32, 208, 209, 211
Anselmo xxi, xxvi, 9, 26, 35, 37, 38, 40, 54, 145, 157, 172, 174, 175, 176, 187, 189
Aristotle xxi, 21
Arnold, Lloyd 2, 5, 7, 8, 9, 26, 27, 28, 47, 53, 85, 111, 122, 123, 135, 138, 148, 149, 157, 182, 200, 202, 203, 207, 209, 211, 219, 220, 221, 223, 224, 225, 227, 229
Arnold, Tillie 20, 28, 29, 84, 85, 157, 165, 207, 219, 220, 221, 223, 225, 226, 227
Ashby, George 6
Ashley, Lady Brett xxi, 16, 17, 18, 19, 20, 33, 34, 72, 73, 74, 75, 93, 108, 110, 114, 116, 130, 146, 184, 185
Atkinson, Chuck 210, 211

B

Barkley, Catherine xxvi, 83, 87, 107, 108, 111, 112, 126, 166, 167, 211
Barnes, Jake xx, 16, 18, 19, 20, 34, 72, 73, 74, 75, 76, 93, 108, 110, 114, 116, 130, 135, 146, 183, 184, 185, 212
Beegel, Susan 45, 53, 54

Bellevue xii, 141
Benner, Dave 7, 47, 123, 182
Bergman, Ingrid 2, 5, 29, 142
Big Wood River 71, 77, 81, 203, 205
Boettiger, Anna 3, 164
Boettiger, John 4, 13, 47, 164, 182
Boulder White Cloud Wilderness 81
Brooks, David xxii, 219
bullfight 16, 34, 75, 130

C

Campbell, Mike 33, 35, 73, 110, 184
Caporetto xxiii, 24, 72, 112, 127, 168, 169
Catholicism 37, 87, 145
Challis, ID 9
Cohn, Robert xxi, 5, 18, 20, 21, 33, 35, 72, 73, 93, 110, 130, 183
Community School xii, 47
concussion 203
Conrad, Joseph 24
Cooper, Gary 2, 5, 138
Count Greffi xxi, xxvi, 26, 107, 111, 112, 113, 114
Count Mippipopolous xxi
Crane, Stephen 24
Cuba 5, 14, 43, 48, 84, 85, 86, 165, 177, 178, 181, 198, 203, 205, 207

D

declarative sentences 59
deer hunt 43
depression 44, 180, 204, 206
Dietrich 3, 5, 30, 48, 138
divorce 2, 20, 28, 37, 84, 87, 115, 154, 156

drinking 42, 70, 107, 108, 127, 143, 149, 174, 193, 198
duck hunting 7, 19, 45, 54, 76, 79, 85, 122, 135

E

El Sordo 157, 161
Emerson 43
Etorre. 128
eulogy for Gene Van Guilder 44, 66, 183

F

"the family" xxvi, 9, 24, 31, 32, 35, 53, 71, 137, 205
Faulkner, William 87
F.B.I. 204
Finca Vigia 85, 178, 198, 207
fishing xii, xiii, 1, 5, 7, 10, 14, 15, 16, 24, 26, 27, 42, 43, 45, 48, 50, 52, 56, 61, 62, 73, 74, 76, 77, 89, 105, 150, 153, 203, 208
Fitzgerald, F. Scott 24, 39, 124, 163, 180
fourth dimension 137
France xii
Frank Church Wilderness 5, 53, 135
Frost, Robert 27
funeral 202, 212

G

Galena Summit xi, 43
Gellhorn, Martha 2, 20, 82, 91, 115, 163, 165, 175
Gooding, ID 48, 138
Gorton, Bill 73
grave (Hemingway's): xii, 157, 200, 212, 216 Gray, Anita 31, 32, 45, 141, 182
Gray, Jed 46, 140, 141, 225
Greco-Turkish War xxii, 142, 211

H

Hailey, ID xii, 3, 58, 209
Harriman, Averell 3, 69, 106, 122, 164

Hemingway and Copper in Idaho: An Enduring Friendship 138
Hemingway, Dr. Clarence 195, 200
Hemingway, Ernest (his works)
  A Clean Well-Lighted Place xxvii
  A Farewell to Arms xii· xxi· xxiii· xxv· xxvi· 20· 24· 26· 27· 28· 40· 69· 71· 72· 83· 87· 96· 107· 111· 113· 125· 127· 131· 133· 134· 142· 166· 167· 168· 177· 195· 201· 206· 211· 219· 221· 222· 223· 224· 225· 227· 228· 229
  A Moveable Feast 68· 124· 158· 177· 178· 179· 180· 205· 224· 226· 227
  A Very Short Story 83· 94· 96· 192
  Big Two-Hearted River 1· 10· 15· 52· 56· 57· 60· 62· 63· 76· 100· 102· 152· 153· 203
  Death in the Afternoon xx· xxiii· xxviii· 20· 50· 58· 84· 136· 149· 163· 219· 222· 225
  For Whom the Bell Tolls xii· xiii· xiv· xxi· xxvi· 1· 2· 5· 9· 19· 20· 21· 23· 26· 35· 37· 42· 45· 53· 65· 75· 83· 85· 111· 115· 116· 131· 145· 156· 159· 161· 163· 164· 172· 174· 175· 187· 190· 193· 194· 195· 219· 220· 221· 223· 224· 225· 226· 227· 228
  Green Hills of Africa 20· 42· 50· 78· 84· 149· 163· 221· 222· 223
  Hills Like White Elephants 83· 104· 106· 108· 169· 170
  Indian Camp 10
  In Our Time xii· xxiii· xxv· 10· 11· 18· 40· 50· 56· 58· 68· 83· 89· 91· 97· 99· 101· 104· 108· 120· 131· 137· 152· 153· 169· 170· 172· 177· 191· 192· 203· 228
  Mr. and Mrs. Elliot 83· 100
  Out of Season 83
  Soldier's Home xxiii· 97· 99· 133· 143· 169· 191

The Doctor and the Doctor's Wife 89, 92, 98
The End of Something 91, 96
The Natural History of the Dead xxvii
The Old Man and the Sea xii, xxvi, 1, 14, 26, 46, 50, 114, 138, 150, 153, 156, 186, 193, 220, 224, 225, 226, 228
The Short Happy Life of Francis Macomber xxiii, 12, 14, 26, 50, 52, 54, 83, 93, 114, 154, 155
The Snows of Kilimanjaro 83, 205
The Sun Also Rises xii, xx, xxvi, 1, 5, 16, 20, 27, 33, 35, 72, 78, 93, 108, 111, 114, 116, 130, 131, 135, 146, 177, 212, 220, 221, 222, 223, 224, 225, 227
Three Day Blow 93, 98, 104
To Have and Have Not 84, 149
Hemingway Festival (Ketchum, ID) xii, 46, 225
Hemingway, Gregory 9, 25, 84, 87, 139, 166
Hemingway, Hadley Richardson 28, 82, 84, 158, 175, 177, 178, 179, 180
Hemingway, Jack 9, 11, 25, 27, 28, 56, 77, 78, 79, 80, 81, 84, 138, 165, 201, 220, 223
Hemingway, Leicester 200
Hemingway, Mary Welsh xii, xxi, 71, 81, 82, 87, 158, 165, 166, 170, 177, 178, 179, 181, 199, 202, 203, 204, 205, 207, 208, 209, 210, 219, 227, 229
Hemingway, Patrick 9, 25, 28, 79, 84, 87, 138, 166
Henry, Frederic xxv, 26, 40, 69, 72, 87, 111, 113, 127, 131, 133, 142, 147, 167
heritage xx, xxviii

High on the Wild 7, 27, 122, 219, 220, 224, 225, 227, 229
Hotchner, A. E. 198, 207, 209, 224

I

Imagiste 58
Irati River 74
Italy xii, 69, 100, 145, 203

J

Jig 83, 105, 106, 107, 108, 169
Jordan, Robert xiv, 1, 2, 9, 21, 22, 23, 26, 35, 36, 37, 38, 39, 40, 42, 54, 65, 75, 76, 83, 85, 86, 89, 111, 116, 118, 131, 132, 133, 134, 145, 149, 152, 156, 157, 158, 159, 160, 161, 162, 163, 172, 173, 174, 175, 176, 187, 188, 193, 194, 195, 196

K

Kansas City Star 24, 59, 136, 222
Ketchum, ID xii, xix, 6, 11, 29, 45, 46, 79, 80, 81, 88, 105, 117, 149, 157, 166, 177, 178, 179, 180, 182, 183, 190, 191, 196, 197, 198, 200, 202, 203, 204, 205, 207, 208, 210, 211, 212, 221
Ketchum Cemetery xii, 157
Key West xii, 5, 28, 29, 43, 48, 84, 87, 177, 201
Krebs xxiii, 11, 97, 98, 102, 120, 133, 143, 169, 191

L

Labrador 3
Life magazine 122

M

MacMullen, Forrest (Duke) 28, 29
Macomber, Francis xxiii, 12, 13, 15, 17, 18, 26, 50, 51, 52, 53, 54, 66, 83, 93, 106, 114, 154, 155

Macomber, Margot 14, 83, 114, 154, 156
magpie 31, 47, 48, 54
Manolin xxvi, 26, 151, 153, 186, 187
Maria 2, 23, 65, 83, 85, 87, 91, 111, 116, 117, 118, 157, 158, 160, 161, 164, 194, 196
Marjorie 91, 92, 93, 96
marriage 14, 20, 41, 82, 87, 89, 92, 93, 102, 104, 107, 111, 115, 145, 146, 154, 158, 163, 165, 178, 179, 185, 186, 211
Mason, Jane 84, 175
Mayo Clinic 44, 58, 204, 206, 207, 208, 209, 210
McCarthy, Cormac 121, 190, 213, 224, 228
medications 198, 204, 206
Meyers, Jeffrey 3, 19, 193, 213
modern poetry 100
monosyllabic prose 99, 120
Moritz, Dr. John 29, 35, 157, 206, 208
Muir, John 56, 222
Mungo Park xxvii, 144

N

Nobel Prize 3, 191

O

Oak Park xxvii, 12, 28, 29, 37, 57, 86, 200, 202, 211
Ordonez, Carmen 25

P

Pablo 9, 54, 132, 145, 152, 156, 157, 160, 172, 173, 174, 175, 193
Pahsimeroi Valley xi, 3, 135, 139
Pamplona 33, 74, 135, 189
paranoia 180, 204, 206
Passini xxv, 127, 130, 169
Percival, Philip 25
Pfeiffer, Pauline 2, 37, 41, 79, 84, 145, 175, 178, 202, 211

pheasant hunting 6, 45, 46, 122
Pilar xxvi, 5, 21, 48, 118, 138, 156, 157, 161, 173, 194, 208
Pinchot, Gifford 55, 77, 78, 221
plane crash 203
Pound, Ezra 24, 58, 59, 172, 222, 227
Priest 26, 69, 112, 114, 115, 156, 211
pronghorn xi, 9, 43, 62, 79, 85, 135, 138
P.T.S.D. xxiv, 61, 76, 102, 104
Purdy, Ruth 29, 32

R

rabbit hunting 30, 48, 138
Regan, Neil 30
Retreat from Caporetto xxiii, xxvi, 24, 65, 112, 127, 146, 159, 168, 169
Rinaldi. xxviii, 129
Romero, Pedro xxvi, 1, 5, 16, 18, 19, 20, 74, 75, 110, 111, 130, 146
Room 206 of Sun Valley Lodge 4, 20, 85, 149, 164
Roosevelt, Teddy 51, 52, 54, 78

S

Safari 53, 56
Salmon River xi, 43
Santiago xxvi, 1, 14, 15, 16, 21, 23, 26, 38, 50, 66, 86, 114, 138, 150, 151, 153, 174, 186, 187
Saviers, George 28, 29, 31, 32, 206, 208
Sawtooth Mountains xi, 43, 80
Scribners 2, 219, 220, 221, 222, 224, 227, 228
Shoshone 3, 30, 48, 53, 138, 139
Silver Creek xii, 3, 5, 13, 31, 45, 47, 53, 77, 78, 79, 81, 122, 135, 148, 150, 164, 182
Snake River 7, 44, 123, 182
Spain xii, 18, 21, 65, 73, 74, 75, 105, 106, 118, 134, 156, 157, 158, 161, 177, 188, 203

Spanish Civil War xxi, xxii, 1, 2, 8, 28, 29, 36, 41, 54, 65, 83, 85, 115, 116, 133, 142, 145, 150, 156, 175, 211
Spiegel, Clara 32
Stein, Gertrude 24
Stewart, Clay 48
suicide 29, 35, 84, 116, 117, 118, 178, 180, 190, 195, 196, 200, 202, 207, 208, 209, 210, 212
Sun Valley xi, xii, xiii, xiv, xxvi, 2, 3, 4, 5, 6, 7, 8, 9, 12, 19, 20, 22, 26, 28, 29, 30, 31, 35, 39, 40, 41, 43, 44, 45, 47, 48, 53, 56, 62, 66, 69, 70, 71, 77, 80, 84, 85, 87, 89, 106, 111, 113, 115, 120, 121, 122, 123, 135, 137, 138, 140, 142, 146, 148, 149, 150, 156, 157, 158, 163, 164, 165, 166, 167, 177, 180, 182, 197, 199, 200, 202, 206, 207, 208, 209, 211, 212, 219, 220, 226, 227, 229
Sun Valley Resort 6, 7, 20, 27, 30, 62, 122, 163, 211
Switzerland 158

T

Tagliamento River xxvi, 72
The Community Library xii, 81, 225
The Elements of Style 59
The Idaho Hemingway 84, 157
Thoreau 43
tip of the iceberg 58, 91, 108, 131, 145, 153, 187
Trail Creek Memorial xii, 66

V

Van Guilder, Gene 7, 8, 14, 27, 28, 30, 44, 47, 53, 62, 66, 123, 146, 157, 182
Von Kurowsky, Agnes 83, 84, 192, 228

W

Warm Springs House 117, 166
Warren, Robert Penn xxiv, xxvi, xxvii, xxviii, 31, 45, 141, 219, 220, 226
Williams, Taylor 5, 6, 9, 26, 28, 29, 31, 32, 122, 135, 138, 166, 183
Wilson, Robert 12, 13, 26, 50, 52, 54, 56, 154, 155, 160
Wood River Valley xii, xiv, xv, 27, 30, 31, 47, 48, 53, 70, 140, 150, 165, 200, 203, 210
World War II xxii
W.W.I. xxii, xxiii, xxv, xxvi, 10, 18, 24, 41, 56, 62, 84, 89, 92, 94, 96, 97, 99, 100, 101, 112, 125, 137, 145, 152, 153, 166, 169, 192, 211

About the Author

Philip Huss is an independent school teacher and writer from Hailey, Idaho, where he lives with his wife, Chrissie, and their two children, Nils and Gretel.

Phil graduated with a BA in English from Amherst College and a MA in English from Boston College.

An English teacher for twenty-five years, Phil has spent twenty of those years teaching at Sun Valley Community School, where he has taught a beloved course titled "Hemingway." In this course, students read Ernest Hemingway's *In Our Time*, *The Sun Also Rises*, *A Farewell to Arms*, *For Whom the Bell Tolls*, and *The Old Man and the Sea*, and they study the local Idaho Hemingway stories. During the unit of inquiry into the local Hemingway stories, students produce documentary-style videos that connect the five Sun Valley area Hemingway sites— Trail Creek Memorial, room 206 of the Sun Valley Lodge, the Warm Springs house, Silver Creek Memorial, and Hemingway's grave—to the local Hemingway stories that bring these sites to life. Samples of these videos are available for public viewing at the Sun Valley Museum of History in Ketchum, Idaho.

Phil has published articles related to his research on Hemingway in *Sun Valley Magazine* and *BigLife Magazine*. Phil is a frequent speaker and discussion leader at the Ernest Hemingway Seminar held each September at The Community Library in Ketchum, Idaho. At the Tugboat Institute in Ketchum, Phil has also presented to business leaders on how the Hemingway heroic code can serve as a platform for codifying core principles of a company.

You can contact Phil for speaking engagements at phuss@communityschool.org.

Visit us at
www.historypress.com